COMPARATIVE POLITICS
A Distributive Approach

COMPARATIVE POLITICS

A Distributive Approach

ALEXANDER J. GROTH

University of California, Davis

THE MACMILLAN COMPANY

New York

Collier-Macmillan Limited · London

PRINTED IN THE UNITED STATES OF AMERICA

The Macmillan Company
866 Third Avenue, New York, New York 10022
Collier-Macmillan Canada, Ltd., Toronto, Ontario

Library of Congress catalog card number: 74-123457

First printing

To the memory of
Jakub, Marian, and Adam Goldwasser
and
Adela, Isaac, and Henryk Hazenfus

PREFACE

UNLIKE many previous studies of institutions, processes, and attitudes, the concern of this book is with the distributive aspects of comparative politics. Its focus is upon the relative benefits and burdens of public policy. How do political systems differ in the ways in which they manipulate resources and gratifications? Why are political "goods" or "pay-offs," other things being equal, differently allocated under different regimes?

These clearly difficult but also important and interesting questions are the theme of this book. What follows is, first, an overview of the politics of democratic and authoritarian states and, second, a discussion of consequent output differences in terms of the several kinds of goods, resources, or gratifications that they mete out.

Our initial model types of regimes are relatively simple—pluralistic democracies, traditional authoritarianisms, and innovative-mobilizational autocracies. Each can be historically and empirically illustrated, and each is distinguished by certain general output characteristics. Yet, the examination of specific policy areas, ranging from the support of popular education to the administration of justice, also shows an increasing complexity in the nature of political systems. The totalitarian (innovative-mobilizational) regimes of Hitler and Stalin had much in common in their exercise of police power but they were sharply divergent in their cultural and educational policies. They shared a certain independence from the pressures of grass-roots opinion but they used this relative independence in some very different ways. Contemporary democracies, too, have differed widely in some of their policies, although none of their constituents have matched either the completeness of power or of powerlessness characteristic of men living under totalitarian regimes.

A perspective on comparative politics in terms of how goods and resources are controlled, manipulated, and divided under different systems provides an additional dimension of understanding. On a modest and relatively rudimentary scale, but with newer information compiled in comparative studies of the last two decades, our quest follows traditional inquiries into the nature of justice and politics from Aristotle to Lasswell. A discussion of the experience of policy outputs, or "pay-offs," under alternative political systems will also increase appreciation of the challenging problems of political development in the decades ahead.

A. J. G.

ACKNOWLEDGMENTS

ACCEPTING sole responsiblity for the shortcomings of this work, the author gratefully acknowledges the assistance and encouragement of many persons. In particular, thanks are due to my wife Marilyn, and my two able assistants, Stevin and Warren Groth, as well as to Professor and Mrs. Oscar L. Gross, to Dr. Genia Goldwasser, and Mrs. B. Wineburg.

The help and advice of Professor L. L. Wade have been most valuable. My gratitude and appreciation are hereby expressed to several graduate and undergraduate students: Barbara Gardner; Robert M. Price at Harpur College, Binghamton, New York; James Clark, Donald Milanese, Donna Turcot, Jay Freeman, Larry Gerston, George Goerl, Michael Jarroff, Barbara Snider, and Larry Wight, all of the University of California, Davis. The efficient and accurate typing of Mrs. Linda Haight and Mrs. Roberta Kenney made a significant contribution to the preparation of the manuscript. Last, but not least, the very capable editorial assistance of Mr. James J. Carroll, Jr., of The Macmillan Company is gratefully noted.

A. J. G.

CONTENTS

CHAPTER 1
A DISTRIBUTIVE APPROACH TO COMPARATIVE POLITICS

THE terminology of politics is rich with descriptive words such as "democracy," "socialism," "fascism," "communism," "authoritarianism," and the like. Political science traditionally has been concerned with the meaning and content of these terms from the standpoint of (1) ideology, (2) constitutional and structural characteristics, and (3) the pattern of power relationships displayed by various species. Recently much attention has been given to the ecology of politics: the operational requisites of political systems. Clearly, all of these aspects of "politics" are part of a pattern that is helpful to the understanding of total political phenomena such as communism, democracy, and so forth. But these approaches, useful and necessary as they are, do not exhaust the range of significant inquiry. In fact, they are but part of a larger perspective.

The prevailing mode of comparative study, traditional and modern, has focused somewhat one-sidedly on what may be termed the *input* side of politics. The emphasis is and has been predominantly on who makes decisions and how, and in what context (historical, political, cultural, or economical). Nation-states have been differentiated mainly on the basis of their ideological orientation and the structures and processes of decision making, rather than on the outcomes of their decision making. It is these outcomes, or *outputs*, that are the focus of our comparisons in this book.

In the nineteenth century, Karl Marx conceived of "politics" and "government" as phenomena shaped and structured by the underlying social and economic realities. There has been a tendency in contemporary political science to revive this approach by linking political systems to levels of economic development—with an obvious plausibility and reasonableness. But if it be granted that much remains to be said for economic determinism in politics, what of the other side of the coin? Is there not evidence that the political-socioeconomic relationship is not merely reciprocal but often dramatically reversed? Are not government policies used to impoverish some and enrich others? Do they not promote the opportunities of some groups and interests while blocking or thwarting other groups and interests? Are they utilized for discriminatory allocations of resources, rewards, sacrifices, and punishments? Are not strikingly different political patterns sometimes imposed on and maintained for long periods of time in polities of a roughly equivalent degree of economic development? Is there not evidence to suggest that political power is frequently employed not to reflect but to change the group structure of society and to reshape social relationships?

We hasten to say that this study is but a brief introduction to a subject on which much remains to be done and on which a great deal of truly comparable empirical information remains to be gathered. Nor is it, of course, a specialized study, empirical or theoretical, such as the recent work by Robert T. Holt and John E. Turner, *The Political Basis of Economic Development* (Princeton, N. J.: D. Van Nostrand, 1966) or the earlier *Politics, Economics, and Welfare* by Robert A. Dahl and Charles E. Lindblom (New York: Harper & Row, 1953), to mention but two outstanding examples. It cannot and does not substitute for the "input" studies of politics that focus on structure and process; it seeks rather to supplement them.

Our concern is with the relationship between different types of political arrangements to which societies are subjected and the apparent consequences to these societies—which may be reasonably attributed to the political arrangements—in *several* significant areas.

We think that one of the most important queries for political analysis to answer is an inevitable "So what?" Granted that, in some countries, there are several political parties and in others only one; that some politicians invoke one set of slogans or ideals rather than another; that different names and even different organs are used for political purposes in different places, does all this really make any practical difference? Are political scientists perhaps simply fussy antiquarians with a penchant for cataloging trivia? Is the political world really something of a game in which a person must actually acquire a taste for the esoteric pastime before he can really appreciate the laboriously established difference between political system X and political system Y? Does this difference have any tangible meaning in his ordinary, everyday pursuits? Or is it no more than mere popular prejudice, a scholarly quibble, or a politician's argument from patent self-interest?

Unless we can demonstrate that the choice among X, Y, and Z has significant consequences of *some* sort, we shall always have great difficulty in justifying to intelligent and well-meaning people, who are *not* especially politically oriented, why a study of differing party systems, for example, is any more worthwhile than one of different colors among butterflies.

On the other hand, if we focus on the nature of the various kinds of results produced by different political regimes—economic, social, cultural, and so forth—we not only can but must revert to the input side of political life. Granted that, under comparable conditions, political system X produces different outputs or value-satisfactions than system Y, how can we *explain* this difference? Obviously we cannot do so without recourse to the inputs, to the nature of the political power, its organization, distribution, orientation, and the like.

This brings us to the problem of the difficulties encountered by a study such as this and the study of comparative politics generally. To make hopefully useful and illuminating comparisons, we first need definitions on the input side of the political systems. How can we compare the social consequences of fascism and democracy, unless we can posit what political characteristics make up fascism and democracy? If we knew the answers to these questions then presumably we could historically examine the performance of all regimes satisfying the specifications of our definitions and—discounting all factors that would make it other than a comparison hedged by an "all other things being equal" proviso—arrive at some conclusions as to system performance differences.

Alas, there are formidable difficulties in our path. We can only, in effect, move toward some approximations in both directions: the definitions of systems and the correlation of system consequences. We can still do more in identifying important problems and in suggesting some general tendencies relative to them than in providing precise answers.

The reasons for the difficulties are threefold: the empirical complexity of the "real world," which one cannot simplify and which is obstreperously and notoriously resistant to generalizations; the inadequacy and ambiguity of the analytical concepts of political study; and, last but not least, the problem of adequate data. These are all interrelated.

One of the basic problems of comparative inquiry is how to compensate, or at least strike a balance, between those phenomena that are general and those that are unique to any particular "country," "nation," "government," "institution" and other relatively complex multipart entities we wish to compare with others. There is always the likelihood that certain phenomena cannot be reduced to satisfactory common denominators. All nations are at least substantially different in such attributes as culture, language, religion, history, geopolitical setting, natural resources, level of technological-economic development, and in many other areas. Ultimately, of course, the argument can be made that not even two *persons* within one culture and one family are ever sufficiently alike so that characterizations applicable to one can be extended to the other without serious modification.

This problem has existed in biology and medicine where significant individual variations among organisms are well known and often require modifications in prediction or treatment; in the area of language and communication there are in fact many idiomatic expressions of one culture that cannot be precisely translated into the language of another culture; in economics the difficulties are illustrated by the problem of comparing popular standards of living among different societies. Obviously what constitutes "middle-class consumption" in the vicinity of Bombay or Moscow or in tropical Africa is not quite the same as in Des Moines or Paris. Different products, different services, and different values are involved in each of these settings.

In political terms, an extreme position emphasizes contextual differences to a point where comparative analysis becomes not a search for common denominators among polities, but rather an exercise in describing unique system A side by side with unique system B and unique system C and so on. The opposite tendency, which sees contextual differences as essentially trivial, is liable to yield a flood of conversion-term comparisons, none of which is informed by sufficient realism (or knowledge) of particular situations, places, and peoples to be of any practical value. This basic problem of comparing phenomena that undeniably contain unique features and that nevertheless also possess important common aspects is one that cannot be settled in an *a priori* fashion. There is no general way of avoiding the discount of the particular and the unique on the common and universal formulae in social inquiry. It must be faced in each comparison often with results that cannot but remain uncertain.

Another crucial problem is that of causality. Implicit to an inquiry such as this is the premise that we can find out whether the adoption of, let us say, fascism is likely to cause retrenchment in the educational outlays by the State, for example, while the adoption of communism will produce the opposite effect. In fact, as David Hume argued in the eighteenth century, all that we can observe with respect to such matters is a correlation: one set of policies has been generally associated with one set of events and another set of policies with different events. *Causality* is inferred by the observer who, in a common-sense fashion is likely to disregard many potentially important factors that in fact may contradict his conclusions. If policy A was correlated with results X, can we be sure that it was not some extraneous cause, other than policy A, that produced X? How can we be sure that in the absence of policy A any other policy, or at least *one* other policy, would not have produced the same results? How can we be sure that a particular "result" that we attribute, say, to an item of agricultural legislation was not, in fact, produced by drought? Obviously many phenomena that have or could have political causes might also have nonpolitical ones. The rate of agricultural output, for example, could be the resultant of factors that easily range all the way from an earthquake—climatic and cultural change—to the political decrees of the rulers.

The difficulties of causality are further compounded by those of "uniqueness." If a political system has apparently produced a set of social results in country X, can we be sure that it would have remotely equivalent consequences in another country very different in at least several significant respects, or even in one? There has been much speculation, for instance, on how the institutions of communism might have developed if they had been introduced first in Germany and then in Russia. Of course, to this interesting question we shall never have an answer because of a certain, already given, irrevocable, and unique sequence of past events.

It is problems of this sort that, even with the most meticulous methods, enable us to do no more than develop approximate, rough generalizations and causal hypotheses.

Let us consider also the further difficulty of adequately describing the structures and processes of a political system. Presumably we need to do this to be able to compare input models with their particular outputs. The task is analogous in complexity to investigating a large and varied landscape.

To begin with, we could study political phenomena by focusing on the number and identity of rulers vis-à-vis the bulk of the population. This could give us a reading on the ancient classical scale between autocracy and democracy. However, the very attempt to find out "who rules" always involves the problem of distinguishing between the "real" and the "apparent" rulers. It goes to the root of the question of what political power really is; and the modern, sociological understanding of power from Karl Marx to C. Wright Mills and Robert Dahl increases the complexity of discovering the true *identity* of the ruling few. Are business managers, and union leaders, and ecclesiastics among the rulers? Or is the circle confined merely to formal political officeholders?

Assuming success in some degree at least on this question, we also need to understand something of the *orientation*, or perhaps even several clashing orientations, within the identified "power elite." We would need to know of the qualitative characteristics of its rule—corresponding illustratively to the ancient theorists' distinction between "tyranny" and "kingship" on the one hand and "mobocracy" as opposed to democracy on the other. We would thus introduce ideological factors to give us an idea of the purposes and goals to which power was ostensibly being used.

We could then focus on *institutions* or, in the modern sociological sense, on certain persistent patterns of behavior and the interaction of stable role structures. Thus, the knowledge of who rules, and to what purposes, could be supplemented with the knowledge of how it is apparently done.

We might also give our attention to the study of the various *attributes* of the participants in the system. We could investigate whom and what they represent—what ethnic or social strata, economic classes, and/or personality types they subsume. This might explain various biases and tendencies implicit in the system that may or may not be overtly articulated.

We could also study the more general *background* or the *context* of decision making: the environmental factors—domestic and international, social and natural—that affect the operations of the political system. These could be explored through studies that range from public opinion surveys and what historians might term "national character" studies to inquiries into the international legal obligations of a state and even to business-management surveys.

Finally, we could employ a developmental-historical approach trying to find out how, and by what stages, the whole political system has come into being. From this vantage point, we could hopefully deduce some functional requisites for both rulers and rules within the context of the particular community.

By multiplying the avenues of approach, we generally add to our total grasp of a particular political system. And although not all approaches may be equally useful in all contexts, reliance on one or a few is invariably bound to be misleading. In this study, for example, we include Great Britain among the models of democracy for purposes of comparison with other, nondemocratic systems. From the input point of view, and in common-sense terms, we do so because Britain has demonstrated over a long period of time a political system in which (1) government has significantly depended on public opinion —for its very existence and for its policies—and (2) individuals and groups not identified with the particular set of power holders, or government leaders of the moment, have been remarkably free to articulate their opposition, simultaneously enjoying the security of life and limb. These attributes might be termed, for the sake of convenience, *majority rule* and *individual rights*. One could readily appreciate that Britain stands in sharp contrast to many other nations with respect to such attributes, both currently and historically. Yet, one could also readily make comparisons in *some* categories to show ostensibly greater "democratism" and "libertarianism" precisely in those polities where in reality these have always been much less.

When the Soviet Union allowed 18-year-old men and women to vote in 1918 it was being more democratic than Britain in respect to sex (until 1928) and age (until 1968). If we considered the observable procedures of electing national leaders, we could well conclude that Britain is occasionally at least a highly autocratic state. Its Conservative Prime Minister may on retirement tell the Queen which of his colleagues ought to succeed him as Prime Minister, whereupon that man is invested with power and his party in Parliament dutifully regards him as its leader. Such, after all, was the ascension of Sir Anthony Eden and of Lord Home. Moreover, once installed as the leader of the British Conservatives, the man chosen need only regard his party's resolutions as gratuitous advice. His own pronouncements are officially statements of policy. In contrast, the leader of the Soviet Communist party is invariably elected to his post by the party's Central Committee, itself elected by the representatives of the rank and file periodically assembled in a national party congress. The party resolutions are said to be, by statute, unconditionally binding on him. Outwardly, what could be more democratic in the one case and more autocratic in the other?

A scrupulous behavioral analysis focused on the USSR would show a large body of men casting ballots or perhaps raising their hands to elevate, let us say, comrade Stalin, to the Secretaryship of the party. In Britain, it would show the Prime Minister and the Queen engaged in various conferences with party leaders but would show no voting by anybody until the decision had been made, ostensibly by the Queen alone. Even though these contrasts are quite real, so far as they go, they are also quite misleading because of what they leave out in each case.

Similar misinterpretations may arise when we compare one-party systems with multiparty systems. Ostensibly, one connotes autocratic rule, for the citizen does not or cannot choose but one party; the other obviously connotes some choice. Actually, during various periods of American history, for example, there have been one-party states in which there existed considerable internal pluralism, represented by many warring factions, and open disputes. There have also been multiparty systems—as under Soviet auspices in Eastern Europe—where if a member of *any* of these publicly had said: "I don't think comrade Stalin is right in everything he says," it would have been enough to get him jailed or worse.

The investigator of political life might be baffled by the structural contrast between the Indian Parliament during the years of Nehru's regime and the Italian Parliament in the early years of Mussolini's rule. Ostensibly, the former was virtually dominated by one party, whereas the latter, in 1924, for example, was to all appearances a multiparty body. Yet, the Indian Parliament has been effectively critical of the regime and in this sense "functional," whereas the Italian was being terrorized and all but destroyed by Mussolini.

Occasionally, the attempt to understand politics through an ideological perspective can be similarly misleading. Anyone who might try to understand French imperial policies between 1870 and 1939 through the ideological pronouncements of the leaders of the Third Republic would be handicapped, among other things, by the disparity in outlook between these men and the actual implementors of France's policy overseas in colonial administration and the armed forces. In fact, in any political system where the bureaucracy is large and not particularly responsive to the nominal rulers of the State, or where great gaps exist between widely shared societal notions about politics and those of the nominal rulers, such an attempt would be seriously handicapped. The policies of the Communist regime in Russia in the immediate aftermath of 1917 could have been accounted for *least* successfully by focusing on the attributes of social class among the rulers, who were mostly of middle-class origins. Examples of similarly misleading or insufficient evaluative criteria in every possible category could be multiplied indefinitely.

How do we explain these analytical ambiguities? First, the numerous components of any political system are multifunctional; that is, often the same tasks are performed by different components of the system and vice versa. No single process or structure, or aspect of structure, can always be taken to have the same meaning as between one political system and another. Moreover, there is comparable fluctuation, from time to time, and place to place, *within* political systems as well.

As Gabriel Almond expressed this:

> If we examine the literature of political science in the past forty or fifty years, we find that one of its great accomplishments has been the demonstration of the multifunctionalism of modern political institutions. Thus it has shown that the courts not only adjudicate but also legislate; that the bureaucracy is one of the most important sources of legislation; that legislative bodies affect both administration and adjudication; that pressure groups initiate legislation and participate

in administration; and that the media of communication represent interests and sometimes initiate legislation.[1]

Projected spatially and chronologically, this kind of fluctation in the relationship of structure to function makes for comparative uncertainties. In a particular period the courts may be the most important legislative organs in system A but not in system B. At another time the significance of a parliament as a legislative body may be wholly preempted by the executive and the bureaucracy whereas at other times it may not, and so on *ad infinitum*.

Any one criterion of a "political system" can be readily deceptive. A large number of interrelated criteria are more likely to be adequately descriptive. But ambiguity and uncertainty attach to all the descriptive schemes of politics, and to all the interrelationships among "things political." The subject of politics, like the subject of justice, is inherently a diffuse, multifaceted human concern. Those who aspire to excessive rigor of definition within it risk irrelevance. It is precisely because of this ambiguity of political terminology that we need to supplement our knowledge of the *input* side of politics, of how the system *works*—ostensibly—with evidence of what it actually *does*. The latter is, in part, an empirical verification of the former.

If our descriptive indices of a system show a "democratic polity," are they matched by performance characteristics comparable to other systems with analogous indices? If, discounting extraneous and environmental differences, they do not match, we have cause to inquire into the "slippages" between appearance and reality that exist within it. Perhaps the regime's control of the bureaucracy is not what it appears to be and for this reason perfectly democratic elections and fair representation in a legislature are largely irrelevant. Perhaps what we *see* happening at a political convention or at a party conference is not at all what really counts. Perhaps the several specified aspects of overt process are all subordinate to some that are not. The recourse to an analysis of system outputs, the operational profile, can help us avoid the pitfalls of a crude nominalism. What, for example, is the meaning of the proposition that country X and country Y are both Communist countries, or that country Z was Communist in 1948 and continues to be Communist in 1970?

To what extent do such comparisons involve the manipulation of equivalent *names* rather than of equivalent *contents* (of conduct)? Are fascism and communism the same thing? Is the regime of country X more like a Fascist or a Communist regime? How can we distill evidence of a genuine intention from mere pretense in political propa-

[1] Gabriel A. Almond and James S. Coleman (eds.), *The Politics of the Developing Areas* (Princeton, N.J.: Princeton University Press, 1960), pp. 17–18.

ganda? In what ways does a regime combine new original characteristics vis-à-vis its other contemporary prototypes? Was Peron's Argentina Fascist? Are Japan and Mexico democratic? How soon, if in fact, did Italy become a democracy after 1943 or Germany after 1945? All these questions require a substantial exploration of regime performance.

On the other hand, let us further consider the nature of the results that our performance or output analysis yields. Let us for a moment optimistically assume that all the facts are at our disposal. As an example, let us say that we can incontrovertibly establish, discounting all environmental differences, the higher propensity of democratic political systems to spend material resources on social welfare projects than is the case with, say, traditional autocracies. What we have discovered is not merely "a fact" but above all a *random value*, a relationship whose worth and significance depend in the last analysis on the perceptions of the beholder.

Some individuals or groups might consider the empirical relationship to be good, others to be bad. Some may consider it one of the desirable "ends" that political activity serves, or perhaps even *the* end; others may look on it as but a means to still other ends or ultimate values. Given a cluster of such value-laden relationships, some observers may regard this particular value-relationship as subordinate to several others.

The relationship is also still comparable to a *random value* in another sense: in terms of its impact on the given political system as a whole. Because we do not really know in an objective, empirical, and universal sense what makes a "good" or a "virtuous" society, we must regard our discoveries with prudence and caution. There are, to be sure, significant differences between different types of regimes in the ways in which they appropriate, regulate, and distribute social resources. But such differences do not necessarily account for the "viability" of these regimes; they do not amount either to universal "good" or universal "evil," nor to any universal "success" or, in opposite cases, "failure." The fortunes of states, good and bad, are all likely to be extremely variable and often are quite unrelated to the values bestowed on the citizenry by their particular governments. Values expressed through sundry institutional arrangements, decrees, exactions, or allocations—however "reasonable" and widely accepted at any given time—are always subject to erosion and failure. Suitable and desirable under some circumstances, they may not continue to seem so even to the same people under changing circumstances. Different values may replace them and the hierarchies of values may change within the system. Institutional arrangements may occasionally become obsolescent in the political process, and the assets of yesterday, like the trappings of monarchy, sometimes appear to be the liabilities of today. Finally, external circumstances, natural and social, can overwhelm even those polities ideally best adapted to the self-perceived needs of the citizenry.

Even within these limits, our inquiry is handicapped by a dearth of data. Obtaining even the most rudimentary empirical information on the performance of past and present political systems is not yet a simple matter. Not all states contribute information to the various United Nations surveys. Not all states collect and report data in the same uniform and therefore genuinely comparable fashion. Some data are rather more suspect than others. Many crucial aspects of "government impact on society" are not yet widely surveyed at all. Some do not readily lend themselves to quantitative appraisal and comparison.

Mindful of all these problems, we have attempted to demonstrate that different political systems tend to distribute social resources in different ways. They disseminate alternative types and degrees of gratification to different people—all other things being equal. These gratifications or values may be looked on as system outputs. Although theoretically, any and all political-system attributes may well be translated into different outputs, we have focused on one basic distinction, that between democracy and autocracy, with a number of subtypes in the latter category.

As one moves on a continuum of popular participation in a political system from "very little" to "very much," one discerns a pattern of change in various other characteristics of that system. Striking increases and decreases in mass political participation have their distributive consequences affecting people's rights in the market place, treatment by the bureaucracy, openness of the educational system, the nature of financial burdens imposed, and many others.

To be sure, in every area of policy we find significant variations from country to country regardless of political similarities. But we also find significant parallels of performance. These are shared by kindred political systems *even* when these exist in countries separated by wide material, economic, and cultural differences.

Democratic polities can be defined in terms of the effective diffusion and openness of popular participation in politics. A reasonable initial set of functional criteria for these polities is provided by the election-oriented scheme developed by Robert A. Dahl in his *Preface to Democratic Theory.*

A high degree of democracy exists where the percentage of participants is high and the conditions of participation are equal and open to all. In every situation the two categories must be in some measure mixed and it is impossible to entirely substitute and discount one by the other. They must be combined. The contrast between the USSR and Switzerland, for example, is one where democratic requirements are met in the first category more fully in the USSR (women vote and the age of franchise begins at 18) than in Switzerland. But the *conditions* of participation are so narrowly circumscribed in the USSR—through one political party and one official doctrine—as to render Switzerland's more limited franchise far more meaningful.

In thus discussing democracy, we address ourselves to what Dahl calls both its Madisonian (libertarian) and its populist (egalitarian) aspects.

The combined construct of these two aspects of democracy, as presented by Dahl in his model of the so-called polyarchy, is relevant both to the discussion of this chapter and to what follows. The construct relies on empirically *observable*, although not always quantifiable, characteristics of democracy.

We thus eschew—reluctantly but necessarily—purely numerical criteria of political systems such as those employed, for example, by Harvey Brazer in *City Expenditures in the United States* (New York: National Bureau of Economic Research, 1959). Without employing indices that are not reducible to numbers we cannot in fact tell, for example, if an ostensibly multiparty system is really more democratic than a one-party system. Is the municipal administration of Warsaw, Poland, under a three-party system more pluralistic than that of, say, Atlanta, Georgia, under one? Analogously, innovative autocracies cannot be distinguished from status-quo autocracies without recourse to non-numerical aspects.

The following is a literal restatement of Dahl's model:

A. *The definitional characteristics of polyarchy*

Polyarchy is defined loosely as a political system in which the following conditions exist to a relatively high degree:

During the voting period:

1. Every member of the organization performs the acts we assume to constitute an expression of preference among the scheduled alternatives, e.g. voting.

2. In tabulating these expressions (votes), the weight assigned to the choice of each individual is identical.

3. The alternative with the greatest number of votes is declared the winning choice.

During the prevoting period:

4. Any member who perceives a set of alternatives, at least one of which he regards as preferable to any of the alternatives presently scheduled, can insert his preferred alternative(s) among those scheduled for voting.

5. All individuals possess identical information about the alternatives.

During the postvoting period:

6. Alternatives (leaders or policies) with the greatest number of votes displace any alternatives (leaders or policies) with fewer votes.

7. The orders of elected officials are executed.

During the interelection stage:

8.1. Either all interelection decisions are subordinate or executory to those arrived at during the election stage, i.e., elections are in a sense controlling.

8.2. Or new decisions during the interelection period are governed by the preceding seven conditions, operating, however, under rather different institutional circumstances.

8.3. Or both.[2]

No political system in the history of mankind has ever completely fulfilled the conditions Dahl specifies. What is of practical significance is the degree to which these conditions actually have or have not been fulfilled in particular cases. According to Dahl, the effectiveness of all the eight norms is dependent on the degree of consensus, or agreement, about them, among the members of the political system. In turn, this consensus is furthered by "total social training in all the norms"[3] in a cyclically reinforcing fashion: Consensus allows members to be trained in norms that are widely regarded as "acceptable" or "valuable," and the training reinforces the tendency to regard them as valuable.

In terms of most, or even all, of the Dahl criteria, the United States as a whole has been a democracy for many decades. This conclusion would emerge, we believe, from a comparison of its participatory performance in relation to that of other national states. On the basis of the exclusion of a large part of their population from participatory rights, the political systems of states such as Mississippi, Georgia, or Alabama have been less democratic than the United States as a whole and much less so than certain other states within the Union. And in general we do expect that output differences between subsystems follow the pattern of differences among systems.[4] The virtually total

[2] (Chicago: University of Chicago Press, 1966), p. 84.

[3] *Ibid.*, p. 76.

[4] The conclusion of Thomas R. Dye in *Politics, Economics, and the Public: Policy Outcomes in the American States* (Chicago: Rand McNally, 1966), that "economic development variables are more influential than political-system characteristics in shaping public policy in the states" (p. 296) is marred by inattention to the one major problem where such differences in political characteristics among the states have been most pronounced: on the racial issue. Beyond this, however, Dye's conclusion accords with the fact that, given a common federal system, pluralistic state politics, and relatively narrow, often imperceptible, ideological differences between American major parties, economic variables are and indeed ought to be "governing" in many policy differentials.

exclusion of 20 to 60 per cent of the population from political "inputs" made some American states closer to repressive traditional oligarchies than to democracies for most of the nineteenth century, and part of the twentieth. Historically, however, the black man's quest for freedom and equality has been significantly aided by the growth of a much more inclusive, open, and procedurally sensitive democratic federal system at the center of national power.

Because valid distributive inferences can probably be made only from the experience of regimes reasonably well entrenched in their respective environments, we confine our "democratic prototypes" or "optimally effective democracies" to those regimes that have maintained their set of interrelated democratic characteristics since before the conclusion of World War II. (See Table 1.)

Table 1
The "Established" Democracies

Australia
Canada
Great Britain
Ireland
New Zealand
Sweden
Switzerland
United States
Uruguay

These may be regarded as the best established of current democracies, but others with shorter continuous histories are referred to here also from time to time. With some exceptions our discussion refers to regimes of the nineteenth and twentieth centuries.

Our general functional or input definition of autocracy is, in one sense, simply the obverse of Dahl's democratic formula. Among the relatively stable types of systems examined are several subvariants of autocracy. These are based first of all on the distinction between innovative-mobilizational and traditional or status quo autocracies.[5] The innovational autocracies include the Fascist Italian and German Nazi regimes on the Right; Communist Russian, East European, Asian, and Cuban regimes on the Left; "mixed" or populist regimes—that is,

[5] See Karl W. Deutsch, "Social Mobilization and Political Development," *American Political Science Review*, Vol. LV, No. 3 (September 1961), pp. 493–514, and Robert C. Tucker, "Towards a Comparative Politics of Movement Regimes," *American Political Science Review*, Vol. LV, No. 2 (June 1961), pp. 281–289.

ones between the innovational extremes such as Nasser's UAR and, recently, Peron's Argentina. Traditional regimes include Spain, Portugal, Saudi Arabia, monarchical Yemen, Venezuela under Perez Jimenez, Duvalier's Haiti, prerevolutionary Russia, and Imperial Germany.

Traditional autocracies are regimes that continue a long-established inherited social order; they de-emphasize popular participation and involvement in political affairs and eschew systematic, rigorous, proselytizing political ideologies. They are oriented to the maintenance of a traditional structure of power and generally do not tamper with age-old customs, beliefs, and attitudes.

Innovative-mobilizational regimes seek to change the inherited social order, popular values, traditional institutions, and the distribution of resources and gratifications in society. They organize and exhort the masses to participate in politics and seek to inculcate them with a new, more or less unified or systematic world outlook. They attempt to develop new bases of political power for themselves—with new identifications, new organizations, and new methods. Within this category the Right regimes, such as the Nazi and Fascist, carry out most of these objectives without simultaneously destroying the socioeconomic elites of *status quo ante*—that is, without massively redistributing economic resources from the old elites to the nonelites. In contrast, the Left regimes are outwardly committed to destroy the perquisites of all *status quo ante* socioeconomic elites and to redistribute economic resources to the heretofore nonelites. Mixed or populist regimes generally seek to destroy some but not all of the inherited elites in the political system with some redistributive effects for the have-nots—less than the Left but more than the Right. Examples of these currently include Nasser's UAR, and in relatively recent history Peron's Argentina, and Sukarno's Indonesia.

The several differing orientations of the autocratic systems are compared with the several common-denominator orientations that characterize the well-established democracies.

Autocracy—the rule of one or a few—includes a virtual infinitude of political orientations. One could multiply our list here and speak of modernizing autocracies, bureaucratic and charismatic autocracies, secular or clericalist ones, and so on *ad infinitum*. But, apart from all these important qualitative variations, all these regimes possess certain input characteristics that distinguish them from the democracies. And, in turn, these characteristics affect the nature of possible policy outputs—that is, the values or gratifications produced and distributed by the system.

The democratic polity is one in which a wide range of a society's interests are afforded access to the input mechanisms of power, to what David Easton might call the value-allocating structures. In an optimum, ideal democracy presumably anyone, with any claim, would have a chance to express his views and have them count in the decision as much as those of anyone else. To the extent that this ideal is even *approached* by some systems, the allocation of values through politics reflects the configuration of many influential publics. Over long periods of time, and over a large number of issues, that configuration is likely to be both widely inclusive and reasonably stable. Issues such as agricultural subsidies, social welfare, civil rights, foreign trade, the equity of taxation, the regulation of labor, and the like, all attract the attention of many different publics.

The attitudes and demands of these publics become generally known and, subject to drastic changes in the whole social environment such as occur in the wake of wars, invasions, physical cataclysms, major depressions, and the like, they tend to be fairly well fixed and stable. Thus, the decision-making mechanisms of a democracy tend to a certain *inelasticity*. Given a pattern of group involvement, the particular policy positions of groups, and the particular distribution of influence or impact among them, the possibilities for policy making fall within a relatively narrow range of more or less.

Unless the participant publics change their views, the opportunity for maneuver in making policy can be obtained by either (1) shedding some publics, (2) bringing in new participant publics, or (3) manipulating the relative influence or impact of the existent participant publics. Actually, the further we move on a continuum of democratic participation toward an "ideally democratic" polity, the more difficult such manipulation becomes. Ultimately, everyone is equally involved in everything, and the influence of each component public is equal to every other. Under such ideal or "optimally democratic" circumstances, the policy choices narrow. In some circumstances, policy outcomes simply register a stalemate, if the participants disagree and if they numerically neutralize one another. Historically, this may be illustrated in the experience of the French III and IV Republics. In any case, the nature of an acceptable compromise or a common-denominator policy emerges in a relatively narrow and fixed form. "All" or "nothing" outcomes are practically impossible. One can exhort and negotiate, but one can neither add to nor subtract from the sum of social interests represented in the polity, nor manipulate their relative weights.

Outward shifts in governmental power, from ostensible control by one party to another, or from one ideological tendency to another, cannot produce really drastic shifts in policy outputs. The shifts taking place among elected officials, parliamentarians, bureaucrats, and the like, represent only a *part* of the decision-making picture in the democracy. Elections may supplement, but they do not displace, other means of representation and impact in the system—those generally associated with the time-honored principle of the right of petition.

By the very nature of the openness of a democracy, the transition from, say, a conservative-clericalist to a Communist-led government *within* the democratic framework (as might conceivably happen one day in Italy) could not produce the really drastic shift in policy outcomes realizable within the framework of a dictatorship by either side.

To be sure, group influence and group politics are endemic to *all* types of regimes. But autocracies tend to "discount" heavily the opportunities for participation, for all the input activities, to those regarded as "enemies of the rulers." The known fact of opposition or disloyalty or any officially declared "undesirability" can be enough to deprive individuals or groups of certain elementary rights—to organize, assemble, express views, use public media of information, investigate, travel, maintain property or employment, or indeed enjoy the equal protection of the laws. Thus, pressure-group activity within the framework of an autocracy is generally likely to be lopsided, much more free and open to those who are clearly identified with the "ins" than to those clearly identified with the "outs." It is, therefore, more *difficult* for those not so closely identified with the official political power holders to exert impact on them. But, over and beyond this greater handicapping of opposition, an autocracy so inhibits political recourse against rulers—by anyone for any reason—that it greatly increases the *costs* and *risks* of opposition in virtually all situations, whether that opposition emanates from within or without the privileged strata.

In a democracy the organization of a strike or a demonstration will generally entail no adverse legal consequences for the participants. In a dictatorship, however, it may well mean the risk of instant death and the cost of far-flung reprisals not only against the participants, but against their families, friends, and associates. Thus, dissent, opposition, or even doubt or mild disapproval can be relatively easily and safely asserted in democratic polities; yet such assertions of open disapproval often require no less than the resolve of martyrs in the dictatorships.

If, thus, autocracies can raise the threshhold of costs and risks for any that would oppose them, they also increase the range of policy choices for themselves. The opportunities for following a zigzag course are multiplied. The ultimate limit (however inconclusive) of "what the people will stand" in a democracy can be tested in periodic elections that one's opponents can win without risking life, limb, or liberty in the process. The ultimate test in an autocracy is revolution, which—although always *possible*—is usually far too risky, costly, and so unlikely to succeed that it is a highly inefficient remedy for the rulers' "excesses" or "abuses."[6] Thus, the autocrat can often pursue a range of policies that alternately lag well behind what the people might want—if indeed there were means of openly ascertaining this—or in fact move much ahead and beyond the attitudes of his contemporaries, as historically Germany's Bismarck, Russia's Peter the Great, and Austria's Joseph II did in various policy areas. In our view here, had the United States been an autocracy in the 1920s, the New Deal might have *preceded* the Depression; or, conceivably, it might have *neither* preceded it, as an anticipation of an influential few, *nor* followed it, as a response to the articulated needs of the many. Given a generally democratic political system, and the specific character of the political public in the United States in the 1920s, the New Deal could only have *followed* in the wake of the Depression and, in a sense, it *had* to follow it.

The prevailing attitudes of "economic individualism" would have made widespread State intervention untenable for politicians dependent on the American electorate—before the stock market crash of 1929. Afterward, public clamor for government-organized and government-financed rescue from bankruptcy and unemployment would have made *inaction* politically suicidal.

Let us hasten to make clear that the greater elasticity of autocratic policy options does not of itself assure either "better" or "worse" outputs. The merit and the effectiveness of a measure always involve value judgments on the one hand and specific empirical circumstances on the other.

All political systems are subject to pressures from their social and physical environments, international and domestic. Doing what the people want may sometimes bring great success or it may bring utter ruin, depending partly on one's outlook (evaluation of what is good) and partly on the circumstances. When Stanley Baldwin, British Prime Minister in the 1930s, confessed that he did not press for rearmament against Hitler because such a policy would have been unpopular with the voters, most Britons in the 1940s looked back on his "responsiveness to public opinion" as shortsighted and disastrous in its consequences.

The relationships that differentiate democratic and authoritarian policy making do not reflect better or worse policies but rather a

[6] See R. L. Curry and L. L. Wade, *A Theory of Political Exchange* (Englewood Cliffs, N.J.: Prentice-Hall, 1968), for an application of economic cost theory to political decisions. The authors describe a revolutionary situation as one in which participants "... do not accept the existing distribution of values and costs ... [when] they [thus] feel that they have little to lose but possibly much to gain [through revolution]." Pp. 48–9.

narrower range of options among the former and a broader range among the latter.

The political process of an autocracy involves narrowing down the sensitivity of the system (or "distributive mechanism") to direct group influences. A relatively small coterie of bureaucratic cliques and interest groups frequently may engage in rivalry with one another, at close quarters, for the favor of *THE* nominal autocrat or decision maker. Such "infighting" generally receives little or no publicity and preserves an image of monolithic unity for the regime so far as the bulk of the people and the world at large are concerned.

Even though *direct* access to government may be completely denied to many interests in a society, the autocratic political system still remains *indirectly* sensitive to its total environment. It can be impacted by foreign intervention, by economic and technological pressures in the world market, by production failures at home, and ultimately, of course, even by the revolt or apathy of its populace. Thus, the need to appease fewer interests in making decisions does not really obviate the need to face up to their consequences. Concessions to demands, anticipated by prudent rulers even if they are not openly articulated within the system, may be necessary to the system's survival. What autocracy can achieve is to raise the cost of opposition for its foes and assure itself a greater range of initial policy options—all ultimately subject to failure.

What we have set out here is admittedly a model based on ideal types—we compare a very "inclusive" democracy with a very "exclusive" autocracy. It is also a *partial* model because there are still other differences between these types of regimes that we do not explore here. In actual experience, most autocracies involve some competitive, pluralistic sharing of power among various groups—for example, bureaucrats and business leaders. Most democracies exclude at least some groups of population from participation on equal terms with all other—whether formally, as by restricting suffrage to those over 21, or informally by the fact that resources for the exercise of influence are not equally shared between the poor and the rich.

The attention and the resources of all *potential* participants are never, in fact, equally focused on all issues that democratic governments consider, as Gabriel Almond has shown in his *The American People and Foreign Policy* (1950). That certain areas of American domestic public policy have been heavily dominated by special interests has been a long-time theme of political scientists, notably E. E. Schattschneider in *The Semi-Sovereign People* (1960) and more recently, Theodore J. Lowi in *The End of Liberalism* (1969).[7]

[7]Peter Bachrach, in *The Theory of Democratic Elitism* (Boston: Little, Brown, 1967),

But if the previously discussed input differences are, nevertheless, even approximated in real political systems, we can expect that—holding economic and cultural differences constant—the greatest divergences and the steepest oscillations in outputs will be found among the autocracies. In fact, this can be empirically demonstrated, both currently and historically, in many policy areas. The allocation of certain resources or gratifications for different purposes and to different segments of the "people" has been more one-sidedly skewed under autocratic than under democratic systems.[8]

Where resource allocations cannot be easily quantified, however, this relationship can be at best suspected and not demonstrated. In some cases, there are overriding cultural, economic, and other non-political output differences among systems; because of these, the allocation of some resources between the most "niggardly" and the most "generous" democracy may continue to differ more sharply than between two comparable autocracies. The low consumption of pork in Israel and of beef in India, because of religious reasons, as compared with the United States, for example, is illustrative. To the extent, however, that there is, as Lucian Pye argues, a trend toward a homogenous world culture, output disparities among the democracies can be expected to continually narrow down. The publics increasingly demand the same things from their political systems.

It is the theme of this work that politics—that is, the character of a regime or a system of rule—does indeed shape various aspects of society, some of them ostensibly far removed from "politics." For our purposes here the subjects (or "aspects of society") singled out for correlation with different types of regimes include (1) political participation; (2) group life, communication, and organization; (3) taxation and budgeting; (4) aspects of economic policy; (5) education and culture; (6) social welfare; (7) social change and mobility; (8) bureaucracy and public service; and (9) justice and police power.

In each of these areas it can be shown that significant political

---

notes that in American politics (1) most people actually do not participate in organized interest groups and that (2) among such groups there is frequently no competitive interaction. See p. 37. Bachrach and various other writers would like to extend competitive participation for the people-at-large to all sorts of decision making. They deplore elitism. The proposition that the American political system is not competitive enough or that it does not supply "the right values" is itself, in one sense, a value judgment of the sort to which we are all entitled. The implications of extending participation in any new policy areas, however, would be to reduce output variations, i.e. promote inelasticity within the given system.

[8] See a discussion of "distributive capability" in different political systems in Gabriel Almond and G. Bingham Powell, Jr., *Comparative Politics: A Developmental Approach* (Boston: Little, Brown, 1966), pp. 28, 198–99, 311.

differences among regimes correlate with significant differences in terms of comparative outputs or performance profiles of the different systems. It is suggested that among reasonably coherent and well-established political systems there are performance "traits" that are, in fact, substantially independent of their material environments. This is true in the sense that we could more readily gauge some specific allocations of resources in a given society if we knew that it was, for example, Communist than if we knew its Gross National Product (GNP), its level of urbanization, or any of its ethnic or geographic characteristics.

It is true that for many political entities the best appellation would be that of mixed or unstable systems reflecting—like modern Nigeria, Ghana, Brazil, or post-Peron Argentina—short-term oscillations between outward forms of democracy and authoritarianism and lacking in well-established, coherent political structures of any one tendency.

But an examination of clear-cut contrasts offers an analytical approximation to the conditions of a biologist's sterilized test tube and the physicist's vacuum chamber. It gives us some basic insights into fundamental relationships and some aids toward an understanding of more complex structures.

In conclusion, our study explores, in a necessarily tentative and generalized fashion, some of the major operational characteristics of divergent political systems apart from the specific, geographic-national and environmental contexts in which they may be employed. It formulates some hypotheses on the impact of such systems on social, economic, and cultural values. (See Diagram, page 22.)

These formulations should serve at least five distinct purposes. They may help to understand more fully the nature of political systems, along with—not in place of—more traditionally oriented inquiries. Secondly, they may contribute to making the problem of political choice among competing political systems more rational and meaningful. Thirdly, an understanding of the emerging or future pattern of politics itself may be furthered, insofar as we are more likely to know the benefits or handicaps to different groups of particular political systems: who may survive and who may disappear. Fourthly, in terms of the distributive profiles developed here, we may offer useful clues as to the actual operative characteristics of "mixed," "marginal" and "unstable" polities apart from mere "structure" and "profession." Finally, we may encourage more detailed and specialized typologies for all these purposes.

Democracies and Autocracies: A Model of Distributive Variations Between Systems.*

The distribution of resources
to particular policy areas in
relation to total resources possessed.

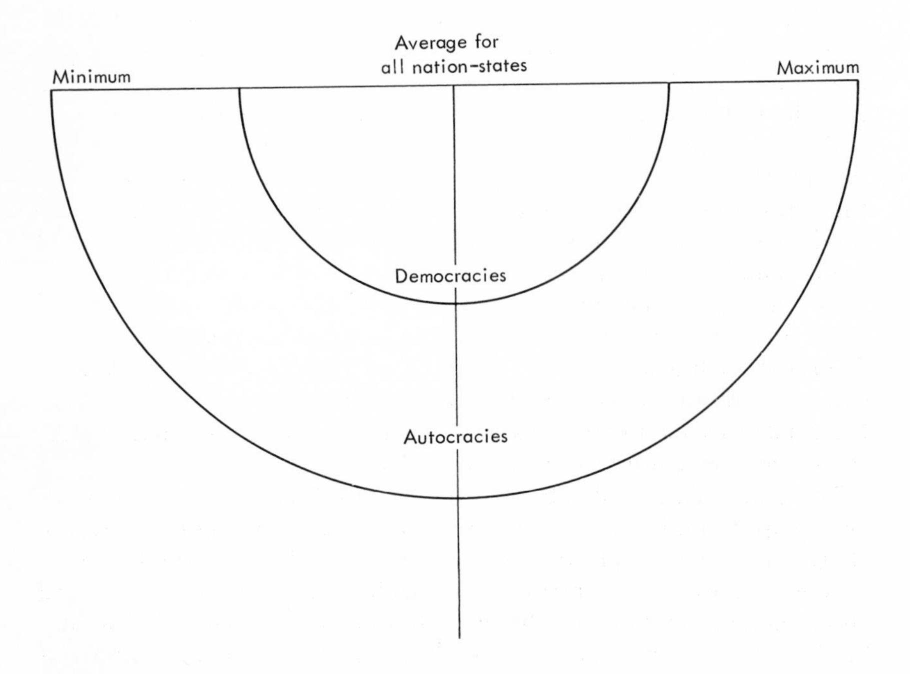

*This diagram is a model of capabilities which are not *always* exercised and observable in the empirical world. At any point in time in any given policy area, some democracies may be either more "spendthrift" or more "frugal" than some autocracies. On occasion, some types of regimes may not even be represented in the world community of states.

It should also be noted that oscillations in outputs are not necessarily indicative of the ultimate satisfactions or economies achieved through them. See A. J. Groth, "Structural Functionalism: Three Problems of Political Development," *Western Political Quarterly*, Vol. 23, No. 3, September 1970.

CHAPTER 2
POLITICAL PARTICIPATION

PERHAPS the most elementary value distribution a political system offers is through participation, which it makes possible, encourages, compels, or forbids. To be sure, political participation is an "input" aspect of government. It involves making claims, organizing action, and working out decisions. But it is also an "output."

As a value meted out, it can be appreciated as a means to an end, as an end in itself, or both. It may be regarded alternatively as "worthwhile" or "pernicious" either instrumentally (1) because of what its consequences are believed to be in terms of some social or individual ends or outputs, or substantively (2) because of its innate psychological attributes. Simply to be involved in it may alternatively confer joy and fulfillment on the individual, or perhaps anger, trauma, and revulsion, quite apart from the ends that the participation promotes or serves.

In terms of these values or "antivalues," as the case may be, what are the differences between democratic and authoritarian regimes?

In the actual experience of some modern nation-states, we find that the opportunity to participate in decisions shaping one's own life and those of one's fellows are reduced to nil for some people; the opportunities of certain others are so enhanced as to confer a standing, discretionary, life-and-death power upon them. This is the stupendous internal contrast posed by the totalitarian regimes of this century.

Essentially, this is the contrast in the participatory rights of a Stalin and a landlord in the Soviet political system, and of a Hitler and a Jew in the Nazi system. Although deep disparities in the participatory rights and *de facto* opportunities of people have characterized *all* political systems historically known to man, the totalitarian autocracy brings that disparity to its ultimate refinement. Here we have a special contrast. A generally defined group in the population—Jews or landlords—is officially consigned to extermination. As such, its members are not entitled even to those general legal protections that traditional autocracies frequently accorded slaves. They are made into *objects* of politics—precisely as if they could be classified with the inert, material objects in their environment—but they are not even given the protections that shelter domestic animals and beasts of burden from inhumane treatment.

The rights of these particular groups under totalitarianism were effectively reduced to the right to die at the discretion of the State. The *de facto* opportunity for participating in the life of society accorded to Jews under Nazi rule in the 1940s amounted to somewhat less than the "opportunity" of beasts of prey. The individual Jew could physically resist or attempt escape. But so far as the regime was concerned, he and all his coreligionists were marked for extinction in any case. The victims possessed no rights against the claims of the State-operated gas chambers. They did not have the right to *vote* on the decision of their lives; more than that, they did not even have a right to *complain*, let alone publicly *discuss, protest*, or *demonstrate* against the fate that was assigned to them by their political masters.

At the opposite pole of totalitarian participation stood the dictator. His power to command death and punishment for any man, at virtually any time, was an overriding fact of political life in the totalitarian regime. And it was not just a roundabout, indirect power that a democratic chief executive might exercise in committing his armed forces to a particular theater of war, for example. This was power to order instant execution, torture, or confinement of a particular person who was suspect or displeasing. And it was a power that, unlike that of a criminal, could be exercised with complete impunity. No court or official could openly seek to thwart it.

The men who served democratic chief executives during World War II knew that they might lose their jobs, and possibly ruin their careers, if they displeased Churchill and Roosevelt. The men who served Hitler and Stalin ran the more acute physical risk of execution. For them, displeasing the chief could bring instant death.

These enormous powers of the totalitarian leader were often exercised for him by his henchmen and lieutenants. The officers and men of such organizations as the Nazi Gestapo or the Soviet NKVD frequently destroyed lives very much on their own initiative. So long as the dictator did not object, or perhaps did not know about a particular situation, the power to decide who would live and who would die inhered in men like Himmler, Heydrich, Eichmann, Yezhov, or Beria. These henchmen, like all totalitarian officials, risked their lives if they incurred the leader's displeasure. But, so long as they continued to possess the dictator's confidence, other men literally trembled in their sight. No office within the gift of a democracy could bestow so sadistically satisfying an experience of total power.

If we look to the other extreme of totalitarian politics, we find that the powerlessness among groups marked for extinction was almost matched by other, ostensibly more privileged, strata. No individual living under a totalitarian regime could claim the right of public protest or demonstration against the State or the State's policies; even the private voicing of complaints to officials could bring death, or imprisonment, against the "offender." It constituted evidence of treasonable disloyalty. Obedience and subordination to orders from above were regarded as mandatory for everyone. To the extent that the ethnic German, unlike the Jew—or the Soviet worker, unlike the landlord—was expected to participate in organized activities, he was expected to obey the leaders. The Nazis called it the *Fuehrerprinzip.*

By and large, the totalitarian political system was so pervasive of the society around it, that the organizational principles of nazism and communism extended beyond governmental, political, and official associations. They were hard to evade in virtually any kind of organizational life to which a person might be exposed: at work, in school, and at play or in professional, charitable, and sometimes even in religious activities.

In the democracies, no one has quite so much power to act as the totalitarian dictator nor so little as the dictator's chosen victims. For the overwhelming majority of people there are all kinds of opportunities to participate in the decisions of their society. For the majority living under autocratic regimes, whether traditional or innovative-mobilizational, such opportunities are fewer. The values maximized by the autocracy are those either of being "let alone," according to the traditionalist view that politics is properly the business of an elite, or of being actively managed. In the innovative autocracy the individual may not have the option of staying out of politics. He is usually compelled to join and to "march with the movement." But he is exposed to participatory experiences in which he is expected, above all, to follow orders: to act out the aspirations and directives imposed on him from without, sometimes in the name of the Leader ("Mussolini is always right"), the party, or the State.

Whether this is good or bad from the standpoint of an individual consumer, as it were, of participatory activity depends on his goals, his values, and his psychological characteristics. According to a typology of support developed by the German sociologist Max Weber, there are four reasonably distinct categories of persons who join up with or give aid to political causes: (1) those with a *value-rational* motivation—that is, those who knowingly support the explicit goals of the party or movement for the sake of these goals; (2) those who are *emotionally-affectually* oriented—that is, who join or give support because some facet of the movement or its leadership produces strong emotional identification and satisfaction in them; (3) the *traditional* supporters who simply continue an allegiance established by their parents, relatives, or most persons in their locality or social group affiliation; and (4) those who support political causes out of direct and *tangible self-interest* in the form of such rewards as jobs or tax rebates on the positive side, as well as to avoid physical and personal reprisals for not doing so, on the negative.[1]

Democracy means elections and legislative assemblies; it means autonomous civic, political, and cultural associations and organs of expression; it means representation, consultation, and debate in municipal and local councils, in local school boards, in industrial advisory and trade union councils, in popularly chosen juries, and in hosts of other bodies whose decisions are real enough and whose activities provide a huge citizenship training ground to thousands of persons.

The right to vote or to participate in legislative assemblies may be seen in part, of course, as instrumental. The vote may be a means for achieving ends that are themselves nonpolitical, including, for example, favorable social legislation, higher wages, the right to strike, the construction of a highway in a particular locality, or the assurance of favorable treatment to a specific religious denomination.

Much of the struggle waged by organized labor, and the political parties representing it in the nineteenth century, was waged with the slogans and weapons of democracy. The goals included the right to organize unions, abolition of child labor, higher wages, a shorter working day, protection of the life and health of workers, job security, and for some at least more far-reaching, millenarian ends of an egalitarian society of universal freedom and abundance. The method was the ballot. If the workers could dominate the legislature and the government they could presumably secure their social objectives.[2]

The widespread acceptance of democracy as a means to various social ends by workers and by organized labor lent a degree of tradi-

[1] See Rudolf Herberle, *Social Movements: An Introduction to Political Sociology* (New York: Appleton-Century-Crofts, 1961), pp. 95–98.

[2] See Mark Hovell, *The Chartist Movement* (Manchester: Manchester University Press, 1950), pp. 1–7.

tional or historical coherence to the behavior of workers in the political arena. Even if many of them cared little about such abstract principles as freedom of speech and association, they nevertheless tended to support, in large numbers and with a high degree of regularity, those leaders and organizations that upheld these principles for "bread-and-butter" reasons. If the leadership wanted to secure the right to association for trade unions, it could not very well be indifferent or hostile to the principle itself. On the contrary, it would generally find it necessary to associate itself with it and to rally wider public support in its name. As long as the rank and file identified with the organization, it was likely to stay loyally behind its efforts.

Democracy allows for a very wide participation of interests, each naturally devoted to its own idiosyncratic, if not selfish, ends. The attitude toward democracy is everywhere structured by group and individual expectations of the likely treatment for their particular values at the hands of the given collectivity. How much change and how quickly is the question confronting the reformers. What price tradition and the status quo is the question confronting conservatives. Those who cannot envision compromise, moderation, or delay in the achievement of their objectives are not likely to tolerate the political market-place mechanisms of democracy.

The participatory process of democracy exposes traditional institutions to hazards, not because the popular will (if allowed to have its way) would always oppose the traditional social, economic, and cultural order, but because the very openness of the democratic process is likely to invite challenges to traditionalism. And what may not succeed today can always seek another chance tomorrow, or on the day after. Thus, to groups or individuals for whom the maintenance of a specific, traditional pattern of social, religious, or economic relationships is *supremely* important, the comforts of a democratic political order are like those of a house whose windows and doors remain wide open through summer and winter, through calm and through storm. If it does not bring about dreaded change, it is at least certain to induce anxiety and insecurity among the extreme traditionalists.

On the opposite pole of political attitudes, those groups that are committed to far-reaching changes in their environment and wish to bring them about as rapidly as possible may justly feel that they could not have the support of popular opinion behind them, that they must either dispense with it or manufacture it first. Those who stand committed to the ideals of militant nationalism in societies traditionally tribal, divided, and decentralized in their political orientations must either sacrifice their ideals or devise experiments in "guided democracy" and other substitutes for popular rule. Those who are committed to ambitious projects of industrialization, at whatever sacrifice, are also unlikely to submit themselves to the judgments of public opinion to whom the present may very well be more important than the leaders' vision of the future.

The autocratic pattern of organization, whether in a party, a movement, or in the society as a whole, offers certain kinds of security that democracy does not and cannot. Autocracy promotes exclusion of the "foe" from public decision making. In totalitarian regimes that exclusion may mean physical annihilation. Under more moderate or traditional regimes it may mean less drastic and even less obvious kinds of exclusion. There may be acquiescence in the physical survival and perhaps even a token public presence of an opposition but always combined with guarantees that the opposition shall remain innocuous. Naturally, to those who feel threatened by an opposition, the security of its formal and *de facto* exclusion is a cherished value of autocracy.

In addition to their instrumental value, however, the participatory rights of a democratic system may be seen as having a certain residual worth, in and of themselves. The case for them has been argued by democratic theorists for a long time. John Stuart Mill made the intrinsic worth of self-rule, and of freedom for its own sake, the foundation of his argument in *Representative Government.* He saw self-government as indispensable to the full development of human faculties, intellectual and moral.

To move from autocratic rule imposed by others to one that was self-imposed, was for Mill a transition from the tutelage of intellectual and moral childhood to the responsibilities and disciplines of adulthood, maturity, and independence. It meant control over decisions affecting one's own life and responsibility for them. It meant involvement in public life that, allowing for differences in distances and population magnitudes, echoed the experience of the Greek city-states and, above all, the experience of Athens. It was training for the mind and the character of man.[3]

In a democracy, the person generally retains the right to draw the line between obligation and pleasure in his political activities; he decides when and if he will be politically active; and where and how he can limit or terminate his activities on behalf of political parties, candidates, or issues. The sanctions for participation, to the extent that they do exist in the democracy, too, are generally social and personal, not legal-punitive. (In Australia and Belgium, however, nonvoting is punished by fines.)

For the individual who *chooses* to be a participant in a democratic

[3] See John Stuart Mill, *Representative Government* (New York: Library of Liberal Arts, 1958), pp. 35–55. "Still more salutary is the moral part of the instruction afforded by the participation of the private citizen.... He is made to feel himself one of the public.... " P. 35.

society, the activity is likely to be characterized by *autonomy, dialogue* and, a measure of *vicarious decision making.*

The content of participation is apt to be oriented toward dialogue in the sense that the individual's interests can be manifested in a discussion and exchange of views between himself and others who may be like minded, but also with those who are not. Much of democratic politics revolves around the theme of persuading people in situations in which they may very tangibly choose *for* or *against*—on an issue, on a candidate, or on a party. This persuasion-oriented activity involves discussion *with* those who are to be persuaded as well as *among* those who set out to persuade. The primary and the general election in American politics is one illustration of this, but the process takes place under very different institutional arrangements in all democracies. The number of sacred cows, of unspeakable and unthinkable political thoughts is generally small. For the man who really likes to think and talk about public affairs, democratic politics offers many forums and opportunities. There is also opportunity for a personal sharing in decisions for those who want to participate. To work for the election of a candidate, to raise campaign funds, attend party meetings, or even to sit in the gallery of a legislature such as the House of Commons, listening and looking at close range at the decision makers in action, can give an individual a strong sense of involvement.

In traditional autocracies the citizen often cannot develop a sense of involvement by seeing the actual decision makers in action. The Emperor, King, or Leader is a secluded figure, little more than a name and a symbol to the average person. There may be no elections at all or no elections with any choices to make. There may be no public forums for the conduct of political discussions. Many subjects are likely to be political taboos. Under the innovative autocracies the opportunities for participation, per se, are likely to be far greater, but these opportunities are also likely to be so rigidly structured that participation in them is more nearly equivalent to military drill than to dialogue. The basic premises of public policy are simply not to be thrashed out by, or before, the ordinary man in the well-entrenched autocracies, whether traditional or innovative-mobilizational.

In the democracies, the outlets to individual expression and self-development that are open through group life are generally far wider and richer. In the political sphere, the individual may participate through a variety of organized groups that make claims upon government, be they political parties seeking to elect candidates to public office or pressure groups bent on securing influence on such choices and on government policies generally. But variety of choices *among* groups represents only one aspect of the democratic system. The character of group life *within* each such entity is another, and often an even more important, aspect.

The specifications of "Dahl's democratic formula" do not necessarily require a multiparty or even a two-party system. But they do require the opportunity for participants in a political system to submit alternatives and to choose from among alternatives. It is precisely in the degree of its openness to choices and alternatives with respect to candidates, issues, and policies that the one-party politics of the American South and at least of several African states since the 1950s have differed from the politics of the totalitarian single party, Nazi, Fascist, or Communist.

Such a party promotes the organizational values of the system to which it is committed. Individual subordination to the leadership, iron discipline and forebearance; the sacrifice of the individual and of his private judgments to the interests of the collectivity as enunciated by the leaders; and obedience and alacrity in the fulfillment of orders or party tasks are the sanctioned norms of group life in the totalitarian political organization. For the average member, the life of the party is the life of a paramilitary organization. It demands involvement that cuts across the distinction between one's public and one's private life, or between one's leisure time and one's other activities. In this paramilitary model, the group life of Communist party members emphasizes somewhat more strongly than the Nazi-Fascist certain politically oriented intellectual values and concerns.

The party member may be encouraged to discuss issues of party policy and to concern himself with the problems of a dialogue between the party and the outer world. He may be expected to engage in "self-criticism" requiring him to analyze how and why his behavior or thinking has departed from the premises of party policy. He may be required to study and discuss the applications of party policy to various problems and situations not per se anticipated by his hierarchical superiors. All of these functions, however, must always be based on the premise of the party's inherent rectitude so far as its rank and file is concerned. It is not a permissible function for the ordinary members to publicly criticize the policy and leadership of the party. Under these circumstances, even the more intellectually oriented Communist parties are not really the forums of open discussion.

On the other hand, politics by discussion, by negotiation, and by compromise, arrived at through bargaining, is highly characteristic of political parties that are democratic and that operate within solidly established democratic systems. True to the pattern of systemic influence, this is the case to a degree even among those parties that repudiate and are committed to the overthrow of the democratic regimes. Unhampered by the sanctions of legal, economic, and physical punishments administered by an autocratic state, the members of minuscule totalitarian parties in democratic political systems can afford to deviate, rebel, and occasionally quit in ways that would be figuratively, and sometimes literally, suicidal for them under the rule of totalitarian regimes.

To be sure, political parties in the democracies are not all open debating societies and the influence of opinion of all the members or participants in them is, in practice, never completely equal. There may be formal and informal sanctions against the propagation of ideas considered traditionally inimical by most members. For example, the organizational structure may not promote the equal opportunity of all the members to express their points of view, let alone to have them count in ultimate party policy. Nonetheless, tendencies that are only partially realized are real and significant enough from a participant's point of view.

It is unlikely that any political system has as yet allowed the free manifestation of *all* the political impulses and expressions of which men are capable. Such a range would need to include even those for whom, all other things apart, politically directed violence is inherently psychologically desirable; perhaps no political system concerned with survival and stability can ever accommodate the complete range of human political aspiration. Democracy allows a wider range than the various types of autocracy both in kinds of orientations to which it accords legalized existence, and in the relative openness of the organizational process within groups that it typically exhibits.

Apart from the force of example, sanctified by tradition, and legislation occasionally compelling it, the democratic system encourages the development of open, egalitarian, and participatory proceedings in political and nonpolitical organizations alike by affording certain social inducements to them. Each organized group, whatever its orientation, faces the problem of dealing with a membership whose general, and prior-to-membership, life experience (not to say socialization) predisposes them to a particular mode of behavior, to certain expectations of procedure, decision making, and type of participation. The necessity of allowing for some discussion of policies and of alternatives *within* any single organization is also likely to be promoted by the availability of competitor groups outside. Dialogue is made virtually inevitable by the variety of the communications media, the dissemination of news and ideas from divergent sources. This requires each group to adjust its policies and even its outlook to stimuli that are beyond its control to regulate. Finally, the relative ease with which one may withdraw or discontinue many group memberships in a democratic political system militates against compulsive relationships within them. It may be everywhere necessary to lead by reason because it is simply impractical to lead by force. The objective of pluralism within groups is also likely to be promoted by the lack of any powerful, State-wielded, political sanctions to punish deviates among the group members.

All these characteristics of the democratic system not only promote openness and participatory tendencies in group life; they also tend to diminish the demands made on the individual in his group associations and activities. Competition in available memberships—as in ideas or life styles—makes it more difficult for organized groups to engage in a monopolistically ruthless exploitation of an individual's time, energy, and resources. The political activist in a democracy may make his party work a hobby. His totalitarian or innovative-mobilizational counterpart is required to be far more single-minded and serious about it. The loss of membership in the party and its affiliated organizations may mean doom for the individual and his family. Such loss has its professional and economic parallels in the democratic experience but, apart from the fact that it is not as easily incurred, it does not involve the threat of physical annihilation.

The dialogue of democratic politics cannot help but be educational in the sense of exposing participants to the rationale of government decisions—in the very necessity all democratic politicians face in having to *explain* and *justify* their actions to a large public. In the area of foreign policy, for example, the citizen has access to information about the policy of his country's adversaries that would be unobtainable and unthinkable to the citizen of a totalitarian or autocratic state. This is undoubtedly true even if the bulk of his information is actually weighted more in one direction than in another. In the United States the conflict in Vietnam has given rise to a public debate the like of which would be inconceivable in the Soviet Union, China, or Spain in that the citizen can inform himself of the position of the adversary and can openly disapprove the position of his own government.

The political *ethos*—the values, orientations, and modes of behavior implicit in the rulers' regime—has its impact even on essentially nonpolitical groups by way of setting a widely imitated, "profitable" social norm. Such norms can be expected to confer legitimacy on a group by their consonance with the prevailing political system. If access to and influence with the rulers is important, even for the ostensibly least political forms of human association, conformity to the rulers' standards is likely to be a practical advantage. If the underlying values of the rulers' political system, through prescription or otherwise, are widely shared by the population at large, conformity to their standards confers social advantage. The conformist group thus appears reputable and worthy in the eyes of a more general public opinion. On the other hand, deviance might tend to isolate and discredit it.

All regimes make use of socializing agencies at their disposal or under their direct control—public schools or the military service among others—to inculcate values in the population. The prolonged and widespread use of such agencies by a regime is likely to affect the attitudes and behavior patterns even of those strata of the population that the regime may regard as hostile, dangerous, and inferior, and that reciprocate that attitude by maintaining a politically revolutionary disposition toward the regime. Thus, the ethos of Prussian rule appears to have had a profound impact on the organizational attitudes of royal Prussia's most uncompromising foes and victims, most notably the Social Democrats and the Catholic Polish minority in Silesia and Pomerania. How the German Socialists behaved in their ideologically antiregime party and trade unions seems to have been profoundly conditioned by the socialization acquired precisely under that regime.[4]

The impact of these factors on individuals is certain to vary from slight (practically even nil in some cases) to what we might well describe as pervasive and profound. Impact differences depend in part on the personalities of the citizens; some are highly "politicized," others are all but indifferent. Social scientists have sought explanations for these disparities of attitude and involvement in factors ranging from the subconscious mind of each individual in the Freudian tradition to the fluctuations of world market prices in the Marxian.

One index of personal propensity toward different types of political participation has been the psychological. Thus, we get a view of a "democratic personality" that is often described as warmly and trustingly well disposed toward people, generally tolerant and open toward them, and autonomous in the sense that it does not have a compelling need to be dominated or to dominate in leader-follower relationships. On the other hand, "an authoritarian personality" exhibits strong traits of

> ... exaggerated faith in powerful leaders and insistence on absolute obedience to them; hatred of outsiders and deviates; excessive projection of guilt and hostility; extreme cynicism; a sense of powerlessness and ineffectiveness (alienation and anomie); suspicion and distrust of others; and dogmatism and rigidity.[5]

[4] On the process of so-called *Verburgerlichung* of the German Social Democrats and some of its consequences, see Richard N. Hunt, *German Social Democracy 1918–1933* (New Haven, Conn.: Yale University Press, 1964), particularly the conclusion, pp. 24–25. *Cf.* Richard E. Dawson and Kenneth Prewitt, *Political Socialization* (Boston: Little, Brown, 1969), pp. 175–178.

[5] See Alex Inkeles, "National Character and Modern Political Systems," in Nelson W. Polsby, R. A. Dentler, and P. A. Smith (eds.), *Politics and Social Life* (Boston: Houghton Mifflin, 1963), p. 184.

According to the noted study made by Zevedei Barbu, personality structures and what the author calls the pattern of individuation determine how a person relates to his political environment and what his propensity for authoritarian behavior is likely to be.

> ... the most important reasons for which someone becomes a Communist or a Nazi lie in the structure of his personality as a whole. Communism or Nazism becomes acceptable to him because his personality is shaped by a specific pattern of individuation. In a sense, he is a Communist or a Nazi before joining one of these Parties.[6]

In this interpretation of political orientation, an individual, through the experiences of childhood and early life, may have become exposed to an environment saturated with insecurity, fear, parental repression, or rejection. These experiences in turn induce feelings of hostility and anxiety toward those in his immediate environment. Such feelings, however, may in some cases be repressed toward the *immediate* objects of one's fear, frustration, and resentment and become transmuted either simultaneously or in later life into political objects. Thus, the individual who could not find emotional satisfaction, love, acceptance, friendship, and a sense of personal worth and security in his face-to-face, primary relationships turns to the public sphere to satisfy his urge for these values and to punish what are in effect imaginary public substitutes for those relatives and private individuals who inflicted real or imagined injuries and deprivations on him.

As Barbu describes it:

> Basic insecurity develops in the individual an excessive need for self-assertion which is discharged aggressively either towards the external world or towards himself. The basic formula of this pattern of individuation is: "If you do not accept me, I will kill you all, or I will kill myself." This is a paraphrase of what Saint-Just once said addressing the enemies of the Revolution, who apparently were the whole French nation minus the members of the Jacobin Club. The process of individuation involves in this case an inner contradiction: the individual's world is sharply divided into two categories, partisans and enemies. The former category embodies the "security" space of the individual

[6] *Democracy and Dictatorship: Their Psychology and Patterns of Life* (London: Routledge and Kegan Paul, 1956), pp. 265–266. See also G. M. Gilbert, *The Psychology of Dictatorship* (New York: Ronald Press Co., 1950); Fritz Stern, *The Politics of Cultural Despair* (Berkeley: University of California Press, 1965). T. W. Adorno, *et al.*, *The Authoritarian Personality* (New York: Harper, 1950); Christian Bay, *The Structure of Freedom* (Stanford, Calif.: Stanford University Press, 1958). For an excellent critique of the psychoanalytic explanation of nazism by F. L. Schuman in *Nazi Dictatorship* (1935) and a Marxian "capitalist plot theory" in Lytton Strachey's *The Menace of Fascism* (1933), see also Theodore Abel, *Why Hitler Came Into Power* (Englewood Cliffs, N. J.: Prentice-Hall, 1938), pp. 186–200.

wrapped up in his love and confidence. The latter becomes a symbol of insecurity, attracting to it all the individual's hatred and suspicion. The individual is utterly incapable of an unemotional, rational relation to the world.

Though possessed by a morbid need to be in relationship with others, this type of personality is incapable of being in dialogue. When he dominates or hates, he annihilates the other; when he submits, he annihilates himself.[7]

The theme of individual temperament and psychology as determinants of different types of political behavior is hardly new. Much of the literature on the subject in the twentieth century has qualified this approach by the interplay of social and historical factors accentuating or inhibiting individual propensity to political behavior.

The term *individuation* suggests that each personality, with its specific properties and dispositions, is shaped by a long and complex process. The immediate environment, one's relations and friends, as well as the individual's genetic make-up, all interact with a more proximate, diffuse cultural environment of one's place and time. The formation of certain personality patterns may be facilitated or impeded by the social and cultural institutions in the environment. Thus the individual is always part of a cycle to which he contributes the impact of his own personality, but he is also shaped by outside forces that tend to perpetuate and reinforce certain personality characteristics within his culture and subculture to the detriment of others.

School, church, military service, youth clubs, workplace relationships, and the content of news and cultural media, all confront the individual with norms of orientation and behavior. Frequently, they can structure his attitude not simply by what they overtly articulate but by the very absence of selectivity in their offerings. In adapting traits and orientations, the personality is analogous to the man who cannot marry a girl he has not met.

It is in the context of these larger considerations that the contributions of psychology travel full circle, and scholars turn to the investigation of environmental factors for the explanation of individual predispositions. Erich Fromm has suggested that the transition from the relatively simple, stationary, and custom-bound mode of life of the middle ages to the complexity, interdependence, and religious-cultural heterogeneity of modern life have produced profound anxieties for the ordinary man seeking to cope with the world and himself as a part of it. In this view the psychological bewilderment induced by social causes gives rise to a widespread craving for escape from responsibility and involvement in social decisions.

The "common man" of the twentieth century has been subjected to so many traumatic influences suggesting his powerlessness and in-

[7] *Ibid.*, p. 167.

competence that temptation to abdicate all responsibility to the "experts" or perhaps to the "genius-leader" who can solve all the seemingly baffling and impossible problems has become very strong in all strata of society. The craving for dictatorship has thus become a form of escapism and imagined security from the turmoil and chaos of one's social environment. In more recent literature, it has been suggested that the technological, social, and cultural changes induced by industrialization have rendered many traditional links between man and man either so obsolescent or so fluid and superficial as to create a mass society of atomized individuals seeking a new and more enduring beacon of identification, faith, and security.

The case histories of Adolf Hitler and Winston Churchill aptly illustrate the linkages between systems, values, and personalities.

The organization with which Hitler identified most closely and that he most admired, as he reminisced in *Mein Kampf* about his own early life and about Germany before 1918, was the Imperial Army. In it, Hitler had found a home and a spiritual fulfillment. As one of his biographers notes:

> Hitler had no use for any democratic institution; free speech, free press or parliament. . . . All his life . . . [he] was irritated by discussion. In the arguments into which he was drawn [in his early years] he showed no self control in face of contradiction or debate. He [would] shout and shower abuse on his opponents, with an hysterical note in his voice.[8]

In 1914, Hitler found "the comradeship, discipline and excitement of life at the Front . . . vastly more attractive than the obscurity, aimlessness and dull placidity of peace."[9] Unlike most other soldiers, he never grumbled about Army life or the war. In *Mein Kampf*, he credited the Army with being the "mightiest school of the German nation. . . . In the face of the Jewish democratic idea of blind worship of numbers, the army upheld the faith in personality . . . courage . . . strength and unity of [one's] own nationality . . . determination . . . idealism . . . devotion to the fatherland." In Hitler's own words, "what the German people owes to the army may be simply summed up in one single word, namely: everything."

Hitler made it quite clear that he liked the German Army both for what it accepted as well as for what it rejected:

> The army trained for absolute responsibility at a time when this quality had become very rare and the shunning of responsibility had more and more be-

[8] Alan Bullock, *Hitler: A Study in Tyranny* (New York: Harper and Brothers, 1952), pp. 35–36.

[9] *Ibid.*, p. 48.

come the order of the day, starting from the model example of all unscrupulousness, the parliament.[10]

Hitler's great World War II adversary, Winston Churchill, on the contrary, identified himself closely with the foremost organizational embodiment of British democracy, the House of Commons.

He delighted and excelled in the art of parliamentary dialogue. The orderly verbal-rational conflicts of a legislative assembly that so repelled Hitler attracted and inspired Churchill. Speaking about his career in the United States in 1942, Churchill said: "I am a child of the House of Commons. I was brought up in my father's house to believe in democracy.... I owe my advancement entirely to the House... whose servant I am."[11]

On his eightieth birthday, in 1954, acknowledged within the walls of the House as the greatest parliamentarian in British history, Churchill recalled:

> I have lived my life in the House of Commons having served there for fifty-two out of the last fifty-four years of this tumultuous and convulsive century. I have indeed seen all the ups and downs of fate and fortune there, but I have never ceased to love and honour the Mother of Parliaments, the model of legislative assemblies of so many lands.[12]

For Churchill the content of democratic political activity was as exhilarating as its rational ends. Analogously, Hitler delighted in authoritarianism quite apart from the ends that he posited for his own political activity. The democratic mode of behavior—with its emphasis on dialogue and persuasion, rather than on suppression and annihilation; with its preference for the open and readily accessible conduct of public affairs, rather than for secrecy and hierarchy; and with its implicit recognition of the ultimate primacy of public opinion, not the judgment of a few—is likely to be appealing in and of itself to the individual whose psychocultural background, upbringing, and life experience predispose him for it.

The confinement of policy-making roles to a relatively small group of leaders frees the individual from responsibility of making his own decisions and from the effort required to formulate them. It may be a psychological easement for the individual simply to fulfill his duties, so long as the scope and direction of his tasks are prearranged for him. To the extent that the individual identifies with the long-range goals

[10] See John Chamberlain, Sidney B. Fay, et al. (eds.), *Mein Kampf* (New York: Reynal and Hitchcock, 1939), pp. 384–385.

[11] Dennis Bardens, *Churchill in Parliament* (London: Robert Hale, 1967), p. 257.

[12] *Ibid.*, pp. 355–356. *Cf.* Byrum E. Carter, *The Office of Prime Minister* (Princeton, N.J.: Princeton University Press, 1956), pp. 62–66.

or values of the ruling group, he may welcome the discipline and control imposed on him from the top because he perceives these as a form of insurance for the achievement of his long-range aspirations. The fanatic and the zealot, whatever his purposes (and these may in some cases be quite changeable) will inevitably suffer frustration in political organizations that are less than ruthless, that are tolerant of opposition, and that are vacillating or hesitant in the brutal use of power. He is certain to be frustrated by any institutional arrangements that would deter or delay him in his activity or that would make it possible for *others* to raise doubts or interfere with the course of action he wishes to follow. Thus, the autocratic system may be satisfactory to a wide range of people: those who are intellectual simpletons; the psychopathic fanatics for whom the particular *method* of political activity is more important than its *goal* or *direction*; and also a variety of perfectly intelligent, psychologically normal individuals whose commitment to certain purposes may, under some circumstances, dictate adherence to autocracy.

On the other hand democracy, no less than authoritarian modes of rule, may be deemed valuable for the purposes it serves even by those who, other things being equal, find it innately distasteful. The calculus of instrumental considerations includes not only the pursuit of what is desirable but also accommodation to necessity. Historically, democracy has had many lukewarm, unenthusiastic, and even treacherous supporters among individuals whose "normal" preferences have been autocratic, such as those of the European monarchs of the 1848 era. They restrained their revulsion in extending democratic rights to their subjects in order to save themselves and their thrones from revolution.

During World War I, democracy won some surprising advocates among German military leaders who, wishing to obtain better peace terms at the hands of the victorious democratic Western powers, believed that the task would be eased by the establishment of "democratic legitimacy" in Germany. Among recent examples of domestic evolution in response to changes in the international environment is the development of the Franco regime since 1939. Possessed of dictatorial power, and having just vanquished the democratic-republican State, General Franco and his autocratic entourage expected a more or less imminent victory for the powerful Axis over the combined, but obviously decadent and weak, forces of the Western democracies and the Soviet Union. Within Spain, the political ideals of the West were being conspicuously consigned to an early and inevitable oblivion. In 1940 or 1941 the country seemed all but a replica of the victorious Fascist and Nazi powers of Europe. Very likely, it would have been imprudent and possibly even unsafe for Spain to be too visibly out of step with the ruling powers of Europe at that historical juncture, *even if* General Franco wished it so. But the tide of Axis military defeats changed the situation. Indirectly, it slowed and reversed the domestic Spanish trend to nazification.[13] After 1945, the Franco regime found it necessary to adapt itself to a very different international environment and to new allies, whose prevailing ideas about domestic politics were also very different.[14] In the decades since World War II, the Franco regime has instituted and allowed changes that, like the quasi-parliamentary assembly and the toleration of at least some forms of public and private opposition, currently give it a much more "democratic" image.

In the 1940s the genesis of the People's Democracies under Soviet auspices in Eastern Europe had its international as well as domestic justifications inasmuch as the Soviets did not wish to alarm the West unduly about the hollowness of the diplomatic pledges of Teheran, Yalta, and Potsdam. The concessions made to democratism after the demise of Stalin, on the other hand, utilized an increased measure of democratic norms as safety valves to accumulated popular discontent.

One of the serious problems faced by the democracies in the 1960s was the apparent failure of traditional political institutions to satisfy new participatory aspirations. The charge that certain political processes or structures had become irrelevant suggests that participatory gratifications are no longer conferred on many people from traditional sources in traditional ways. To the extent that student protest movements, for example, are oriented to the greater involvement of youth in political decision making, they are indicative of a new and yet traditional democratic demand for more inclusive participation. This time it is by the young rather than, as in the nineteenth century, the poor. On the other hand, the charge of irrelevance or meaninglessness levelled against specific organizational, parliamentary, or bureaucratic structures suggests another familiar theme of political study. Social change inevitably promotes and accentuates the obsolescence of traditional political forms and their interrelationships.

[13] See Carlton J. H. Hayes, *Wartime Mission in Spain, 1942–1945* (New York: Macmillan, 1945), particularly Chs. 6 and 8.

[14] *Cf.* Benjamin Welles, *Spain: The Gentle Anarchy* (New York: Praeger, 1965), pp. 117–120, 174–177.

CHAPTER 3
GROUP LIFE, COMMUNICATION, AND ORGANIZATION

JUST as we can discern different participatory values available to people under different political systems, we can also recognize different values accruing to groups and organizations. Here again, group life can be seen as both an "input" and an "output" of politics. We can say, for example, that what the political system is, is largely or partly determined by the distribution of power among various groups in the society. But there is also an important reciprocal relationship. The nature of the system, once well established, impacts the ways in which groups can and cannot function. And, thus, without prejudging the interesting problem of causality—how did political system X come into being and what keeps it going—we can correlate its existence with certain kinds of organizational values that differ from those realized under other types of political systems. Well-established democracies are characterized by group life that more frequently parallels their political qualities—the salient features of which are pluralism, autonomy, and diffuse decision making characterized by bargaining and by significant popular rank-and-file participation.

In autocracies we find less pluralism in group life: first, in the sense that a narrower range of existent social interests is allowed the basic right of public, legally sanctioned association; and secondly, in the sense that, within the associational groupings themselves, the range of permissible manifestations of interests is also narrower—that is, less representative in relation to the total potential clientele of the given group than is the case in a democracy.

Regimes bent on forcible, large-scale social engineering seek to move farthest away from pluralism, autonomy, and open decision making in the group life of society. Democracies, on the other hand, tend to maximize these values; more moderate, traditional, or moderately innovative oligarchies occupy a middle ground between these extremes.

These distinctions need not be taken as inconsistent either with an oligarchical-elitist critique of democracy and democratic organization, such as those of Roberto Michels and Gaetano Mosca, or the pluralist critique of totalitarianism as propounded by more recent writers.[1] Whether in application to democracy or to dictatorship, pluralism and monism and autonomy and dependence are terms differentiable by degree, and rarely, if ever, as "absolutes."

For our ordinary man in the street, however, the significance of all these differences in degree is enormous. It relates to the quality of life he lives, to a whole range of experiences and opportunities for self-expression and participation that begin in infancy and do not cease in his earthly life. These differences structure a man's experience in school, on the job, in military service, and even in his use of leisure time. They shape his character and personality and determine the way in which he will relate himself to others. Moreover, the treatment of organized interest groups, different under different regimes, has a profound impact on such bread-and-butter issues as a man's ability to earn a livelihood, to keep abreast of inflation, to receive an education, or to change his job.

From time to time interest-group influences within autocratic regimes fluctuate sharply, from high to low and vice versa, depending on the group's standing with the ruler or ruling clique. Finally, by the very nature of the autocratic political system, the maintenance of access or influence by any collectivity must occasionally require the outright sacrifice of its individual members. The principle of "one for all and all for one," so characteristic of trade union disputes in a democracy, is difficult to invoke against a dictatorship. These system differences can be illustrated with reference to specific examples in recent history.

The German Army, the so-called *Reichswehr*, was an influential and

[1] Among others, see A. J. Groth, "The Isms in Totalitarianism," *American Political Science Review*, Vol. 58, No. 4 (December 1964), pp. 888–901.

widely respected interest group under the Weimar Republic (1919–1933). It successfully pressured the government to help it in, as yet, "modestly" evading and exceeding the limitations imposed on Germany by the 1919 Versailles Treaty. But the Reichswehr was limited to a size of 100,000 men under the treaty, and few German officers were satisfied to operate within the basic framework of its limitations. Many wanted to see Germany revived as a great power with a great army. Visions of grandeur and empire abounded, both in personal-professional and political terms. To the German military, the recovery of territories that had been German for decades before the disastrous defeat in World War I seemed not only a reasonable, patriotic objective but one that, aided by rearmament, would yield a flood of new commands, promotions, perquisites, and opportunities for the officer corps.

The establishment of Hitler's dictatorship, by and large, was viewed sympathetically by the military, because Hitler vigorously espoused militarism, expansionism, and, concretely, the repudiation of the Treaty of Versailles. Moreover, the German Officer Corps, reared under the Wilhelmian empire, had very little sympathy for the democratic values of the Weimar Republic. If, in order to fit into Hitler's new order, the Army had to show that it was anti-Marxist, anti-liberal, and anti-Jewish in its membership, organization, or views, this did not require much change from pre-1933 days.

From the standpoint of the military, Hitler could act decisively on their behalf where the Republic would not and could not. Hitler would be free from the "nonsense" of political opposition by Left-wing and pacifist elements; free from parliamentary inquiries into "delicate" matters; and free from exposure by a hostile press. In fact, the Army (Wehrmacht under Hitler) succeeded in all these objectives. Virtually all pacifist and anti-militarist influences lost direct access to the chief decision maker—the Fuehrer.

The benefits to the Army were obvious and well-nigh immediate. Within months of Hitler's accession to the chancellorship, Germany was well on its way to economic mobilization for war. The clandestine buildup of the armed forces grew by leaps and bounds. By 1935, in fact, Hitler defiantly publicized his massive rearmament program. On June 30, 1934, nevertheless, two generals who had incurred Hitler's wrath and suspicion, Kurt von Schleicher and Kurt von Bredow, were simply gunned down by Hitler's SS executioners in their own homes; coincidentally, Hitler had also liquidated hundreds of his own SA (storm troop) leaders whom the Army chiefs regarded as military rivals.

The recourse that the Army would have had against the murderers under the Weimar Republic, with its parliament, courts, and press, was no longer available to it under Hitler's regime. The generals were still in a good position to use, or perhaps threaten, violence against him; yet, in view of the "basic soundness" of Hitler's policy, was it really worth so much risk and trouble? The overwhelming majority of the Wehrmacht's leaders did not think so. If the Nazi regime did not have readily available "brakes," this still appeared, over all, as an advantage to the military.

Meanwhile, Hitler continued his efforts to eliminate individual officers whom he regarded as dangerous or insufficiently pliable. Following an elaborate criminal frame-up in each case, he removed Field Marshal Werner von Blomberg and General Freiherr von Fritsch early in 1938.[2] He wrested command of the Army for himself and steadily whittled down the political autonomy and influence of the Wehrmacht. To be sure, policies that he pursued between 1936 and 1938 enhanced the material strength of the armed forces, but they were also regarded as too risky and too adventurous by many generals. Many of them feared that Hitler would drag Germany into a disastrously broad, worldwide conflict exceeding the military-economic capacities of the nation. Some had qualms about the moral qualities of a regime that stooped to the murder and persecution of innocent victims for the achievement of its goals. In 1938, on the eve of Munich, these oppositional stirrings finally found the only outlet possible under the circumstances, a conspiracy to oust Hitler from power in a *coup d'état.* But by 1938 the ante of revolution had risen still higher. The more entrenched Hitler became in power at home, and the more successful in foreign ventures abroad, the more difficult grew the task of uniting the Army for revolution against him. No attempt was made.

After the defeats in Russia and North Africa, as Hitler's war gradually turned into disaster, more and more Wehrmacht officers had second thoughts about his power. The generals no longer saw eye to eye with Hitler on the means and ends of policy. When in June 1944, however, Colonel Von Stauffenberg's plot to kill Hitler failed, the Nazi system was used to inflict summary, cruel, and haphazard punishment on hundreds of Army leaders. (Field Marshal Von Witzleben was hanged on a meathook and films of his and other executions were shown to German troops.) With the aid of the SS and the Gestapo, Hitler all but reduced the once proud German Army Officer Corps into a hapless rabble. Hitler's control of the media of communication, the refinement of his espionage system, the infiltration of all strata of society with Gestapo and party agents, and the great risks attaching

[2] See John W. Wheeler-Bennett, *The Nemesis of Power: The German Army in Politics 1918–1945* (New York: St. Martin's Press, 1954), pp. 383–455. *Cf.* Gordon A. Craig, *The Politics of the Prussian Army 1640–1945* (New York: Oxford University Press, 1956), pp. 381–503.

to any kind of oppositional activity all made it very difficult to organize even "a dialogue about opposition," among German Army officers, let alone opposition itself. The inducements to passivity—reinforcements to doubt and vacillation—were enhanced, even in the face of a colossal defeat for Germany; and the inducements to oppose were minimized. Thus, the Army evolved from the role of a powerful veto group in 1933–1934—a kingmaker in the view of many observers—to a mere tool, a body of terrorized clerks in late 1944–1945.[3] Under a genuinely democratic regime, the Army could not have expected to maximize the values of militarism in German society as it did in the 1930s and 1940s; but, by the same token, it would not have suffered the butchery and degradation to which Hitler ultimately subjected it.

In democratic political systems "the rules of the game," in David B. Truman's phrase, generally preclude a precipitous rise and fall of interest groups in response to coercion by the government of the day. An electoral victory for one party or another may change the political atmosphere—that is, it may lessen the access and prestige of one interest group and enhance another. But it rarely destroys the internal autonomy, membership, or outlook of particular interest groups. Moreover, a basic ability to communicate and to act among and within groups, toward the general public and toward government itself, is also substantially maintained. *To the extent* that interest groups remain untouched by election results (the American Medical Association, the U.S. Army Corps of Engineers, or the National Association of Manufactures could all serve as examples) the political system, as a whole, operates with considerable stability.

In fact, in some areas of policy the rights of the democratic rules of the game produce not only "stability" (or, as some would argue, "stalemate") but, paradoxically, even a kind of "segmental oligarchy." For as long as citizens are protected in the right to devote their unequal interests and resources to the arenas of their own choosing, many lasting imbalances are likely to be perpetuated. The involved, organized, articulate, and resourceful minorities may thwart the fitfully participant, amorphous majorities. In Great Britain in 1945, the solid majority the Labour party received in the General Election was not enough to ride roughshod over the British Medical Association's objections to Labour's socialized medicine bill. The Minister of Health, Aneurin Bevan, had to negotiate and compromise on numerous issues in order to implement a workable program.[4]

The politics of terror and intimidation that Hitler and Himmler could use against so powerful a group as the German Army could not

[3] *Cf.* Wheeler-Bennett, *op. cit.*, p. 694, and Craig, p. 496.

[4] See James B. Christoph, *Cases in Comparative Politics* (Boston: Little, Brown, 1965), pp. 3–43.

be invoked by Attlee and Bevan against a relative handful of physicians. The latter, unlike famous German generals, could oppose the government at little personal risk to themselves. They could meet, communicate, and plan with one another without fear of the secret police. Personal reprisals against them or their families would have been an unthinkable scandal. The change from Tory to Labour rule did not destroy the doctors' capabilities for opposition, and the decision of the electorate did not convert them to socialism. They would continue to "count" under any democratic regime.

In contrast, by acquiescence in the substitution of totalitarian rules for democratic ones in the 1930s, German militarists risked their professional and corporate perquisites on the anticipated pay-offs of Hitler's policy. The system worked against them, as it turned out.

For the average person, the innovative, totalitarian experience of this century has been a study in contrasts, a paradoxical combination of participation and repression. The regimes established by the Fascists, Nazis, and Communists have in all cases extended the opportunity for people to belong to organized groups far beyond the levels attained by the regimes that they displaced. In some cases they have compelled people to become joiners, either in terms of membership in a political party or its affiliates or in terms of regular activities designed to immerse the individual in the totalitarian way of life, in the ruling creed, and in the implementation of party policy.

In each case, the totalitarian party has been the central mobilizing agency, at once extending the organization of a totalitarian society into various sectors of human activity and simultaneously assuring the centralized regimentation and control of it by the totalitarian leadership. In each case the totalitarian party has assured a *quantitative* leap combined with a *qualitative* change of popular participation. Germany before 1933 possessed an impressive network of communications and a relatively high incidence of organized group membership among the population. Millions of adult Germans were members of labor unions, political parties, trade associations, churches, farmers' guilds, and the like. News media, particularly newspapers, were among the most abundant in the world and Germany possessed one of the world's most avid reading publics.

The Nazi experience saw an extension of these communication and organization networks within the framework of the new order. Trade unions independent of the regime were abolished, but in their place came the party-directed National Socialist German Labor Front, which actually combined and extended previous labor union membership under one roof. The labor welfare program, *Kraft Durch Freude* (Strength Through Joy), provided benefits and activities for more employees within a single organizational framework than had ever been accomplished before in German history. Many other organizations representing diverse interests were either merged into new, Nazi-controlled bodies or allowed to remain substantially as before the Hitler take-over, on condition of their explicit and implicit fealty to the Hitler regime. Organized groups that were allowed to exist after the Nazi seizure of power ranged from those that openly declared their support for the new regime to those that, like the churches, maintained officially an air of benevolent neutrality toward it. Those groups whose hostility to the regime was a matter of public record were not allowed to continue, being either banned or replaced by new Nazi-oriented organizations.

Independent and oppositional press organs were gradually liquidated; but this surgery, too, under the leadership of Dr. Goebbels' Ministry of Propaganda, was combined with a consolidation, replacement, and augmentation of the media and not their diminution. The opportunities for political involvement and for the reception of political information were everywhere increased. The so-called *Gleichsschaltung* was extended to children of prekindergarten age, to women and teenage girls, to all institutions of learning, to the entertainment field, and to many other spheres of activity that under the Weimar Republic and the Empire were only slightly affected by attempts at organized, institutionalized politicization. The Nazi principle of authoritarian, hierarchical leadership, the *Fuehrerprinzip*, was extended by the party to all organizations that came under its direct control, notably to business enterprises, labor organizations, and trade associations.

No group that hoped to maintain itself could publicly flout Nazi organizational principles, even if its members were so disposed. To the Nazis, parliamentarism was one of the dirtiest words in the dictionary. The organizational notions connected with it, such as leadership elected by and accountable to the rank and file, open deliberations, member initiative in the formulation of policy, and the like became anathema.[5] Even those organizations, like certain manufacturers' groups, that were not formally reconstituted anew by the Nazis, de-emphasized and even abandoned the pre-1933 procedures for election of officers and for the periodic public rendering of accounts to the membership. In each organized group, even those most resistant to Nazi penetration, as was in some respects the higher officer corps, the Nazi members within them, aided by the powerful machine of the State wielded by Hitler and the party outside, attempted to render them miniature organizational ideological replicas

[5] What Zbigniew Brzezinski and Samuel Huntington call the "bubble up," as opposed to the "trickle down," process of policy formulation in their *Political Power: U.S.A./U.S.S.R.* (New York: Viking Press, 1964), pp. 202–204.

of the Nazi vision of society and politics at large. Ultimately, each such organization was to be but a suitable cog in the all-embracing machine of Nazi political power, its wholly obedient tool and replica.

Discounting for the moment the obvious fact that the Nazis faced formidable difficulties in establishing total assimilation of all organized German life into the mold of the party, and that they never *wholly* succeeded, the attempt itself was a reinforcement of the hierarchic, autocratic patterns of group life throughout German society. It molded the life of the average person in the fashion of a military barracks.

Part of the extremist or totalitarian character of Nazi autocracy was the suppression of public dissent in any form—even mild and indirect—from newspapers, radio, cinema, and all *ad hoc* public meetings (the latter could only take place at the discretion of the Nazi authorities). Oppositional, antiregime ideas and opinions were limited primarily to informal, word-of-mouth channels. They went underground in the shape of rumor, clandestine leaflets, and undercover humor. Even a trivial anti-Nazi joke whispered to the wrong person could result in imprisonment, and under some circumstances even in execution. Church pulpits and academic chairs remained among the relatively few places around where people might publicly and regularly assemble to hear discussions of moral, social, scientific, and cultural questions from a non-Nazi point of view. Only infrequently could one find discussion from an overtly anti-Nazi point of view, and then only at a considerable peril to the priest or the lecturer, and in some cases even to his audience.

The Italian Fascist experience was a close replica—and before 1933 a forerunner—of the Nazi pattern of communication and group control. The differences between these regimes could be summed up under the somewhat greater laxness of fascism, with its less extreme totalitarianism. As in the Nazi case, organization and communications networks were greatly augmented along with extended control by the Fascist party of the content and nature of both.

On the other hand, the sanctions meted out to opponents of the Fascist regime were, on the whole, neither as numerous nor as severe as in Hitler's Germany. The legally sanctioned and *de facto* autonomy of groups that could be classified either as allies or benevolent neutrals toward fascism was greater in Italy than in Germany. This was reflected in the continued maintenance of a substantial Catholic educational system, along with the public lay schools, and in the continued circulation of journals of Catholic opinion, albeit under restraints of censorship. Criticism of the regime and outward ideological diversity could manifest themselves, as in Germany, only through (1) underground and word-of-mouth channels and (2) within the framework of organized groups that enjoyed the sanction of the regime, although they were subject to censorship and reprisal.

Both the Fascist and Nazi regimes can be said to have restricted and narrowed down pluralism and autonomy of group life in their respective societies. There was hardly an organized entity—social, professional, or cultural, let alone political—that did not experience *some* regimentation or *some* organizational ideological deprivations at the hands of nazism and fascism. This is a fact. How these deprivations were perceived by their victims, however, is another problem. No matter what the facts of the case are, it would require the interposition of other people's perceptions, and values, to determine that the regimentation of A was *worse* than that of B.

Nevertheless, a reasonable case based on known facts can be made to show that fascism and nazism inflicted far greater damage on the autonomy and self-perceived interests of those whom they relegated to the category of enemies than of those whom they considered allies or neutrals. A case in point is that of business and labor under nazism.

In Germany trade unions had always represented a favorite target of Hitler's attacks and of Nazi propaganda generally because of their permeation by Marxism and social democracy, which Hitler had vowed to destroy root and branch. The merger of the formerly independent trade unions after 1933 into the German Labor Front was no mere change of symbols or nomenclature. The unions in their new organizational form lost the crucial right to strike and could no longer manage their affairs through officials elected by their own rank and file. Their officers were appointed by a minister of the Reich. These official leaders were party men, not union men, and their primary concern, both officially and unofficially, was not to represent the claims and grievances of the workingmen under their control, but to supervise workers' affairs in such a fashion as to secure the most efficient functioning of the Nazi economy. To the extent that this supervision involved taking up workers' grievances against employers, compulsory arbitration through the labor courts represented the ultimate recourse for the workers. The labor courts were, like the unions, presided over by Nazi party functionaries, and so far as we can judge from the character of their membership and the extant record of their decisions, they were generally weighted in favor of employers over the employees.[6]

Hitler's attitude toward employers, businessmen, and landed pro-

[6] William Ebenstein, in *The Nazi State* (New York: Farrar and Rinehart, 1943), p. 297, observes that "legal power of economic superiority" over employees, embodied in the 1934 Law for the Regulation of National Labor, was unprecedented even among "Fascist countries." *Cf.* Gaetano Salvemini, *Under the Axe of Fascism* (London: Victor Gollancz, 1936), pp. 67–98 and 245–388.

prietors was, at least since the time of *Mein Kampf*, a striking contrast to his abject hatred toward all things Marxist. By 1933 Nazi propagandists had long since discarded the vague threats aimed at bankers in the party's 1920 "unalterable program," which had promised to end "interest slavery" in Germany. To the Hitler of the 1930s, the only "bad capitalists" were Jewish and foreign capitalists. As early as 1925 he had specifically endorsed the principle of hierarchic leadership, from the top down, for business as much as for politics.[7]

The practical consequence of that recognition was to be found in Nazi labor legislation, which declared the employer to be "the leader" of his particular enterprise. The prohibition of strikes was in itself a major concession to employers, who in turn were prohibited from engaging in lockouts against the workers—a rather doubtful *quid pro quo* under the circumstances. Employer associations, although reorganized to some extent, did not undergo the upheaval of trade unions and, above all, continued under the leadership of men who really *did* represent business. Where in the unions workers' choices—that is, the pre-1933 officials—were simply removed and replaced by Nazi party functionaries, employer associations' leaders were generally furnished with party membership—that is, co-opted. The procedure of appointment of leaders from above, by the party-controlled government, rather than through election by the rank and file from below, was sensitive to the facts of business influence. Generally speaking, the men who dominated German industry and business before 1933 continued to do so after 1933. The same could hardly be said about organized labor.

Some of the restrictive regulations imposed on the population—even if theoretically applicable to all—in fact had a rather selective impact on different groups and strata of German society. For example, restrictions applicable to changes of employment made it increasingly difficult for German workmen to maintain physical mobility. On the other hand, Nazi passport regulations remained sufficiently lax until the outbreak of World War II, so that most German citizens who had the means adequate to the purpose could travel freely abroad. The various political restraints and disabilities imposed on the membership of organized groups and on the expression of opinion had, in fact, a similarly differential impact.

Organizations whose clienteles consisted of Junker landowners, ranking officers of the armed forces, industrialists, or senior bureaucrats were virtually unaffected by the disabilities imposed on Jews or Marxists, or by campaigns against ideologies and beliefs that they

[7] See *Mein Kampf*, Ch. 4, "Personality and the Conception of the National State," and Ch. 12, "Trade Union Question," *op. cit.*

regarded as alien and pernicious without having to be told so by the Nazis. In fact, it would be more appropriate to view the reception of such restrictions by nazism's (or fascism's) allies as wholesome and useful, notwithstanding their *outwardly* blanket character. And it is precisely in the light of the shared values between nazism (and fascism) and some of the interests in the surrounding society that we can better appreciate their greater autonomy vis-à-vis the regime.

This autonomy seemed mutually justified by a substantial community of outlook, although in some respects it was also an adaptation to the necessities of power by each regime. All considerations of intent and purpose apart, it was considerably easier for Hitler to begin the construction of his Thousand Year Reich by intimidating Jewish shopkeepers than the men who had led the German armed forces. Mussolini, understandably, displayed similar prudence in the restraints that he very differentially imposed after 1922 on Italian society.

Broadly speaking—the bulk of the bureaucracy, the military, and the business and the ecclesiastical elites—were not destroyed by the Fascist and Nazi revolutions. They were subjected to increased controls, in addition to suffering some limited casualties. These groups corresponded to the ally and neutral categories for the Nazis and the Fascists. Drastic and immediate physical removals, mass punishments, and thorough reorganization under direct State control were reserved for the enemy category, whose largest and most conspicuous examples in both cases were the trade unions and the oppositional political parties.

Under Communist rule, the destruction of group autonomy was not nearly so measured and so limited. To begin with, the principal foes to the Bolshevik regime were to be found precisely among those elements whose benevolence the Fascists and the Nazis had cultivated so assiduously. The Bolshevik Revolution was aimed directly against them. The men who controlled Russia's industry, commerce, land, and bureaucracy before 1917 were swept away by the wave of revolution. To be sure, during the decade immediately following 1917, the Soviet regime, hard pressed by the economic and military needs of waging a civil war (1917–1921) on the heels of Russia's enormously costly and destructive involvement in World War I (1914–1918), made use of economic, technical, and military personnel inherited from the Tsarist regime. Tsarist officers, at the point of a gun and under the control of party commissars, were used by Trotsky to lead the Red Armies in the civil war. Dispossessed factory owners were kept on as managers of industrial enterprises, sometimes their own and sometimes others', in the period of the so-called New Economic Policy, between 1921 and 1928.

But countless thousands of persons in these formerly privileged categories had already been physically "liquidated" in the course of the revolution and the civil war. Thousands more had fled abroad leaving most of their possessions behind them. Those who remained were branded as class enemies and officially marked for no uncertain extinction in one way or another by party propaganda. No chambers of commerce or industry or landlords' leagues were allowed to exist, let alone function. No old-time officers' associations survived the revolution of 1917. Foes were physically and organizationally pulverized by the revolution, if not totally destroyed. By 1930 the party controlled the economy, the bureaucracy, and the armed forces not because it had reached some mutually satisfactory *modus vivendi* with its prerevolutionary masters, but because it had almost completely eliminated them.

In the Communist experience, beginning with the Soviet, organized groups representative of "friendly" strata, above all workers, invariably have been the first to be assimilated into the mechanisms of party control. The cadre of the party invariably became the cadre of the trade unions. In the process, the demands of the party in effect displaced the demands of the unions. The party-ruled State became the principal, almost exclusive, employer. To strike against the party, against "the socialist system" became legally unthinkable. Opposition to the party, whether viewed as the State or as the employer became similarly untenable. Demands and grievances by workers would still be voiced and represented by union leaders. But the range of demands that could receive public articulation from the party-controlled union leadership has tended to be limited, even innocuous, and the ultimate recourse of a strike or similar overt action by workers has been denied.

The unions became, by and large, organizations to maximize and coordinate production with the corollary and subordinate function of minimizing worker discontent. The latter function has been fulfilled by the appearance of worker representation, group catharsis through the voicing and appeasement of minor grievances, and finally through the administration of various social welfare, cultural, and entertainment tasks by the union organization. The basic bargaining function of trade union leadership on behalf of workers' claims for higher wages, shorter hours, and better work conditions has been eroded. As in the case of other organized groups, the range of permitted claims, the means to express them, and the sanctions to implement them, have all been emasculated. It would be as inconceivable for Communist trade unions to conduct a genuine public debate on the government's foreign trade policy, even though it might affect unions, as it would be to argue the desirability of a right to strike. Nor could organized labor find room in its ranks for those who would publicly oppose forced labor camps, any more than organized religion under communism could find room for conscientious objectors in its public life.

If we can generalize that Communist regimes have been at least as thorough as Nazi and Fascist ones in the destruction of foes, but even more thorough in the "ingestion" of allies, religion is an anomaly. Communist regimes have been generally unable either to destroy or absorb it.

On ideological grounds, with its avowed atheism, the party has not been able to make the leading cadres of the churches simultaneously the cadres of the party. Nor could any religious organization, however pliant and docile, publicly identify itself as a branch of the Communist movement. These disabilities of cross-affiliation have made possible no more than the politics of religious alliance and subordination to the party rather than a merger with it.

On the other hand, the hold on public opinion exercised by the churches has made the direct and immediate abolition of organized religious life practically untenable for the Communists. In all cases, there have been efforts by the ruling parties to limit, control, and emasculate the content of religious group activity and communication. These efforts have been variously successful and differently conditioned by environmental constraints. In the countries of East-Central Europe, where the indigenous support for the party regimes was scant in the aftermath of the Red Army's occupation (or "liberation") in the 1940s, the measures undertaken against the churches were initially cautious and mild; in Russia they were at the outset brutal and sweeping.

In consequence of its ideology and its supportive propaganda we might expect communism—far more than fascism or nazism—to have sought the abolition of religious institutions. In fact, however, every Communist regime since 1917 has represented a pattern of accommodation between Church and State.[8] The diffusion of popular support for and identification with religion in Russia and in all the subsequent Communist-ruled systems has been much too general among the people to allow for any such immediate frontal assaults. The churches were a far more powerful opponent than a handful of landlords or even hundreds of thousands of bourgeois proprietors and bureaucrats. They represented the deep feelings and age-long habits even of the

[8] On Soviet legislation of January 1918, see M. Spinka, *The Church in Soviet Russia* (New York: Oxford University Press, 1956), pp. 14–47. *Cf.* Robert Conquest (ed.), *Religion in the U.S.S.R.* (New York: Praeger, 1960); Constantin de Grunewald, *The Churches and the Soviet Union* (New York: Macmillan, 1962), Ch. 3; Walter Kolarz, *Religion in the Soviet Union* (London: Macmillan, 1961), Ch. 1.

party's indispensable mass clientele—the workers and peasants, the poor, the underprivileged, and the disinherited. If the party viewed religion as an ailment, it had to face the fact that it was present in virtually every limb of the body politic. Surgery would be not merely impractical but conceivably suicidal.

In the ensuing pattern of accommodation between regime and religion, the party set about controlling and limiting the influence of churches instead of proscribing them. Unable to ignore the Russian peasant's habits of attending church, offering donations to the priests, and adhering to the basic customs of church rites on the great occasions of life (in birth, marriage and death), the regime's policy restricted the availability of such religious gratifications without wholly removing them.

Churches destroyed in the civil war were rebuilt in fewer numbers; many were converted from places of worship into state museums. Seminaries for the training of priests were similarily limited. Various religious orders and charitable institutions were abolished. Priests were subjected to close political surveillance and allowed to preach and perform ceremonies only if they evidenced "quietist" attitudes toward the regime. The priest who would denounce communism as godless to his parishioners was liable to severe and swift punishment. On the other hand, by the total abolition of religious education in primary and secondary schools, by the official encouragement of atheist views, by the dissemination by the party of antireligious propaganda, by the substitution or at least widespread availability of civil ceremonies for the religious in every occasion of life, and finally by the party's concerted campaign to picture religiosity among the people as a barely tolerated relic of the past, not worthy of the best Soviet citizens, the foundations of religious institutions were being steadily undermined.

To be a believer and a party member was an official incompatibility. The party constituted the vanguard of the ruling worker-peasant alliance. No one could reasonably hope, under Soviet rule, to rise to any position of importance in secular life if he remained, outwardly at least, religious.

In the case of Russia, the Communist regime was assisted in its effort to establish the subservience and quietism of the religious elements that survived the Revolution by the legacy of Church-State union under the Tsars in the predominant Greek Orthodox Russian Church. The issues of ultramontanism and of an international religious hierarchy implicit in nations with large Roman Catholic populations were virtually absent there, and during World War II, the Stalin regime actually mobilized the State-controlled Russian Church in behalf of its then more broadly based national patriotism.

Ideologically, the claims of fascism in behalf of the indisputable total primacy of the State were viewed by devout Christians as ultimately incompatible with the moral and spiritual teachings of religion. Fascist militants, on the other hand, believed that the support given the State by the Church was much too lukewarm and qualified. Above all, in the field of education, there were doubts on both sides whether the ruthless, blindly responsive warrior type of man and citizen, posited by Fascist ideology and propaganda, could ever be produced under the auspices of Catholic moral and religious instruction. These doubts, on the Fascist side, led to sporadic attempts to exercise greater control over Church schools.

Under Mussolini's regime, there was no doctrinal Fascist parallel to the Communist position that religion is "the opium of the people." There was no call for the destruction of the Roman Church. On the contrary, Fascist ideology and propaganda professed to see a rightful place for religion as a constituent element and a bulwark of the State and claimed to take national pride in Italian Catholicism. There might be occasional "bad" or "mistaken" priests, to be sure, but fascism sought no overt quarrel with the Church or religion. What it sought, however, was "cooperation" which could be, and from time to time was, regarded as unacceptable subservience by many Catholic priests and laymen.

The position of the Nazis under Hitler's leadership, so far as party ideology and propaganda were concerned, bore some resemblance to Mussolini's fascism. Religion and churches were never officially declared the objectives of a policy of extinction. Hitler never publicly attacked either Catholicism or Protestantism. Unlike Mussolini he never identified himself—even privately so far as we know—as an atheist. In his speeches and writings, notably *Mein Kampf*, he never tired of favorable references to spirituality and denigrations of materialism. Like Mussolini, he appeared to many Christians (Catholic Vice-Chancellor von Papen among them) in the attractive guise of a ruthless opponent of communism and one not without religious instincts.[9]

On the other hand, the Nazis went farther than the Fascists in attacking various selected aspects of religion. Hitler's official ideologist, Alfred Rosenberg, for example, directly challenged and abused a variety of Christian teachings and traditions claiming that they were, in fact, "Jewish misrepresentations" of the true heroic (and somehow miraculously Aryan) Christ. He particularly abused Saint Paul as a purveyor of a false doctrine of humility, meekness, and submission

[9] See Franz von Papen, *Memoirs* (New York: Dutton, 1953), pp. 278–282. See Guenter Lewy, *The Catholic Church and Nazi Germany* (New York: McGraw-Hill, 1964), p. 263.

rather than the "true doctrine" of heroism and martial grandeur. In addition, specific Nazi policies, including State control of education and racism, contributed to Church-State conflicts and the persecution of many priests and ministers.

For those who wanted to involve themselves in politics and public affairs directly there was only one organizational-ideological outlet in Germany and Italy alike: the totalitarian party, Nazi and Fascist. In both cases, individual membership in the party involved not merely the unquestioning acceptance of a set of dogmas about the authority of the leaders and the ideology and the mission of the party, but it provided activity that minimized the individual's opportunity for deliberation and discussion of issues and policies and for the choosing of alternatives and of leaders. What it did confer was an intimate sense of belonging, heightened by a continuous process of propagandistic exhortation, public ceremonies, insignia, uniforms, and the like, and by the performance of hierarchically prescribed party chores.

The unique status of the party, as a *de facto* molder of society and chosen instrument of the Leader, conferred prestige on membership and frequently assured material preferment and spoils. Party members regarded themselves as rulers who could claim the best of everything —united as they were by a common mission and possessing a pervasive political influence not shared by their countrymen in general. Under fascism and nazism the totalitarian party visibly strove to substitute itself for the power of a whole electorate in the democratic systems and to become an organized group in charge of all other organized groups, public and private, governmental or not.

For those who enjoyed a unique sense of power over their fellows, for those who craved a sense of disciplined obedience to authority on a grotesque military model, and finally for those who wanted to secure themselves preferential treatment and career opportunities, party life offered considerable satisfactions.

The effect on the individual German or Italian, insofar as we could abstract him, of the manipulation of organization and information by fascism and nazism was to reduce the diversity of social experiences, of cultural-intellectual stimuli, and of personal choices available to him. It also increased his need to conform to politically manipulated group standards enforced by the regime. These standards generally emphasized and reinforced autocratic modes of behavior in virtually every walk of life.

In the Communist experience, too, the party has been the chosen instrument for the destruction of pluralism and autonomy in group life and in social communication. The parties of all the Communist-ruled states to date have followed the Russian, as well as the Nazi and Fascist, experience in the attempt to subordinate all functional, indigenous group interests—whether economic, social, cultural, or otherwise—to the overriding unifying directives of the party.

In the Russian case virtually all organized groups became "transmission belts" for the advancement of the party's objectives and for the more effective maintenance of its power in the society at large. In other Communist systems, in Eastern Europe and even in China for a number of years after 1949, the party's guiding role appeared to some extent camouflaged and diluted by the deployment of several other political entities as auxiliaries, or front organizations, for the Communist party itself. The common minimum of the Communist experience, however, has been participation for people in public life *only* under the leadership of the party and in conformity to its principles and general policies.

The differences among individual Communist systems make it impossible for an individual in Russia to participate in any party but the CPSU, but in Poland he may also be a member and activist in the so-called United Peasant party or the so-called Democratic party. Each of these parties, however, is pledged to cooperate with and implement the tasks set forth by the ruling Communist United Polish Workers party. Thus, the individual has no chance of undertaking legal opposition to the regime through *any* party affiliation that is open to him, nor even any right of voicing occasional dissent. He is simply assigned "another sector of the front," as it were, by the regime; he is expected to act as a loyal supporter of the Communists among strata such as the peasantry or the intellectuals where the difference of label and the appearance of diversity and autonomy are believed by the party to be transitionally helpful.

A notable social difference among the totalitarian regimes stems from their different orientations toward science and culture. We have noted that one of the common denominators of group life in all innovative-mobilized systems has been the increased volume of affiliation and communication made available to and even imposed on people, combined with a decline in the variety and the indigenous autonomy of the content of both. We have also noted the tendency to hierarchic subordination of the members to the leaders in organized groups within these political systems. Nevertheless, the Communist regimes, while upholding the authority of the party in virtually all walks of life, have made concerted efforts to—if we may borrow the language of the party—"raise the cultural level of the masses."

Extensive resort to censorship and the preference of particular interpretations in art, literature, music, and even science, notwithstanding, the *popularization* of art, literature, music, and science has been far more consistently and assiduously promoted under communism than under either fascism or nazism. One effect of this tendency on social communication and group life has been analogous to the impact of education.

Although the range of overtly or even implicitly political experience for the average individual has been decreased in all these systems, communism has afforded the individual the compensation of a generally richer cultural existence. If it has decreased the stimuli of political diversity, it has increased the stimuli of cultural communication and participation hitherto available to most people in territories under its rule.

Unlike Fascists and Nazis, the Communist oligarchs have promoted a cultural as well as a political mobilization, to which the only, and at that but partial, exception has been China's current Great Cultural Revolution. Through the media of the publicly financed printing presses and vastly augmented performing arts, and through theatre, opera, ballet, concerts, lectures, and exhibits, there has been an appreciable enrichment of the lives of people who under pre-Communist regimes simply could not afford to partake of such things.

Under each of the Communist regimes, with the recent Chinese exception, there has been a State-promoted revival of interest in folklore and the traditional classics of national literature, music, and the arts generally. There has also been an extensive promotion of foreign literature and art, albeit subject to political-ideological manipulation, such as the inordinate emphasis on the diffusion of the literature and drama representative of social protest abroad, along with the more politically neutral classics of the arts. The increased exposure of the peasant and the manual worker to the cultural stimuli of plays and concerts and of museums and libraries has been a significant feature of life under Communist rule. In this respect, the policies of Communist regimes, even China's, have been markedly different from the Nazi-Fascist totalitarian prototype.

The latter did not emphasize any diffusion of intellectual-cultural values to the population, or specifically to the poorer strata. The volume of political communication increased, but culturally Nazi and Fascist policies were socially quiescent, if not reactionary. Hitler and Mussolini adhered to the time-honored formula that what the masses needed was "bread and circuses." They were not interested in promoting culture or intellectualism among their workers and peasants. They were willing to provide recreation to the masses of a more primitive, physical rather than intellectual, character under the party auspices. Only those who had the means and the taste for more refined pastimes could enjoy them under these regimes—subject, of course, to political censorship, which excluded the works of Jews in Germany and also of many foreign and indigenous writers, artists, and composers under both regimes.[10]

[10] See George L. Mosse (ed.), *Nazi Culture: Intellectual, Cultural and Social Life in the*

Oligarchies that are overtly committed to the "uplift" of their societies away from traditional modes of life, regardless of direction, invariably commit political controls to impinge on the pluralism and the autonomy of group life around them. This is true paradoxically even in those cases in which the regime seemingly intends to *create* greater social pluralism than it has inherited. Autocratic innovation implies an inevitable subordination of economic, social, cultural, and possibly religious groups through which the regime either hopes to promote new popular orientations and modes of behavior, or through which it hopes to curb the undesirable traditional patterns of outlook and action.

Illustrative of such innovative autocratic regimes, deeply regimenting the society around them, was Turkey under the leadership of Mustafa Kemal. As Arnold J. Toynbee has recorded, Kemal

> . . . carried into his interregnum of administration a reforming zeal seldom shown in such spectacular fashion; and made a unique place for himself in the annals of history as the great iconoclast of the Islamic tradition and the builder of a new Western state out of an Oriental people.[11]

One of the first steps in the establishment of the Kemal regime was the founding in 1919 of the so-called National Organization, a political movement ultimately converted into the Popular Republican party, which wielded considerable mass following to a revolutionary-ideological direction under the leadership of Kemal.

Turkey's new regime was the very antithesis of a "power-for-its-own-sake" ideal. It began its rule with what Toynbee has called an "amazing series of abolitions" which to

> . . . the eyes of the world . . . seemed an orgy of iconoclasm, the breaking of ancient idols, the repudiation of national traditions and customs, the renunciation of Turkish institutions.[12]

Among the destroyed structures of the old order were the monarchical Sultanate and the religious-temporal caliphate; polygamy; the seclusion of women; mosque schools; and numerous age-old customs affecting basic matters, including dress, language, and family relationships.

Even though the objectives of the regime were those of republican, egalitarian, and democratic institutions for Turkey, the process of sweeping social change combined with resistance and, from Kemal's point of view, backsliding by the Turks, led to institutionalized autocracy on a very complex scale.

Third Reich (New York: Grosset and Dunlap, 1965), pp. 235–240.

[11] *Turkey* (New York: Charles Scribner's Sons, 1927), p. 135.

[12] *Ibid.*, p. 189.

One expression of this autocracy was the curtailment of the freedom of the press. In December 1923, the Kemalists instituted a system of special tribunals with sweeping powers for trying those accused of treason.[13] Kemal pledged himself to a policy of pervasive vigilance against counterrevolution, implying wide-ranging censorship and repression of opposition, and to the effective centralization of both the educational and judicial systems of the country under the authority of the ministries of the national government under his direction. Kemal resorted to new nationally run State economic monopolies in industries, ranging from salt, tobacco, and alcohol to various branches of banking. In 1926, he adopted a new revenue system emphasizing the graduated income tax, death duties, and other levies on the pattern of the modern, Western democratic powers. The regime also sponsored large-scale population exchanges with Greece and drastically altered the privileged pre-1919 positions of resident foreigners in Turkey (the so-called capitulations). "Ecclesiastical seminaries were confiscated for State purposes, and their vast properties and endowments made over to the national treasury."[14]

Kemal abolished religious schools in 1924. In place of these, he provided a universal system of publicly supported and centrally run secular education. Governmental controls of curricula and of teaching were generally increased. Scholarship aid was greatly increased by the State. Notwithstanding all the traditions of Islam, Kemal advanced the emancipation of women beyond any contemporaneous Muslim precedent from Algeria to India.

> The University of Constantinople opened its doors to women, and for the first time admitted the principle of coeducation. Women entered the professions of teaching, of medicine, and of law. They began to work for the further enfranchisement and education of their sex by writing, lecturing and political agitation. Khalideh Khanum . . . first Turkish woman to take a University degree had distinguished herself as a writer [and] aide-de-camp to . . . Kemal.[15]

It is of interest to note that insofar as the Kemalist reforms represented a thorough secularization of society, they were not as extremely innovative as the Communist because they did not aim at the *abolition* of religion. As K. H. Karpat wrote in 1959:

> The Republic did not want to depart from Islam and accept a new faith, as was thought by some, but wished to rid Islam of those features thought, rightly

[13] *Ibid.*, p. 228. "The first act of the Constantinople Tribunal was to arrest the editors of the three leading newspapers of that city, and to suppress their journal."

[14] *Ibid.*, p. 243.

[15] *Ibid.*, p. 254.

or wrongly, to contradict the modernistic spirit of the new regime; that is dogmatism, exclusiveness, and primitiveness. The Republic sought a purified, reformed Islam which was both modern and Turkish.[16]

Above all, however, the political development of Turkey under an innovative autocracy required increased penetration of society by the state: the subordination of various ostensibly nonpolitical institutions to political-governmental ones. The regime, which had itself introduced institutionalized political opposition in Turkey as a means of westernizing and modernizing the nation, moved to abolish it within a decade of its accession to power. The so-called Liberal party and other minor parties were dissolved because Kemal's Republicans charged them paradoxically with serving as "covers" for "religious reactionaries."[17]

Characteristic reforms included labor legislation in 1936 that "denied the workers' right to organize and declared strikes illegal." In 1938,

> ... political parties and Masonic lodges were dissolved. The police were given full authority to seize and hold "indefinitely" without warrant any persons considered dangerous. Government officials could not be held accountable before the courts for acts committed in the course of their duties except with the approval of those highest in the government hierarchy. The press was most tightly controlled, both in its daily work and in permission for founding new publications.[18]

Peron's rule in Argentina was similarly a type of innovative-mobilizational regime. Not satisfied to hold supreme power on the basis of traditional institutions and inherited beliefs, Peron promoted an innovative ideology. His amalgam of *justicialismo* (nationalism and authoritarianism) was an attempt to anchor his dictatorship on the allegiance of the poor urban workers, in particular; but in fact he sought the allegiance of all who could identify themselves, in Peronista language, as *descamisados* (shirtless ones). In common with the ideology of nazism and fascism, Peron's orientation employed the language of class discontent venting it in large measure on "foreign exploiters" of the Argentine people—the Americans and the British, above all. With its emphasis on national self-determination, autarky, denunciation of international capitalism, and of the financial oligarchy at home, Peronism provided at once a verbal substitute for the radicalism of Argentina's traditional anti-status quo Left and also some remarkable parallels to the ideological orientations of nazism and

[16] *Turkey's Politics: The Transition to a Multi-Party System* (Princeton, N.J.: Princeton University Press, 1959) p. 60.

[17] *Ibid.*, p. 67.

[18] *Ibid.*, p. 74.

fascism. The Peronista orientation could be described as demagogical inasmuch as Peron did not move to wipe out the Argentine oligarchy, urban or rural, as the tone of his propaganda might have suggested. He did, however, sponsor various new measures of social protection for workers and employees of Argentina, and he extended the domain of State economic enterprises in various areas of Argentine business and finance.

The structural counterpart of Peronismo was the Peronista party with which the dictator attempted to saturate and to integrate the social, cultural, and political institutions of the entire nation between 1946 and 1955. Like Hitler and Mussolini before him, Peron was initially cautious and circumspect, notwithstanding all his verbal radicalism, to respect the interests and integrity of powerful status quo groups—the Church and the armed forces, in particular. The two major components of Peron's power were simultaneously the urban workers and the Army. In 1955, conflict with the Church and the armed forces proved to be Peron's undoing.[19]

But while his regime lasted, it attempted to subordinate most hitherto independent, autonomous institutions to political direction from the center. George I. Blanksten has called this "institutionalized lockstep." The press, the trade unions, the universities, and business—and ultimately even the armed forces—all felt, in varying degrees, the Peronista attempt at close regimentation. Peron's carrot-and-stick policy resulted, most strikingly perhaps, in the conversion of organized labor into an adjunct of the regime. The dictator made the unions accept State-appointed (Peronista) officials; eschew strikes in favor of compulsory, government-provided arbitration; refrain from (unofficial) political activity; and submit to militaristic organization and hierarchic discipline imposed from above.[20] Even the traditional autonomy of the universities was trampled by Peronism, as "politics" continued its conquest of "society" in the Argentine State of the 1940s and 1950s.

In Indonesia, the transition from a would-be constitutional democracy in 1956–1958 to an outward dictatorship under President Sukarno was accompanied by similar innovative-mobilizational measures, precariously shared between the president and the armed forces.

There was an ideological mobilization, largely handled by Sukarno himself, hand in hand with an effort to make the military into a control-

[19] See Frank Owen, *Peron: His Rise and Fall* (London: Cresset Press, 1957), pp. 102–103. See also George I. Blanksten, *Peron's Argentina* (Chicago: University of Chicago Press, 1953), pp. 390–391. *Cf.* Arthur P. Whitaker, *Argentine Upheaval* (New York: Praeger, 1956), pp. 3–8.

[20] Owen, *op. cit.*, p. 32. *Cf.* Blanksten, *op. cit.*, pp. 322–323, who quotes Eva Peron as follows: "The Argentine labor movement . . . is a Peronista movement. It cannot exist without the doctrine of General Peron and the doctrine cannot exist without [it]." P. 322.

ling political movement behind the president. In the end, the organizational efforts of the Army proved more substantial than the ideological ones put forth by Sukarno. From the standpoint of the innovative pattern of autocracy in Indonesia created in the late 1950s and mid-1960s, both are of interest. According to Herbert Feith:

> Throughout this period the president repeatedly fashioned new symbols of state, new formulations of the meaning of the present and of the goals to be sought in the future, and these immediately dominated virtually all mass communication. His central ideological theme from 1959 onward was Manipol-USDEK, Manipol standing for the Political Manifesto (President Soekarno's speech of August 17, 1959) and USDEK being an acronym summarizing the five essential points of this Manifesto: the 1945 constitution, Indonesian Socialism, Guided Democracy, Guided Economy, and Indonesian Personality or Identity. Among his other slogans were Gotong Rojong (Mutual Help), NASAKOM (the Unity of Nationalists, Religious People, and Communists), Building the World Anew, and the Message of the Suffering of the People.[21]

Meanwhile, the armed forces under General Nasution pursued a policy of depluralizing and deautonomizing the whole field of Indonesian politics. The Army began to "supervise the activities of ex-soldiers and all sorts of youth organizations," through its Veterans Legion and a Youth-Military Cooperation Body.[22] It used its martial-law-decree power to regulate property and educational institutions. A large number of political parties—although not all—were dissolved by the Army; many politicians were arrested; and the press was rigidly censored. Even Boy Scout groups came under "unified government control."

> Subsequently, disbandment orders went out to a number of internationally linked organizations said to be out of conformity with the Indonesian national personality including the Freemasons, the Rosicrucians, and Moral Rearmament.[23]

In the cases of Algeria and Egypt in the 1960s, we have still other regimes that are innovative and autocratic but whose goals and the political machinery for the realization of them are neither as explicit nor as far-reaching as those of the Communist states. In both cases, political movements, analogous to the party, extend control over nongovernmental and overtly nonpolitical groups as well as over the formal structure of government. Trade unions are movement affiliated and government controlled; so are all the media of communication.

[21] *The Decline of Constitutional Democracy in Indonesia* (Ithaca, N.Y.: Cornell University Press, 1962), pp. 594–595.

[22] *Ibid.*, p. 593.

[23] *Ibid.*

Censorship is a prime fact of life, and the right to strike is denied. The *de facto* pervasiveness of these controls, however, is dependent partly on the apparatus that the autocracy can provide for their enforcement, and is a function of the claims made by the regime.

Neither Algeria nor Egypt, each with its version of Arab socialism, has developed full-fledged equivalents of "Socialist realism"—for example, compelling the production of particular types of art and effectively proscribing others or demanding a particular philosophy of science and life. They have punished and repressed specific overt acts and utterances aimed against the respective regimes. They have not yet committed institutions of learning to an official secular ideology with as universal an applicability as Marxism-Leninism. They have not embarked on a campaign to exterminate religion among the people.

The transition from innovative-mobilizational to the traditionalist regime generally involves movement in the opposite direction: deemphasis of official ideology and increased autonomy or independence for the overtly nonpolitical institutions in society. This was the development in Spain between 1939 and 1941 and the 1950s, when the Fascist-minded Falanga gradually lost its outward preeminence in the autocracy of General Franco. On the other hand, the ideological and organizational autonomy of social, cultural, and civic associations —of students, workers, professionals, municipalities, and universities— all appreciably increased from the days when Franco appeared as a Spanish replica of Mussolini and Hitler. Similar developments appear to have taken place since the passing of Salazar in Portugal in 1968.

Generally speaking, traditional autocracies maintain a relatively pluralistic group structure primarily benefiting those interests and organized groups whose political salience is low and those whose relationship to the regime belongs to the ally and neutral category. Such interests may be allowed very considerable internal autonomy and freedom of expression. At times their influence, directly and indirectly, on the State may be greater than the State's on them. Like the Spanish Church under Franco, the institution may be a barely disguised ruling alliance, a major influence on the autocrat's decisions. On the other hand, organized interests and communications media representing enemies of the traditional autocracy are likely to be dealt with far more harshly and summarily (if not necessarily illegally in the narrow terms of positive law) than would be possible under a democracy. The disparity between the rights and the autonomy of organized religion, allied to the regime, and of organized labor suspected of being an enemy to it is strikingly wide. This disparity of rights—unlike the analogous if much lesser disparities among the democracies—is never openly umpired or sanctioned by the judgment of the whole community. It may be the product of a dictator's predilection, or perhaps of a "deal" behind the scenes or, more likely yet, it may be based on an informal understanding of mutual interests. Any or all of these may then be readily translated into "laws" and into administrative practice.

For the autocratic bureaucrat, his professional-economic interests are subject to self-effacement. They cannot be openly articulated. We find artists, writers, or designers in autocratic regimes for whom various modes of expression are strictly taboo; who cannot voice grievances against certain aspects of their professional lives because of the basic challenge to official doctrines implicit in them; and who, thus, can express only a part of their total, *de facto* professional aspirations, interests, and problems in the very associations that are ostensibly devoted to these purposes.

Many innovative as well as traditional autocracies simply do not match the *intensity* of characteristics exhibited by the extremely innovative autocrats—the totalitarian regimes—in three qualities: the design for total power, whatever its overt purpose; the aspiration to drastic institutional change, that is, to change in the behavior and orientation patterns of people under one's rule, regardless of its avowed direction; and the capacity to implement these with formidable technological and organizational weaponry.

Where the regime, although autocratic, asserts only moderate claims to power and to change from the status quo, politically disadvantaged and persecuted groups are likely to be treated more leniently. The Tsarist regime in Russia was brutally repressive toward political opponents but nowhere nearly as systematic, thorough, and effective as the Soviet regime. The Tsar and the interests influential in his government did not care to create anything analogous to the "new Soviet man" or to fundamentally alter the existent political or economic institutions around them. They wanted rather to preserve a status quo, with perhaps small and piecemeal accommodations, if and as inevitably necessary. They did not care to remake minds and souls. They resorted to censorship but not to the mass dissemination of propaganda. And the censorship that they did use was so full of administrative loopholes as to be frequently ineffective and even flagrantly self-defeating. Similarly, the surveillance and repressions applied through the secret police (*Okhrana*) and the penal system were neither well organized nor systematic. Some political offenders suffered the penalties of hanging or flogging, but countless others were allowed quite tolerable conditions of exile. In Stalin's case in 1912, this allowed not only for the survival of the individual but even for the maintenance of all his old, anti-regime, revolutionary contacts, and activities. Such persecution, by its crudeness and ineffectiveness, has been thought to be more a stimulant to revolution than an obstacle to it.

Analogously, the persecution of Catholics, Poles, and Socialists under the Wilhelmian Empire was mild and ineffectual as compared with the totalitarian punishments meted out by Hitler's machinery of terror, propaganda, and intimidation. Ideologically, the struggle did not need to be so total from the regime's point of view because total power was not its objective, only an equilibrium of the status quo. Materially, the resources for a totalitarian type of purge could not be found without raising the level of political claims, and thereby impairing the traditional autonomy and perquisites of interests on whose benevolent support the monarchy had rested.

One of the consequences of system differences on group life is the greater ability of organized interests in the democracies to represent a wider range—if not the total range—of the aspirations of their members. Political salience is generally relevant here in the sense that even democratic systems impose increasing disabilities and regulations on groups and on group affiliations in proportion to the "security sensitiveness" of the individual's role in the government's estimate. But even among the highly salient government bureaucracy, for example, the democracies have generally recognized the legitimacy of an economic and professional self-interest of their civil servants. The right to collective bargaining, to representation of grievances, negotiated settlements, and in some areas of service even of strikes against the rulers have been widely recognized by the effective democracies. Such rights have not been acknowledged by the innovative-mobilized regimes and, generally speaking, there have been no parallels among the autocracies either to the right to strike for public servants or to bargain openly as through the so-called Whitley Councils in Britain.

The propensity of autocratic regimes to fluctuate widely in their treatment of organized groups, and of the media of public opinion and communication, presents a paradoxical contrast with the democracies. The individual who identifies security for his particular interest with autocratic rule exposes himself to a greater potential danger of eventual betrayal and disillusionment than his democratic counterpart. The alleged fickleness of public opinion is buttressed in a democracy by substantial numbers and by procedural safeguards. One's interest may not always prevail in the democratic forum but no loss, no fall from grace, need be final, irrevocable, or the cause of shocking mistreatment, legalized or otherwise, as under various autocratic systems.

A group founded in the United States for the purpose of promoting recognition of the merits of President Thomas Jefferson could never hope to achieve either total and obligatory adulation for their hero or the banishment of his detractors. An analogous society of Stalin's admirers in the Soviet Union would likely undergo an all-and-then-nothing-at-all sequence of development.

CHAPTER 4
TAXATION AND BUDGET

IN the great conflicts of history, taxation and finance have had many memorable pages. In the Cromwellian revolution in seventeenth-century England, King Charles I lost both his throne and his head largely because Parliament and the people considered his taxes arbitrary and onerous. The removal of taxation from the sphere of royal prerogative by the Bill of Rights of 1689 was one of the chief accomplishments of the constitutional history of Britain and of the Glorious Revolution in particular. The right to levy taxes also figured prominently in the American and French Revolutions of the eighteenth century.

Other things being equal, are we not entitled to expect that in fiscal matters, a government by the poor would differ greatly from one by the rich? Or that, more generally, the burdens and rewards of the public treasury would be shouldered differently in different political systems?[1]

What is more reasonable than to expect that politicians in power,

[1] The great theorist of democracy, Alexis de Tocqueville, believed that "Universal suffrage . . . in point of fact does invest the poor with the government of society," but also that democracy would encourage the proliferation of a middle class as profoundly concerned with preserving the rights of property as with acquiring more wealth. See M. Zetterbaum, *Tocqueville and the Problem of Democracy* (Stanford, Calif.: Stanford University Press, 1967), pp. 78 and 78–80.

whether "democratic" or "totalitarian," should be more generous to their own causes, interests, and supporters than to their adversaries or to any random interests?

The political system does influence the nature of a State's budget—where and how it gets the revenue, who profits by it, and how—but it is never the only influencing factor. Nor can we expect its influence to be of a constant magnitude. A drought, an earthquake, a foreign war, or an abundance or lack of certain forms of wealth may in some circumstances be more significant in shaping government revenue and fiscal policy than the political orientation of the rulers. The political factors may be under some circumstances modified by phenomena in no way dependent on the political organization of the society. Only a case-study approach could adequately account for all these additional factors and their relative weights in any given case. In most nations tax systems have developed piecemeal, over long periods of time, in response to various circumstances not always "political" in the sense in which we use this term.[2]

Among the numerous "discount" factors that render comparisons of national fiscal systems difficult are lack of data; widely differing reliability of such information as is actually reported; absence of internationally uniform classifications of various types of government revenues and expenditures; lack of adjusted price-cost information that would enable the observer to judge to what extent apparently equivalent expenditures on the same general purposes are in fact so (for example, does $100 million buy the same quantity and quality of school buildings in India as it does in Japan?); the degree to which certain kinds of revenue and expenditure of national governments are duplicated or preempted by their subdivisions on state, local, and municipal levels; the degree to which private spending supplements certain types of expenditures (a matter of key import in comparisons of spending for educational purposes in the United States and the USSR, for example); subsidies accorded private interests from the public treasury; and, very significant, secret budgetary allocations.

We must consider taxation in fact rather than in name to which governments can resort. Deliberate inflation of the currency and the freezing of wages, but not prices, for example, can be used by governments to produce effects analogous to those of taxation. A realistic approach to available information must recognize the interrelatedness of certain problems. Put in the simplest terms, the burdens of taxation cannot be fully judged without simultaneous reference to the uses of

[2] See, for example, the discussion of these problems in W. S. Woytinsky and E. S. Woytinsky, *World Commerce and Governments* (New York: Twentieth Century Fund, 1955), Ch. 15; see also, J. F. Dewhurst, *et al., Europe's Needs and Resources* (New York: Twentieth Century Fund, 1961), Ch. 13.

the proceeds. The government may in fact rob Peter to pay Paul. High or low levels of taxation, whether in terms of a particular GNP, or in international perspective, must all be related to the nature and amount of spending that results from it. Resources drawn from one segment of the economy may be poured into others at rates so unequal as to make A fully comprehensible only in light of B.[3]

If we assume that in *all* political systems there is a tendency to distribute the fiscal burdens of government and its benefits in such a way as to maximize the advantages and the purposes of those who effectively control the political system, this "maximization" can only be defined and discerned in a relative sense—that is, in the light of such claims and values as the power holders themselves have, not in an absolute sense. We must distinguish, therefore, between the proposition that a certain mode of taxation or budgetary allocation *really* serves the interest of a particular segment of society, or indeed the whole society, and the proposition that such taxation or allocation corresponds to traditional claims and widely acknowledged interests of various groups. Socialists and conservatives differ in their conceptions of effective and just taxation, and the validity of their claims is the subject of philosophical and/or practical disputes. But the claims afford us a basis for judgments of the prevailing realities of fiscal practice.

Among the characteristic tendencies of democratic budgets are (1) progressive taxation—that is, emphasis on an equitable sharing of the fiscal burdens of government in terms of the citizens' ability to pay; (2) relative openness of the whole budgetary process, allowing various segments of society to know what is being collected, how it is spent, and the opportunity to publicize and object as restraints to graft, corruption, and misuse; (3) the employment of assessment and collection procedures that impede arbitrary gifts to some groups and outright expropriation of others; (4) the balancing of income and outgo in

[3] We believe that, according to the old maxim, it is better to light a single candle than to curse the darkness. It is worth noting that the problem of comparative analysis becomes even more formidable where different historical periods as well as systems are compared. "... it is extremely difficult to compare the volume of governmental activities and public finances in relation to all economic activities and total national income in periods remote from one another or in nations of different economic types. There is no way to decide, for example, whether or not a modern democratic government, with all its agencies, absorbs a larger part of national income than was exacted from the people in the Middle Ages by what then represented the governmental system—the Church, the King, and the nobles combined. It is difficult to determine whether the administration of modern Egypt has disposition over a larger share of Egypt's income —in products and services—than a Pharaoh controlled in the second millennium B.C., or whether the cost of government in Great Britain represented a heavier burden for the people in 1950 or 1815, after the Napoleonic wars." Woytinsky and Woytinsky, *op.cit.,* p. 684.

response to conflicting and fluctuating societal demands for publicly provided services and amenities, on the one hand, and minimal burdens on private incomes and wealth of individual taxpayers, on the other. All these tendencies, maximized among the more solidly established democracies, are subject to extreme variation among autocratic regimes.

Insofar as democratic political systems involve popular pressure on decision makers not all strata of the population—not all groups and individuals—have equal capability for exerting it. What is known of the impact of wealth, education, status, and organization on individual and group capabilities within the democratic political systems suggests some significant differentials.[4] These differentials are likely to mitigate in favor of the haves rather than the have nots within the democratic political system. Nevertheless, the democratic political mechanism brings a wide mix of interests to bear on policy making. Those who are primarily interested in increasing public expenditure for their own ends are pitted against those who, above all, wish to minimize their tax burdens. The democratic political mechanisms and procedures encourage concern with the question of whether everyone carries his fair share of the burdens. Advantages to one group or another may be disputed, but for taxation to become *either* arbitrary expropriation of the rich *or* to be wholly supported by the poor would be well-nigh inconceivable.

On the other end of our political scale, oligarchical political systems, without competitive elections and institutionalized oppositions, have greater leeway to pursue discriminatory and arbitrary tax and appropriation policies.

The ideal of direct taxation, proportionate to income and increasing in burden with rising ability to pay, was characteristic of socialist and reform movements in the nineteenth century in Europe and throughout the world. It has generally accompanied the ideal and the slogan of universal suffrage. It has been embodied also to some extent, both in law and practice, in all of the effective democracies that are also highly industrialized and in which the workers and employees are significant constituents in the population.

Let us consider how one economically marginal democracy, Ireland, fits into this pattern. Ireland's case is particularly relevant because as T. P. Coogan has recently written:

[4] See, for example, Lester W. Milbrath, *Political Participation: How and Why Do People Get Involved in Politics?* (Chicago: Rand McNally, 1965), Ch. 5; Robert E. Lane, *Political Life: Why People Get Involved in Politics* (Glencoe, Ill.: Free Press, 1959), Ch. 16. *Cf.* Gabriel Almond and Sidney Verba, *Civic Culture* (Princeton, N.J.: Princeton University Press, 1963), Ch. 3 and *passim*. See also Mancur Olson, Jr., *The Logic of Collective Action* (New York: Schocken Books, 1968), especially Ch. 5.

Table 2
Percentage of Total Tax Revenue Drawn From Direct Taxation of Central Governments in the Long-Established Democracies (Figures c. 1959)*

United States	85.5
New Zealand	65.7
Uruguay	65.2
Canada	59.0
Australia	58.9
Great Britain	55.5
Sweden	55.3
Ireland	32.5
Switzerland	27.9

*This table is based on Yearbook of National Accounts Statistics (New York: United Nations Statistical Office, 1959). Switzerland's low ranking in the proportion of direct taxation is explained, in part, by the strength of Swiss federalism in which the cantons consume a large share of public expenditure, and the character of the population, still made up of many small producers. (*Cf.* remarks on Ireland.) See also John F. Due on the redeeming (progressive) qualities of Switzerland's indirect taxation in "Sales Taxation in Western Europe," *National Tax Journal*, Vol. 8, No. 2 (June 1955), Part I, pp. 171-185.

> . . . in European terms, Ireland is small and among the poorer countries of the "developed" world. Its economy is more dependent on a single market (Britain) than any European country. It has a high ratio of dependents to producers: seventy-four to every 100, as compared with fifty-three in Britain, fifty-seven in Italy and forty-eight in Germany. The country is still heavily reliant in balancing its budget on the universal popular indifference to cirrhosis of the liver and lung cancer. Without the revenue from alcohol and tobacco taxes (which in 1963–64 accounted for 30 percent of budget income), the Irish exchequer would totter. Because of the proportion of the labor force in agriculture as opposed to industry, the tax basis is so low that in 1961–62 tax on personal incomes brought in only 4 percent of the nation's income.[5]

The Irish tax structure is outwardly far more regressive than that of

[5] *Ireland Since the Rising* (New York: Praeger, 1966), p. 150.

In making comparisons of economic development, we refer here either to GNP (Gross National Product) per capita or national income per capita. The first of these figures generally connotes the value of all goods and services produced in a country during a year per each inhabitant. The second figure allows a deduction for depreciation and taxes. Both figures can serve only as rough approximations of wealth per capita, inasmuch as nation-states differ considerably in their accounting and reporting practices.

the other established democracies. It relies on revenue drawn from consumption and transaction taxes as well as from assorted imports and duties to a far greater degree than from direct income and/or corporation taxes. In fact, Ireland appears to be behind such authoritarian oligarchies as Spain and Portugal in these aspects of its tax structure.

But the bulk of Ireland's population is not made up of workers and assorted industrial employees. The backbone of the Irish economy continues to be agriculture, and the traditional demands of farmers, particularly small owners, may be reasonably expected to have shaped the Irish fiscal system. There are, thus, both economic and political reasons why one could not really expect analogous tax structures in Ireland and the United States, Britain, or Sweden, where industry and workers count for so much of the wealth and the population. Historically, independent farm owners have not been enthusiastic proponents of the income tax. The collection of both corporate and income taxes in an economy made up of many relatively poor producers is also, of course, far more difficult and expensive than in the opposite case.

On the other hand, we should note that even though the Irish tax structure can be said to correspond to the traditional demands of a very substantial segment of its population, this is much less so in the case of authoritarian states like Portugal and Spain. Here indirect tax structures are imposed on populations where the ratio of workers and employees to owners and the self-employed is considerably higher. Granted traditional tax orientations of constituent populations in all three states, it seems evident that what is more or less to be expected in Ireland is being maintained artificially by the authoritarian regimes of Portugal and Spain. Thus, as of 1959, the share of principal sources of the central government's revenue in Ireland included 67.5 per cent in indirect taxes.[6] The Portuguese intake included 60.7 per cent in indirect levies. In Spain the relevant figure was 61.0 per cent as of 1958. But population ratios of employers and families to employees in the 1950s showed that in Ireland the former accounted for over 42 per cent of the total labor force. In Spain they accounted for about one third. In Portugal they constituted only about one quarter of the working population.

More important still, however, are the uses made of tax revenues in each case. Here it turns out that democratic Ireland with the smallest proportion of employees has been far more responsive to the traditional demands of labor and the economically underprivileged than

[6] M. H. Bryden, "Fiscal Figures: Tax Mix in Various Countries," *Canadian Tax Journal*, Vol. 10, No. 2 (March–April 1962), p. 114.

either Portugal or Spain. This is clearly evidenced by spending for education, health, welfare, insurance, pensions, public assistance, and the like. In 1955, Ireland's public spending on education amounted to 2.5 per cent of her GNP, a higher percentage than that of France and in Western Europe exceeded only by Sweden, Finland, Iceland, and the Netherlands. The Portuguese government spent only 1.2 per cent of the GNP on education; Spain spent only 1.4 per cent. In 1934, Ireland spent 2.9 per cent of her GNP out of the public treasury on medical care and cash benefits to the population, Portugal only 1.4 per cent, and Spain a mere 0.3 per cent![7]

In 1955, Ireland ranked third highest in Europe, outside the Soviet Bloc, in her percentage of the working force covered by compulsory unemployment insurance (behind Britain and Belgium). Spain and Portugal ranked among the lowest in Europe.[8] Ireland's spending for unemployment insurance in 1953–1954, as a percentage of her GNP, was twice as high as the average for Western Europe and was outranked only by Denmark. Spain and Portugal spent virtually negligible sums. As of 1957 more than 55 per cent of Irish citizens over the age of 65 received old age pensions. In the extent of coverage, the Irish outranked Italy and France in Western Europe. Spain covered barely a quarter of her oldest citizens; Portugal less than 2 per cent.[9] Where the Spanish and Portuguese total allocations of revenue to pension payments under social insurance programs amounted to 0.6 and 1.3 per cent of the GNP, respectively, the Irish figure was 3.3 per cent.[10] The Irish, similarly, spent more on family allowances.

Insofar as government contributions to the social security funds are concerned, the Irish treasury contributed 72.7 per cent; the Portuguese only 12.0 per cent, and the Spaniards a bare 1.7 per cent. Total national spending for social security was 8.7 per cent of the GNP in Ireland in 1954; it was only 4.6 per cent in Portugal and 1.8 per cent in Spain.[11]

Obviously, no *single figure* cited here need be taken as *the* decisive comparison. But their total import, taken together, can hardly be denied. If anything, the Irish tax system is outwardly more regressive and "backward" than either the Portuguese or the Spanish, but the governments concerned spend their proceeds with very unequal generosity.[12]

[7] Dewhurst, *op. cit.*, p. 383. On relevant population figures see p. 433.

[8] *Ibid.*, pp. 3 and 5. As of 1962 no actual figures on Spain and Portugal were available.

[9] *Ibid.*, p. 390.

[10] *Ibid.*, p. 391.

[11] *Ibid.*, p. 399.

[12] See Woytinsky and Woytinsky *op. cit.*, Table 250, p. 702.

How do we explain these differences? Insofar as we can construct an ideological profile of the Spanish and Portuguese oligarchies during the past thirty years or so, these regimes are socially conservative or quiescent. They have not enunciated conspicuous programs of social and economic upheaval aimed at enriching the poor or, conversely, impoverishing the rich. They have, rather, emphasized the values of stability, order, and tradition in their domestic policies. This relative quiescence of their outlook is reflected not only in the kinds and amounts of spending for social welfare purposes, but in the relatively low share of taxation in the GNP of their economies. In Ireland in the late 1950s, taxes represented about 23 per cent of the GNP; in Portugal they represented only 17.4 per cent and in Spain just under 17 per cent.[13]

Finally, by the very closeness of the budgetary process in the two authoritarian regimes we would be precluded from an effective appraisal of the subsidies that these governments make to various private interests and how these differ from the Irish case or that of any other democracy. This involves substantial sums. The Spanish government has expended more than 10 per cent of its outgo on "subsidies" to private interests and nongovernmental organizations since 1950, and more than 6 per cent annually during the past decade.[14] Who gets what, and why, is not open to parliamentary or press scrutiny in Spain. In Portugal during the past decade, subsidies have fluctuated between 6 and 10 per cent of total expenditure under analogous circumstances.

We do know, in retrospect, that subsidies to powerful business and landed interests were very significant features of the economies of the authoritarian regimes of Fascist Italy and Nazi Germany.[15]

Finally, we can note that indirect taxation, per se, is not *always* regressive; it depends on what is being taxed and at what rates. A more detailed comparison of these tax systems would actually enhance Ireland's case even further.

Another financial aspect of political systems involves tax assessments and tax collections as contrasted with formal rates and levies. In some systems the disparity is a major fact of life. It is also a prime *clue* to the effective distribution of political power, an indication of what "is" rather than what is being claimed.

[13] M. H. Bryden, "Fiscal Figures: World Tax Burdens," *Canadian Tax Journal*, Vol. 9, No. 3 (May–June 1961), Table, p. 202. See also, H. T. Oshima, "Share of Government in Gross National Product for Various Countries," *American Economic Review*, Vol. 47, No. 1 (March 1957), p. 382.

[14] United Nations, *1964 Yearbook of National Accounts Statistics* (New York: 1965), pp. 273 and 249.

[15] *Cf.* Maxine Y. Sweezy, *The Structure of the Nazi Economy* (Cambridge, Mass.: Harvard University Press, 1941), and Gaetano Salvemini, *Under the Axe of Fascism* (London: Victor Gollancz, 1936).

A degree of corruption has attached to most human institutions. Cheating the tax collector has occurred in *all* political systems. Even though a great deal remains to be learned about this important problem before we can fully judge who really pays what and who really gets what, there is nevertheless, political salience in tax evasion. It is probably much more significant and systematic under some regimes than under others. It is frequently diagnosed by scholars and observers under the French term *incivisme* (lack of civic spirit among the citizens)—in some cases a response of the citizenry to a rule of force imposed on them by an authoritarian or illegitimate regime.

In France, at least two significant political causes underlie widespread tax evasion. The first stems from the low level of legitimacy accorded by the populace to the successive regimes of the nineteenth and twentieth centuries, reflecting the unhealed breach created by the Revolution of 1789. To many Frenchmen the regime of the day is merely an irksome impostor of "rightful" authority. Secondly, there is the inability of governments, lacking any sizeable and lasting popular and parliamentary support, to carry out consistent, thorough reforms that would give firm control of the personnel and procedures in the field of fiscal administration. The net effect has been for weak and short-lived regimes, parliamentary or otherwise, to let the various branches of the civil service conduct fiscal affairs with a minimum of political leadership and maximum concessions to prescriptive, let-sleeping-dogs-lie procedures. The description given by Carl S. Shoup accurately summarizes one aspect of this French problem:

> From the time of the French Revolution to the mid-twentieth century, the task of tax administration had been divided among four divisions, or bureaus: the bureau of direct taxes, the bureau of indirect taxes, the customs bureau, and the bureau of registration and stamp taxes and public domain.
>
> These bureaus became self-sufficient, exchanging little or no information with each other, and disinclined to ask for advice from the outside. Taxpayers were harassed by multiple inspection of their books. Each tax bureau became conscious of its own importance, and resisted proposals that would diminish the role played by the "particular taxes under its jurisdiction." This sense of autonomy was strengthened by unions of tax officials in the several divisions. The personnel, able technicians, developed a taste for complicated refinements (uncharitably refined complications).[16]

In still other cases, it is difficult to escape the conclusion that tax evasion represents the regime's own way of squaring certain profes-

[16] "Taxation in France," *National Tax Journal*, Vol. VIII, No. 4 (December 1955), pp. 332 and 325–344. See also his "Some Distinguishing Characteristics of the British, French, and United States Public Finance Systems," *American Economic Review*, Vol. 57, No. 2 (May 1957), pp. 187–197.

sions that common language would describe as hypocritical—that is, designed simply to give an outward appearance of rightfulness, or legitimacy, in the national and perhaps also international contexts, while concealing very different realities of power and privilege. Such clearly appears to be the case in the majority of the Latin American republics, where traditionally the pretense of democracy has resided in the constitutions and laws and the *de facto* oligarchy in the practices.

In 1954, a United Nations' survey of tax and fiscal policies unearthed some highly revealing practices in several Latin American states, all of them with histories of chronic dictatorial rule.

In Bolivia, for instance, it was found that assessments of land values were so hopelessly outdated and vitiated by inflation as to render the liability of the land-owning sector of Bolivia's economy a small fraction of what could be originally and reasonably regarded as the intent of the law. Thus, the UN experts reported that:

> Urban real estate is subject to municipal taxes of 0.2 per cent to 0.8 per cent of assessed values. The national income tax as it applies to real estate amounts to 0.32 per cent of assessed values. [But] the last assessment . . . took place in 1940–41. A good part of urban property has not been assessed and pays no taxes. Owing to inflation, average property values in mid-1950 were said to be three to five times those of 1940–41.[17]

Interestingly enough, the UN inquiry found Bolivia to be spending 57 per cent of its national budget on political purposes—that is, for the maintenance of its bureaucracy, police, and defense forces.[18] But the organization and practices of authorities charged with the collection and spending of revenue were found singularly lax and inadequate to the purpose.[19] Similar findings were made elsewhere. In Chile, for instance, the experts concluded that "excessive use [was being made] of tax exemptions and preferential rates. While some groups of taxpayers have been favored by inefficiencies in the system of assessment and collection and by the inflationary process, low income taxpayers and foreign and domestic corporations carry a considerable tax burden."[20] Even in Colombia, where direct taxes accounted for a larger share of government revenues than in most of Latin America, the system of tax administration was found to be entirely inadequate.[21] The UN mission reported this inadequacy as the result of a lack of

[17] UN Technical Assistance Administration, *Taxes and Fiscal Policy in Under-Developed Countries* (New York: 1954), pp. 47–48.

[18] *Ibid.*, p. 43.

[19] *Ibid.*, p. 44.

[20] *Ibid.*, p. 54.

[21] *Ibid.*, p. 61.

staff and trained personnel and expressed the view that government tax yields could be increased by more than a third with better administration. In pre-Castro Cuba, the UN investigators found that tax and budgetary operations had been carried out without any legislative oversight or even approval, with one exception, since 1937–1938.[22] Typically, it concluded that "one of the most serious defects in Cuban budgetary practices is the lack of control," and widespread tax evasion exists throughout the system.[23] In Guatemala, the UN mission found real estate and land taxes in 1950–1951 to be based, in the overwhelming majority of cases, on assessments carried out in 1921 and revised upward in 1931. In Nicaragua, the UN found no income tax of any kind, whereas direct property taxes yielded only 3.4 per cent of total government revenue in 1950–1951. Such examples could be readily multiplied in this and other studies.

A politically significant avenue of tax avoidance and evasion in the Latin American states has been the exercise of very considerable discretion in both assessments and collections given to administrative agents of government. Tax laws have been traditionally vague and imprecise,[24] leaving it to administrative officers and interested parties to arrive at a very wide range of possible settlements. The latter are frequently based on arbitrary assessments of taxable income.[25] The door to collusion between various segments of the ruled and the representatives of the rulers has been thrown wide open.

A complete summary of all the aspects of tax evasion in Latin America would be clearly beyond the scope of our brief and introductory treatment. We can conclude here, however, with this salient example provided by a leading authority in the field of public finance:

> One of the biggest loopholes in the income tax legislation of most Latin American countries is the favorable treatment meted out to profits from the sale of movable property. Since recurrence, or periodicity, is considered to be one of the essential characteristics of income for tax purposes in Brazil, Chile, Colombia, and Mexico, only profits from the sale of depreciable property are subject to an income tax. In this latter country, a tax of 20 percent on [occasional] commercial transactions is a dead statute. In Chile, profits from the sale of immovables are specifically exempt, and in Brazil, cumbersome legislative enactments to tax transfers of real estate have been completely ineffective. Only in Argentina is there a full-fledged capital gains tax, and that, at least until recently, has been spottily administered. Thus, governments which have been paying lip service to the promotion of productive investment and the discour-

[22] *Ibid.*, p. 64.

[23] *Ibid.*, pp. 64 and 66.

[24] Joseph P. Crockett, "Tax Patterns in Latin America," *National Tax Journal*, Vol. XV, No. 1 (March 1962), pp. 93–104.

[25] *Ibid.*

agement of speculation have hitherto failed to discourage speculation through taxation because of an unwillingness or inability to introduce capital gains taxation.[26]

The example cited by Froomkin is a clear testimonial to the effective power and behind-the-scenes influence of the landed interest in Latin America, an interest that traditionally has probably come closest to embodying the region's ruling class.[27] Although it is granted that tax evasion is not always wholly accounted for by political factors, what can we reasonably infer from it in purely political terms?

To the extent that taxpayer attitudes simply represent recognitions of the *legitimacy* of the particular regimes in the eyes of their peoples we might well find that the subjects of at least some authoritarian states would be as dutiful taxpayers as any. Illustrative of this, there is no reason to doubt that the citizens of Royal Imperial Prussia were on the whole as good taxpayers as they were obedient subjects.

But this represents only one side of the coin. Widespread recognition of the legitimacy of their rule merely makes it possible for authoritarian regimes to conduct their operations in an aboveboard fashion without fearing the consequences and without sacrificing any material interests dear to them. This indeed was the case in Prussia where taxation was traditionally very lopsided and regressive but relatively honestly and effectively enforced. The relative equivalence in citizen compliance between the effective democracies and some authoritarian states could be attributed to this common factor of legitimacy. But this still leaves a striking gap in the distributive features of the system complied with.

Latin American states have been generally as consistent in their taxation as in their politics. Their façades of political liberalism embodied in the letter of the law, constitutions, and symbols of public authority have been traditionally matched by a reality of very limited diffusion of power within the mechanisms of government. Analogously, in the area of public finance, liberal and egalitarian laws have been administered in such a fashion as to correspond much more closely with the realities of *de facto* political power than with constitutional-legal-symbolic pretense.

The instruments for enacting, enforcing, and controlling taxation and spending have reflected the reality, not the pretense. The practice may be seen as a systemic compensation for the pretense. What cannot be done under openly spelled-out "letter of the law" can nevertheless be accomplished by administrative action, particularly inas-

[26] Joseph Froomkin, "Some Problems of Tax Policy in Latin America," *National Tax Journal*, Vol. X, No. 4 (December 1957), pp. 372 and 370–379.

[27] *Taxes and Fiscal Policy*, *op. cit.*, p. 73.

Table 3
Latin American Central Government Tax Receipts—1958*

	Direct Taxes on Individuals, Corporations, Property (%)	Indirect Taxes (%)	Customs (%)	Total (%)
Argentina	47.8	47.3	4.9	100.00
Bolivia	23.7	26.3	50.0	100.00
Brazil	34.2	52.8	12.9	100.00
Chile	29.4	54.2	16.5	100.00
Colombia	53.3	5.4	41.2	100.00
Ecuador	24.6	35.8	39.7	100.00
Paraguay	55.6	26.2	18.2	100.00
Peru	54.8	17.3	27.9	100.00
Uruguay	65.2	28.1	6.7	100.00
Venezuela	79.9	5.5	14.7	100.00

*This table is based on Yearbook of National Accounts Statistics (New York: United Nations Statistical Office, 1959). Figures given in Table 3 actually understate Uruguay's advantage in direct taxation since World War II. Tax reforms in Colombia, Paraguay, Peru, and Venezuela all took place in the late 1950s. In Venezuela the bulk of direct taxes represented corporate taxes (over 97%) largely levied on foreign corporations.

much as the institutions, channels of information, and popular skills are wanting to render such obvious maladjustments untenable for those who daily engage in them. The scale and variety of practices that support tax evasion and avoidance in Latin America on the administrative side are such that the conclusion of substantial "willfullness" on the part of the power holders is inescapable. For it is certainly clear that the neglect, disorganization, and inefficiency—not to mention dishonesty—have served to benefit the well-to-do in a historically prolonged, consistent, and substantial fashion. Tax evasion has been an integral feature of the political system.

Another problem connected with taxation is that of government intake of material supports in ways that historically may be less conventional or generalized than taxation but that are supplementary to it. These exactions can be examined under the heads of acquisitions into the public domain. The significance of such acquisitions to government operations varies from place to place and time to time. The method, however, is highly salient politically. These acquisitions may range from brutal and violent wholesale confiscations of goods and property to the most legally complex, remunerated, and variously safeguarded proceedings.

On the latter score, the most far-reaching contrasts can be seen between the effective democracies and the innovative-mobilizational autocracies, as well as some very significant differences among systems in the latter category. Authoritarian regimes of the twentieth century have significantly supplemented the resources available to them through taxation by large-scale confiscation and expropriation of private resources. Both in extent and method such appropriations have far exceeded anything realized by any of the effective democracies.

On the other hand, depending on the ideological orientations and circumstances of these regimes, there have been significant differences in terms of *who* was being pillaged for the benefit of the State's treasury; *how* the proceeds were allocated; and, therefore, who benefited thereby.

We must hasten to add that the difference between democracy and autocracy with respect to the acquisition of resources does *not* center on the question of legality. Within the narrow confines of positive law *any* act of the duly constituted authority may be generally regarded as legal. The decrees of an absolute King or a totalitarian dictator may be legal in the sense that they represent binding decisions of a State as much as, say, the enactments of the United States Congress or the British Parliament. The difference rests not in legality but in the degree of involvement of public opinion behind the decree.

Authoritarian regimes tend to limit the impact of public opinion on the making and implementation of policy, including, of course, fiscal and tax policies. General Franco and Emperor Haile Selassie do not have to divulge their decree proposals to hostile critics in advance of promulgation, much less consult them or provide them with a forum for attacking such proposals. In the *de facto* authoritarian Bismarckian empire, military expenditures were formally approved by the national legislature; in fact, ever since 1862, at least, the approval of military estimates had been largely perfunctory. Questions relating to the military and to defense policies were treated as a virtual prerogative of the Crown and of the military themselves.

Backed by the procedural advantages of their systems, various totalitarian regimes have, from time to time, employed the extremes of outright violence and crass confiscation to accumulate resources. The experience of modern Communist regimes affords some examples of this practice. The Russian prototype of the Communist state made its debut almost literally by confiscation. On the second day of the Soviet regime, November 8, 1917, large-scale landownership was abolished in Russia, and estate owners were summarily expropriated without compensation. The following year, by decree of June 28, 1918, all large-scale industry was similarly expropriated—and nationalized. During the period of so-called War Communism (1918–1921), the Soviet regime obtained its most important single resource—food–by confiscation often with little or no payment in kind.[28] This policy, temporarily abandoned in the so-called New Economic Policy period of 1921–1928 under the pressures of a collapsing economy, was resumed by the Soviet regime, ruthlessly and dramatically, in the violent liquidation of the kulaks actually beginning sometime in early 1930. Not only were these peasant holders subjected to outright and summary confiscation of property, but millions of lives were physically liquidated in the process as well.

Passing on to the more constantly used and orthodox means of appropriating resources in the USSR, we find that the tax base from 1930 onward has been anchored in heavy consumption levies, primarily the so-called turnover tax. This tax, levied on food, clothes, and virtually all the perishable and durable commodities that the Soviet citizen consumes, yielded 46.4 per cent of total revenue in 1931, whereas income taxes contributed only 1.2 per cent. In the sixteen peacetime years from 1931 to 1951, the turnover tax has contributed on the average more than 60 per cent of the Soviet government's total revenue.[29] In 1960, it still accounted for 41 per cent of the State's income, although since the late 1950s the turnover tax has been increasingly supplemented by a profit tax imposed directly on commercial, industrial, and agricultural enterprises. The significance of the income tax continued to be completely marginal from the 1930s until the 1960s.[30]

In the eyes of Soviet policy makers this basic tax is justified in terms of the ultimate planning purpose of constructing a Communist society. This in turn requires consumer sacrifices and adequate incentives to the indispensable technological, administrative, and scientific elite without which productive successes could not be achieved. It is a matter of fact that high taxes on bread, milk, vegetables, tobacco, and clothes impose far heavier burdens on the man who earns 400 rubles a month than one who earns 4,000. Workers' parties *outside* the Soviet domain have traditionally regarded such taxation as regressively unfair and inequitable. But Soviet tax policies, like those of Nazi Germany or Fascist Italy, and like those of many other Communist and non-Communist oligarchies, have been substantially shielded from the impact of public opinion.

To the extent that tax and budget decisions are genuinely debated and quarreled over, the process is confined to a relatively narrow

[28] Harry Schwartz, *Russia's Soviet Economy*, 2nd ed. (Englewood Cliffs, N. J.: Prentice-Hall, 1954), p. 106 and Ch. 4 *passim*.

[29] M. V. Condiudem, *The Soviet Financial System* (Columbus: Ohio State University, 1951), pp. 84–85.

[30] Nicolas Spulber, *The Soviet Economy* (New York: W. W. Norton, 1962), Ch. 10.

forum maintained by the Communist party of the Soviet Union. *It* largely determines who may and may not discuss and determine such questions. It also carefully circumscribes the ground rules, as it were, of such discussion. The conception of Soviet democracy, so-called, never envisaged the right of the kulaks to participate in national tax policies equally with all other individuals in the political system. And it has not and does not acknowledge the right of the workers to so participate except insofar as they may do so under the leadership of the vanguard of the proletariat—the party itself. There are significant parallels between the USSR and the other Communist-ruled states.

One recent study concluded that:

> The experience of communist China in financing its programme of development has demonstrated that it is possible to increase tax collection in a relatively poor country on condition that little attention is paid to the progressiveness of the tax system, equity among tax payers and incentives in the private sector by improvement in tax administration. The fiscal experience of communist China in this regard may not commend itself to a poor country planning its economic development through the democratic process.[31]

In all cases of Communist rule, confiscation with no or minimal participation, let alone consent, by the victims has characterized State intake of resources. Tax systems have been regressive and heavily burdensome to the consumer. The opportunities for the disadvantaged elements to press for changes have been minimized if not altogether eliminated.

Where Communist states have differed from their Fascist and Nazi counterparts has been in the *social choices* of their discriminatory policies. All of the so-called innovative-mobilized authoritarian regimes of this century have imposed heavy taxation on consumers: workers, peasants, and employees. But where Fascist and Nazi oligarchies have subsidized, exempted, or at least tolerated the socioeconomically privileged groups in their respective societies, Communist tax and appropriation policies have generally tended to destroy the inherited socioeconomically privileged groups. Tax policies of the Communist dictatorships have tended to reward most the political, administrative, cultural, and scientific managers of the new Communist-ruled societies, not landlords, industrialists, or entrepreneurs.

Another different and, in part at least, compensating feature of the Communist fiscal systems has been the considerably larger allocation of resources to social, cultural, and educational objectives. These allo-

[31] R. N. Tripathy, *Public Finance in Under-Developed Countries* (Calcutta, India: The World Press, 1964), p. 93. See also, J. Froomkin and Ronald Hsia, "Public Finance in Communist China," *Public Finance*, Vol. 10, No. 1 (1955), pp. 83–102.

cations, both in relation to the respective GNP's and to the apparent accomplishments in consequence of them have undoubtedly done more for the welfare of the common man in terms of certain values and criteria than was the case under the Fascist and Nazi oligarchies. Recent studies, like those of the economist Arthur Schweitzer, show that the Hitler regime greatly increased government revenues from taxes and all other sources in the 1930s by considerably and one-sidedly increasing the burdens of wage earners and consumers, as compared with employers and large-scale producers. They also show that the budgetary allocations of these increased revenues to military purposes were largely hidden from public view.

Where in 1933 German national income was 46.5 billion marks and taxes 10.6 billion marks, by 1938 the national income had risen to 82.0 billion while taxes went up to 22.7 billion. Where in 1928, the last year of pre-Hitler prosperity, under a democratic regime, indirect taxes accounted for 30 per cent of the total tax revenue, the proportion became 41 per cent by 1936. The proceeds were being increasingly expended under deceptive, vague, and innocuous labels such as public works, construction of highways, modernization of railroads, and the like.[32]

A whole plethora of laws, rules, and regulations was devised by the Hitler regime for the accumulation of resources in the hands of the State and the perpetration of material deprivations on certain groups of citizens; these measures included donations forced on all citizens by the Nazi party, in fact, if not even always by law or decree. Certain citizens, notably Jews and those who can be broadly categorized as political enemies, were deprived of property rights and specifically of the right to appeal State confiscation and expropriation through judicial or administrative channels.[33]

As Nazi Germany expended an ever-larger share of its resources on war purposes, the share devoted to social welfare—cultural, educational, and other expenditures catering to the material needs of the people at large, and particularly the lower income groups—declined.

[32] *Big Business in the Third Reich* (Bloomington: Indiana University Press, 1964), Ch. 7, pp. 326–329, particularly.

[33] For an account of the arbitrarily obtained windfalls in the Nazi economy from confiscation of Jewish property, amounting to several billion marks' worth and similar acquisitions from other sources, see Gustav Stolper, *German Economy 1870–1940* (New York: Reynal and Hitchcock, 1940), Part V. *Cf.* M. M. Zarchin's *From Constantine to Hitler* (San Francisco: United council to combat anti-Semitism and nazism, 1936), pp. 85–171. According to Raul Hilberg, confiscation and various other arbitrary measures taken against the Jews netted the Nazis several billion reichsmarks between 1933 and 1942. But in the actual mass killings begun in 1942 "receipts no longer balanced losses." Hilberg estimates about three billion marks as the net value of Jewish war production lost to the Nazi economy through the Final Solution. *The Destruction of the European Jews* (Chicago: Quadrangle Books, 1961), pp. 644–646.

In relation to the GNP, the democratically organized Weimar Republic was more generous in this respect in the years 1919–1933 than was Hitler between 1933 and 1939.[34] Through what political processes were these drastic changes brought about under the aegis of Hitler and the Nazis?

The party leaders, the generals, and the business tycoons who supported the Nazis were shielded from the public forum of any parliamentary inquiry or scrutiny; or any debate that open and honest elections would have required; or such compromising disclosures and painful dialogue that the existence of opposition parties and a reasonably free press would have certainly imposed on them. From the very beginning, Hitler's Third Reich excluded from political participation precisely those elements that, logically enough, were hardest hit by the impact of Hitler's fiscal policies. Thus, in drafting his budgets, Hitler consulted and sometimes deferred to the pleas and the advice of the military and the business representatives. But the economic and political leaders of the workers, small businesses, and agricultural laborers as distinguished from owners—not to mention Jews, of course—enjoyed far fewer opportunities, formal or informal, of pleading their cases let alone of vetoing the decisions. Insofar as the Enabling Act of 1933 required him to discuss his legislative proposals with the cabinet, we note that the latter included, besides Nazis, only Right-wing Nationalist party members; and even this body soon became all but a ceremonial relic. For practical purposes, from 1936 onward, the decrees of the Nazi regime did not require the advice and consent of any national organs of public opinion.

Similar tax and budget policies—that is, highly discriminatory against certain strata of the population and largely shielded from public exposure and debate—were conducted in Italy under the aegis of Mussolini. Governmental subsidies of various private firms out of the public treasury in the 1920s and 1930s were so heavy as to prompt Gaetano Salvemini, a foremost Italian student of fascism, to conclude that "... the taxpayer... has become responsible for private enterprise.... Profit is private and individual. Loss is public and social."[35]

[34] See Maxine Y. Woolston, *The Structure of Nazi Economy* (New York: Russell and Russell, 1941). "Despite growth in population, total expenditure of all kinds under all provisions for social insurance was 4 per cent less in 1938 than in 1929."... "The reduction in old age pensions [was] spectacular." P. 227. *Cf.* Otto Nathan, *The Nazi Economic System* (Durham, N.C.: Duke University Press, 1944), p. 338. Jurgen Kuczynski, *Germany: Economic and Labour Conditions Under Fascism* (New York: Greenwood Press, 1968), notes that an increasing rate of industrial injuries during the thirties was accompanied by drastically decreased compensation payments to workers. P. 123. For comparisons with Soviet policies see e.g. Alec Nove, *Economic Rationality and Soviet Politics* (New York: Praeger, 1964), pp. 220–230.

[35] Salvemini, *op. cit.*, p. 416.

But in Italy the extent and significance of such operations could not have been known to broad segments of public opinion. The apparatus of Fascist rule—structurally analogous to the Nazi in many crucial respects—made it impossible for the aggrieved to know their fate, voice their case, or do anything effective about it.

The democratic experience has been very different. Appropriation of material resources in the democracies has always required either direct or indirect sanction in the laws—that is, an ultimate authorization and consent of the legislature. In cases where, as often occurs during time of war or national emergency, appropriations of resources have occurred by virtue of administrative decrees, these have generally involved certain typical safeguards. Authority delegated to the executive would, first of all, require an original statutory authorization by the legislature. The instrument of delegation of such authority typically would describe the conditions and limits under which it could be invoked, and possibly also specify a time period during which it could be exercised. Above all, such instruments generally have provided avenues of appeal and redress to the citizenry: political (review by parliament), judicial (appeal to courts), and/or administrative (resort to administrative courts).

The net impact of these procedural characteristics is that governments in the democracies generally do not and cannot appropriate any resources to the public domain—be it land, taxes, or any valuables whatever—without involving themselves in a complex process of exposure to public opinion. Not only the persons or institutions directly affected by government tax proposals but the public at large, political parties, news media, organized interest groups, legislators, and all interested citizens usually become involved to some significant extent in the deliberative and evaluative processes that attend the passage and the implementation of such measures. A scrutiny of the government's original fiscal proposals—common to all the democracies—is inevitably followed by continuing public criticism and frequently private litigation during their implementation. In all the democracies, legislative bodies exercise *post facto* audit and control functions forcing the disclosure of government uses of public revenues.

Among the outstanding illustrations of the financial watchdog functions performed in the democracies is the British House of Commons' Public Accounts Committee. Before the Reform Act of 1832, parliamentary approval was required for government expenditure. However, there was not as yet any institutionalized means by which Parliament could check up on the government's uses of the appropriations. In 1862, the House of Commons made the Public Accounts Committee one of its few permanent or standing committees. As Sir Ivor Jennings has described it:

[The Public Accounts Committee] consists of fifteen members. By convention, it represents the parties of the House in proportion to their voting strength. By convention also, a member of the opposition is always elected chairman. Usually, in fact, the Financial Secretary to the Treasury in the last Government formed by the Opposition has been appointed chairman.[36]

The committee is advised by an independent professional staff headed by a comptroller and auditor-general, and the committee:

. . . has the usual power "to send for persons, papers and records," and its proceedings usually take the form of examination of witnesses. Occasionally, the Committee sends for a minister; but more often it examines as witnesses senior officials from the departments. . . . The Committee reports to the House from time to time. It publishes also most of the evidence it receives."[37]

A recent comparative study of the audit procedures employed by modern governments has concluded that:

Questions of finance are questions of power, and from the openness and quality of accountability and control the political fate of a state can be read as if from a barometer. . . . The budget which is completely under an uncontrolled executive is exposed to all kinds of abuse. It has no real defenses against the underground influences of "the courtiers, the clique, the gang, the lobby clientele, the notables and the favorites" . . . .[38]

In the light of what we have said so far in this chapter, we would only add that the "cliques" and "gangs" differ in the nature and objectives of their appetites from one autocracy to another.

The careful public scrutiny and procedural safeguards involved in the democratic appropriation process were strikingly illustrated by the British in the passage of the nationalization acts proposed by the Labour Government of 1945–1950.

The British Socialists had pledged themselves long before the election to an extensive program of public ownership for basic industries including coal, steel, power plants, rail transport, and the Bank of

[36] *Parliament*, 2nd ed. (Cambridge: Cambridge University Press, 1957), pp. 333–336 and Ch. 9 *passim*.

[37] *Ibid*.

[38] E. L. Normanton, *The Accountability and Audit of Governments* (New York: Praeger, 1966), p. 402. This British author deplores, incidentally, the lack of adequate accountability in Britain's nationalized industries but finds it ample "where national funds are spent." P. 411. See also Paul Einzig, *The Control of the Purse: Progress and Decline of Parliament's Financial Control* (London: Secker and Warburg, 1959), pp. 318–331, an appreciative but critical estimate of the Commons' control of government expenditure.

England. The party obtained a sweeping majority in the House of Commons. Nevertheless, the Labour Government took its time in submitting actual nationalization bills to Parliament. First, virtually all of the interests and groups directly or indirectly affected by the government were consulted. These consultations helped the government determine, among other things, what compensation might be acceptable to those whose enterprises were to be taken over. When the legislation was at last introduced in the House of Commons, it was debated and challenged by the Conservative opposition and members of the Liberal party. The debate was extensively reported and substantially duplicated in the nation's press, at public gatherings, and in the news media.

The whole discussion took several weeks in the House of Commons alone and, for each major object of nationalization, was then repeated in the House of Lords. On several bills the government made some substantial concessions with respect to compensation for the former owners, the procedures of take-over, and the forms of actual public control. Characteristically, the compensation paid to mine owners and other entrepreneurs generally came to be regarded as fair and equitable. Some critics, and not only those on the extreme Left of the Labour party, criticized the amounts as actually excessive. Moreover, in the face of strongly voiced public opposition, the government simply dropped a number of its nationalization proposals for the time being.

In all those instances where nationalization plans were carried out, provisions were made in the legislation for the interests affected, whether those of labor or the consumer, to enjoy statutory, continued, and institutionalized access to the administration of the particular industry or program.[39]

The care and consideration employed in implementing Labor's nationalization programs are all the more remarkable in view of the clear mandate the party was able to claim by its decisive 1945 election victory. It was remarkable in view of the relatively simple, streamlined legislative procedures any British Government with a disciplined party majority behind it has at its disposal. There are no checks in a written constitution, buttressed by judicial review. There are no territorial or functional limits to the power of the central government embodied in parliamentary legislation. There is no absolute veto in the House of Lords that could thwart the will of the Commons.

But although we can say that in Britain the essentials of democratic procedure are arrived at informally, in large measure from a generally

[39] See, for example, E. Eldon Barry, *Nationalization in British Politics* (Stanford, Calif.: Stanford University Press, 1965), Ch. 15 particularly; see also R. A. Brady, *Crisis in Britain* (Berkeley: University of California Press, 1950), and Herbert E. Weiner, *British Labour and Public Ownership* (Washington, D.C.: Public Affairs Press, 1960).

accepted force of habit or tradition, these essentials are not absent in the other established democracies. They are, rather, realized through somewhat different channels in each case.[40]

In time of economic crisis, however, this democratic process is virtually certain to bring into the open popular pressures for tax and budgetary changes designed to relieve mass suffering such as typically brought on by large-scale unemployment. In the 1920s in Italy and in Germany of the 1930s, what many businessmen and landowners feared was not just "Communist take-over" but the more or less natural, it seemed, fiscal consequences of parliamentary democracy operating in conditions of acute economic crisis and deprivation for the masses of the people. How would economic recovery be financed? Fascism and nazism openly appealed to the privileged strata with the notion that solutions to economic problems would be sought "above the mere sum of class interests" and not in response to direct popular pressures. Indeed, solutions would be sought through the superior moral and intellectual insight of the charismatic leader. If this leader was not really hostile to the privileged, might he not be preferable for them to social democracy, let alone communism, as the nation's chief assessor and spender?

Clearly, the *process* by which a government acquires resources can be seen as at once an "insurance" against certain hazards for those in power, and as an economic weapon (regardless of the particular use to which it may be put at any point in time) against possible contingencies.

An inkling into fiscal practices of autocratic regimes is provided by the contemporary experience of Saudi Arabia's traditionalist oligarchy. No one is quite sure how and for what purposes the vast revenues from the country's oil resources have been or are being spent.

As one writer observed in 1959:

> The late king, Ibn Saud, had little use for budgets in handling the financial affairs of his kingdom; he understood neither their purpose nor their structure, much less the need to publish them.
>
> Until World War II, the pattern of income, expenditures and financial administration had remained essentially unaltered since the eighteenth century. During his reign, King Ibn Saud made the major financial decisions . . . .[41]

Apparently the King's generosity, however lopsided, knew few bounds so that

> . . . every personal fancy, which ran the gamut from a railroad to flashy mechanical gadgets and automobiles, was indulged. Royal hospitality and opu-

[40] On analogous processes in the United States, see R. A. Wallace, *Congressional Control of Federal Spending* (Detroit: Wayne State University Press, 1960), and particularly Aaron B. Wildavsky, *The Politics of the Budgetary Process* (Boston: Little, Brown, 1964).

[41] George A. Lipsky, *Saudi Arabia* (New Haven, Conn.: Hraf Press, 1959), p. 184.

lence went to unbelievable lengths. If the money ran out, the payment of obligations was postponed and the royal family bought on credit.[42]

An example of similarly uncontrolled large-scale, public spending in an innovative-mobilizational regime can be seen under the Perons. Here, Evita Peron, the dictator's wife, had established in 1947 a foundation for dispensing charity to the poor. The so-called Maria Eva Duarte de Peron Social Aid Foundation soon became the sole disburser of public charity and reportedly amassed at least two billion pesos by 1950 from donations often collected under thinly veiled pressure of the dictator's power of reprisal.

> Evita never gave, up to the day of her death in 1952, any public accounting whatsoever as to the disposal of the enormous funds involved; indeed as far as is known Evita did not keep any books.... In fact, Evita handled the monies ... "like a bride with a new banking account." [But] ... famous public figures in Argentina's political and social life were hounded into exile, and lesser-known men disappeared entirely after making indiscreet remarks or inquiries about the disposition of those otherwise so well-advertised charity funds.[43]

The acquisitions by Hitler's lieutenants—Alfred Rosenberg, Martin Bormann, Hermann Goering, Julius Streicher and various others—of world famous art treasures, estates, jewels and assorted valuables during the 1930s and the 1940s ran into multimillion dollar figures. The distinction between private and public domain was blurred by these subautocrats on a gigantic scale.

At this point we conclude our discussion here with a tentative summary. There is no one index, numerical or otherwise, that could give us a rank order of fiscal systems describing their respective total impacts. We must perceive governmental tax and budget systems as interrelated. If we simultaneously consider who actually pays what and how it is spent, a strong case of relative equity can be made for the democracies. Among this kind of political system we find a high incidence of direct and essentially progressive taxation, relatively low tax evasion, and also relatively high amounts of spending on the people's social, cultural, and material needs.

Both in the intake and in the spending all democracies are in considerable measure responsive to claims of the have-not groups in their societies. On the other hand, this responsiveness is limited both in intake and outgo. It is certainly not as generous as some critics of

[42] *Ibid.*, p. 185.

[43] Frank Owen, *Peron: His Rise and Fall* (London: Cresset Press, 1957), pp. 126–127. According to reports in the American press, Rafael Trujillo's thirty-odd year dictatorship in the Dominican Republic netted him a private fortune of more than one quarter billion dollars. This in a country of three million inhabitants whose per capita income was only about one-twelfth of the United States at the time of Trujillo's demise in 1961!

democracy in the nineteenth century feared that it might be (Mill or Bagehot, for example). In all the democracies, the propertied interests have been vocal and reasonably effective in their self-defense. The agitation for more and better public services—at public expense—has always been countered by the concern over the costs. And thanks to the procedural safeguards of the democratic process, the citizen's interest as a beneficiary of the State has always been countered by his interest as a taxpayer and a benefactor of society. The one has never completely yielded to the other, however these interests may have fluctuated over time. Groups that have made themselves the spokesmen of spending in the name of compassion, justice, and right have invariably found opponents in other groups emphasizing thrift, solvency, and equity—also in the name of justice and right.

Without the benefit of worldwide, uniform statistical information we can only guess at some of the dollars-and-cents relationships that distinguish the democracies in general from authoritarian political systems.[44] We find that the democracies tend to spend more generously in proportion to their GNP's on the needs of their respective lower strata than do these regimes that conspicuously exclude such elements from the ruling oligarchies. And "favoritism" or "punishment" in the direction of any social group or category does not go quite as far in the democracies as it does in the oligarchies. There are no counterparts to either Jews or kulaks in the fiscal policies of the democracies. Admittedly, some autocracies, notably the Communist ones, have spent more of their wealth on such social projects as education than have some democracies (contrast Britain and the Soviet Union, for example). They have spent much more, proportionately, than the Fascist, Nazi and various other dictatorships or oligarchies (Ethiopia, for example). But in doing so they have victimized and denied all legitimacy to the interests of a great many people. This, as a fact, must be explictly weighed in any equation of equity, regardless of which values one chooses to apply to the whole process.

The heterogeneity subsumed under terms such as *autocracy* and *democracy* is such that it obviously suggests many further subtypes. Communist and Fascist fiscal systems have widely differed in terms of the identity of their principal victims and their chief beneficiaries. Democracies have differed depending on whether the bulk of their citizenry has consisted of independent farmers, craftsmen, and merchants or urban-based factory workers. The Swiss and the Irish have thus differed from the British and the Americans.

Yet, a basic distinction between *all* democracies and *all* autocracies seems substantiated by empirical inquiry. It relates to the openness of

[44] Dewhurst, et al., *op. cit.*, pp. 412 and 422.

the entire fiscal process from appropriation to expenditure; the degree of popular participation and consent required for the promulgation of fiscal measures; and, finally, the tendency to direct and progressive taxation as the principal source of government revenue in the democracies.[45]

The tendency to indirect and basically regressive taxation characterizes many autocratic systems. There are also certain fiscal traits that afflict *some* autocracies but not the democracies—at least not nearly in the same measure. Such a trait is represented by widespread government misapplication or nonapplication of tax laws, combined with large-scale tax evasion. This phenomenon is not a major one in those political systems where effective public scrutiny and accountability exist and where there is a widespread identification by citizens with their government.

Before proceeding to other complementary aspects of our study, we may note with specific reference to taxation that in the period since World War II there has been a constant increase of *international* factors promoting fiscal changes and tending to blur certain differences that might otherwise be perpetuated. In Latin America, for instance, the effort to obtain backing in the Alliance for Progress, arms, and economic aid from the United States, as well as the effort to deal with communism as a domestic and an international danger, has led Latin American oligarchies to modify and reform their internal fiscal policies. In Europe, the most striking example of internationally promoted domestic change has been taking place within the Common Market. The tax policies of nations there are now becoming increasingly synchronized.[46]

[45] See Ira Sharkansky, *The Politics of Taxing and Spending* (Indianapolis, Ind.: Bobbs-Merrill Company, 1969), pp. 8–32 and 146–149. The author reports that self-interest is more frequently recognized by respondents with higher rather than lower educational attainments in U. S. surveys of people's attitudes toward taxes. P. 17. *Cf.* R. L. Curry and L. L. Wade for a perceptive discussion of theories explaining fluctuations in the production of public goods, *A Logic of Public Policy* (Belmont, Calif.: Wadsworth, 1970), Ch. V.

[46] See A. G. Davies, "Fiscal Revolution in Europe?," *Canadian Tax Journal*, Vol. 11, No. 1 (January–February 1963), pp. 12–18. Also on the subject, but treated in a more general way, see Andrew M. Scott, *The Revolution in Statecraft* (New York: Random House, 1965).

CHAPTER 5
ASPECTS OF ECONOMIC POLICY

THE dichotomy between democracy and autocracy has its economic consequences. And in some respects these are more important than the traditional contrasts between a market economy and a planned economy. The crucial question is not how much of the economy is "owned" or "controlled" by the State, but what the nature of the State is that does the owning and the controlling.

Because the political processes underlying the State are substantially similar—as between Sweden, the United States, and Great Britain—the *outputs* of the two so-called Socialist economies (Sweden and the United Kingdom) and the free enterprise economy (United States) are more alike than those of, say, Sweden and Yugoslavia, or Hungary and the United Kingdom.*

Democracies experience the problem of reconciling and adjusting pressures and demands that are local, particular, and related to specific industries with the more general demands of voters, consumers, farmers, or workers; occasionally, the balance of policy reflects local and special interests over more general, national ones. Regulation of utilities in the United States is illustrative of this. Political democracy

* See for example the interesting data on income distribution cited by Karl W. Deutsch, *Politics and Government* (Boston: Houghton Mifflin, 1970), pp. 88–95, Figs. 4.6, 4.7, and Table 4.1.

allows a variety of economic pressures to register with the decision makers: the pressure to offer a wide assortment of goods at low prices to the consumer; the opposite pressure to protect the prices of domestic manufacturers over cheap imports from abroad; the pressure for generous redistributive outlays for the poor; and, alternately, demands for thrift, low taxes, and cuts in public spending. Autocratic political systems can and do weaken the representation of certain claims in society (different ones in each case) to a point where the economy registers a corresponding distortion.[1]

One of the characteristics of traditional autocracy is an economy in which few resources are allocated to redistributive purposes for the uplift of the masses through welfare, education, and assorted public projects. On the other hand, the regime insures the *de facto* conspicuous consumption by relatively small privileged strata of society; coincidentally, it refuses to commit the society's resources to a massive capital investment program and, frequently, maintains a large military-bureaucratic establishment for purposes of domestic restraint. Policies of this type have been exemplified by assorted Latin American, Iberian, and Middle-Eastern regimes.

At the other extreme, stand the innovative systems of the Communist variety that emphasize redistributive social welfare expenditures; destroy the consumption patterns of the old privileged strata; and commit resources to a massive economic-industrial uplift of every society under their control (often with very disappointing results).

Taking democracy as our point of departure, we might reasonably look for some degree of equivalence between the generally existent political rights and the economic rights in the society. In other words, such decision making as might be taking place in the realm of the economy, whether private, public, or governmental, would have to be informed by the general rights of association, expression, petition, and the guarantees of security both in persons and property that underlie the exercise of the franchise in the democratic systems. None of this could tell us much about the specific kinds of decisions that were being made in the economy. However, it could tell us something about the way in which these economic decisions could and could not be made. The implications of the democratic process for taxation and

[1] Among output extremes that occur between opposite types of autocracies (holding GNP per capita constant) are (1) Newspaper circulation per capita: Mongolia (1956), highest; Kuwait (1960), lowest. (2) Radios per capita: East Germany (1961), highest; South Africa (1961), lowest. (3) Inhabitants per hospital bed: Mongolia (1956), lowest; Taiwan (1960), highest. See Bruce M. Russett, et al., *World Handbook of Political and Social Indicators* (New Haven: Yale University Press, 1964), pp. 108–110, 120–122, and 208–212. Other comparisons include school enrollments: Mongolia (1966), highest and Saudi Arabia (1966), lowest. Automobiles per capita: People's China (1966), lowest and Union of South Africa (1966), highest.

budgeting that we discussed here earlier have their parallels and counterparts in certain even larger and more inclusive issues of economic policy. Thus, a British employee of a nationalized steel mill and his American counterpart who works for a private mill owner are both free to strike, boycott, picket, quit their jobs, move away, organize political and economic action, or publicly protest and denounce their employers and/or public authorities. Both individually and through their unions, the British and the American workers can denounce unfair management or government inspectors to independent and willing news media and thus, indirectly, appeal for the support of a larger public. Most of these rights, however, are lacking for workers either in the nationalized enterprises of, for example, the USSR or in the capitalist enterprises of Spain, Paraguay, or Saudi Arabia.

The Swedish program of socialism or welfare state interventionism to provide full employment, to secure a redistribution of incomes, and to assure certain minimal conditions of livelihood, health, and welfare to all citizens may be regarded as extremist, mistaken, costly, doomed to failure, and so on, depending on the outlook of the observer. But however it is perceived, it is unlike Soviet economic policy, because it is based on full recourse to the judgment of public opinion. If it is a socialist folly, it has not been imposed and maintained by force and it is subject to change without notice because the rights of the participants to change it, if they wish, have not been jeopardized, let alone abolished. Economic policy favoring the views of labor and trade unions has not been coupled with a denial of any participatory rights to agriculture or business.[2]

The future of Swedish economic policy has not been and cannot be foreclosed by government, so long as political democracy continues to be maintained. In the Soviet Union economic policy has fluctuated from less severe to more severe treatment of certain sectors of the economy and certain strata of the population. In the 1920s, for example, larger investments were allocated to the private sector, to agriculture, and to consumer goods' industries than after 1928. Open commodity markets for farmers and townspeople were allowed by the party. In the 1930s, the private sector was all but wiped out. Even between 1921 and 1928, however, we note that some of the elements

[2] As Robert A. Dahl and Charles E. Lindblom have pointed out, the distinction between public and private ownership or management of economic agencies is by no means equivalent to the distinction between compulsion on the one hand and freedom on the other. A closed-shop trade union of today, or a medieval guild of yesteryear, is a more restrictive type of organization than some publicly owned utilities, for example, to which there may be other available alternatives. Such private bodies may be more "compulsive" in their decisions than many fact-finding, mediation, and advisory boards occasionally set up by the United States Federal Government, for example. See *Politics, Economics and Welfare* (New York: Harper & Row, 1953), pp. 11–16 and Tables 3–4.

that clearly profited most by the relatively "liberal" policies were simply recipients of hand-me-down favors. They never had participant standing in the Soviet policy-making process.

The kulak and the merchant were being used by the party to promote what it considered an expediency, an indispensable "breather," and this involved some significant easements and concessions to the kulak and the merchant. Some Western observers actually saw the USSR on the way back to prerevolutionary capitalism! But, in fact, middle-class elements in the Soviet economy never ceased to be officially regarded as class enemies and essentially as "outsiders" to the policy-making process. The proletarian worker-peasant State had to take cognizance of them in the sense in which one discerns and adapts one's course to obstacles blocking the road ahead. The middle class of Russia—whatever remained of it after 1914–1921—was not a comaker, but rather an object, of Communist policies. It would have been sheer heresy to suggest to the party leaders that the question of how to deal with the urban and rural middle class could only be settled with its own participation! It would have been an unthinkable betrayal of the proletarian revolution; not even Bukharin ever advanced so "preposterous" an argument! It would have been analogous to suggesting the participation of Jews in the making of Nazi decisions affecting the Final Solution.

Even though men are entitled to entertain grim forebodings with respect to the future, as Hayek did in his notable *Road to Serfdom*, there is no empirical evidence whatever to indicate that any Swedish entrepreneur's political-legal rights have been lessened or destroyed by the Socialist regime. Only the judgment of Swedish public opinion stands between the current and recent welfare state orientation of the Swedish polity and another, presumably more laissez-faire, free-enterprise-oriented policy. And the businessman is as free to appeal to that judgment as ever he was. In this sense—the greater capacity of economic policy to change in accordance with the changes of public opinion—democracies differ from dictatorships, whatever the ideological orientations of the latter may be and whatever the circumstances.

Wartime operations, with their tendency to subordinate all economic activity to the political-military interests of the State, actually illustrate, rather than negate, different system responses under analogous circumstances. Totalitarian regimentation of economic agents reached its apex in wartime. The labor discipline maintained by the innovative-mobilized autocracies of World War II was in many respects more a throwback to slavery than to feudalism. Absenteeism or lateness to work, leaving one's job without official authorization, disregard of instructions by one's supervisor, appearance of neglect or slackness at work, or a touch of "defeatism" in one's remarks to fellow workers all were subject to drastic and summary punishments often equivalent to the penalties inflicted on deserters, saboteurs, and traitors.

Management personnel at various levels was saddled with a responsibility for the performance of production and service tasks that was not merely personal but criminal, collective, and generally blind to the issues of intent or willfulness on the part of the offender. A factory manager was liable to summary execution by administrative agents (Ovra, Gestapo, or NKVD, that is), without a trial in court, on the mere suspicion of serious malpractice, sabotage, or theft occurring somewhere within the structure of the organization of which he was formally in charge. The issues of foreknowledge, *de facto* capacity to control events, and even proof of the allegations themselves (did sabotage really occur?) were left to the discretionary decisions of police organs. The managerial attitude toward labor was thus structured by the indifferent cruelty of the political system. It became a matter of kill or be killed; perform by whatever means feasible or literally go under. The employer or manager was able to render his existence somewhat less precarious only if he could cultivate influential contacts with, and even bribe, some of his administrative-political overseers, or if he could occasionally profit from their ineptness in the exercise of economic vigilance.

The restraints on the consumer under the totalitarian regimes featured long-term prison sentences, exile to concentration camps, and even execution for offenses as trivial as petty theft of produce, fuel, or building materials; the falsification or misuse of rationing cards; the unauthorized use of scarce materials for food, clothing, or for any other consumer purpose; and the sale or purchase of goods on the black market. The powers of police and administrative organs in dealing with consumers were generally as wide and arbitrary as those exercised against producers.

In contrast to these extreme autocratic practices, labor, management, and consumers among democratic participants in the war all retained a remarkable measure of personal, professional, and organizational freedom. In essence, much of the job of economic mobilization for the war rested on the voluntary efforts of economic agents, on agreement and consensus rather than on punitive sanctions. Trade unions in Britain, the United States, Australia, New Zealand, and Canada often agreed to no-strike policies without compulsion by the State. The unions remained free to negotiate labor contracts and make demands on employers. Notwithstanding some forms of antistrike legislation, labor conflicts were never violently suppressed. Controls on production and consumption were to a large extent voluntarily enforced, and violators of wartime regulations were not deprived of legal and administrative rights that—so far as activities by civilians behind the front lines were concerned—would have been available to them in peacetime.

In the democracies, men and women could change jobs, move to different locations, and express dissatisfaction with their work, their bosses, or the conduct of the war, often without suffering so much as a reprimand, let alone imprisonment or execution. The *de facto* effectiveness of the vast plethora of controls, regulations, and ration cards designed to curb private consumption and to husband scarce resources did not depend in Britain, the United States, or in the other democracies on a vastly increased network of police agents and surveillance systems. It rested on the force of public opinion, without recourse to extended coercive machinery. In fact, at the height of the war crisis in Britain, the general incidence of crime and lawbreaking appears to have declined.[3] The commitment of British resources to a victory over nazism was in the profoundest sense the decision of the British people themselves.

The bread-and-butter significance of democracy is found in the right of the consumer and the producer, worker, farmer, and entrepreneur to voice his claims in the market place of goods, services, and ideas. What it means to the public is that if things go terribly wrong, there will be cries for redress and reform; that so long as government policy is made by elected officials, those cries, if loud and long, will have to be heeded, whether the source of abuse is public *or* private, governmental, corporate, or individual.

This safety valve of control by public opinion has a number of practical consequences. In the democracies, even essentially private business operations are within the domain of public news reporting and of public discussion: as to their desirability, propriety, or usefulness. Individuals can always undertake public action against businesses, whether by boycotting, picketing, denunciation, exposure of malpractices, or the petitioning of political-administrative organs urging corrective action. In the autocracies, the information about business operations, whether government owned or private, is frequently unpublicized; any individual action against them, beyond a purely private petition or a suit in the courts, if that, may be treated as a political offense.

[3] The evidence here is admittedly impressionistic and tenuous. See Joseph Treneman's *Out of Step* (London: Methuen, 1952), Appendix A, p. 205. According to his data, the number of males convicted in all courts in England and Wales rose steeply between 1940 and 1941 but declined in 1942, 1943, and 1944, exceeding the 1940 figure in 1945. The seriousness of the offenses committed, changes in public policies on prosecution, and the relative effectiveness of detection and reporting all complicate comparisons.

The restrictions on consumers, employees, and other interest groups in using the channels of political communication and association for economic objectives are characteristics of autocracy that help to maintain featherbedded, vested economic power. In some cases, these bastions may be private, as in Spain today or in Russia before World War I. In other instances they may be publicly owned, as under the current several Communist regimes of Europe and Asia. In both cases, press censorship, limitations on public meetings, strikes, and demonstrations—as well as the absence of any real institutionalized opposition in many cases—all help make public response to abuse from existent economic institutions muffled and ineffective.

The recourse to court action alone—which is permitted in many autocracies—is not nearly as effective as organized public action: First, because it narrows down the liability of business enterprises from something that may be widely regarded as undesirable or unfair to proving specific legal wrong—which is nearly always more difficult to sustain, even where no collusion exists between the accused interests and the judiciary; and secondly, the absence of publicity which makes every individual case, whether handled in the courts of law or administratively, so much less important from the standpoint of its impact on nationwide economic policy. No one can effectively generalize from quasisecret proceedings, even if the results are adverse for the particular enterprise before the bar of justice. Whatever the outcome of the case, it cannot be readily made into a *cause célèbre* by the corporation's opponents, because it cannot be freely reported and subjected to a public debate.

The propensity of the State to intervene in economic affairs may be subject to changes, and at least some of these, like wars, may not be wholly or even significantly controllable by any one particular State. But the rights of economic agents depend on the political character of the system.

The functions of public relations and of advertising performed by private business organizations in the democratic systems illustrate consequences of these rights. In a viable democracy, no private empire, however extensive, could long sustain its existence if the public at large became convinced that it constituted a conspiracy against the public interest, that its practices and purposes stood in conflict with some basic values of the society. If such a conception did take firm hold, political, legislative, administrative, and legal action would readily destroy it. This is well understood by managers of business enterprises in the democracies for whom the functions of advertising and public relations are not limited to selling products and services. Business must also appeal to the electorate on issues that in a neutral sense might be subsumed under the term *the general good*. Such appeals are made to convince the electorate that the profits of business are just and beneficial from the standpoint of a larger public interest.[4] Under an autocracy, such activities would be superfluous. Under a democracy, the failure to pursue them could lead to tangible consequences ranging from adversely increased business taxation to outright nationalization. The need of government-owned enterprises for a satisfactory public reputation is, if anything, no less urgent.

One of the reasons for widespread disenchantment in Europe with the policy of nationalization has been the shabby image built up by the nationalized enterprises in the years since World War II. Nationalization, once regarded as a touchstone of Socialist hopes for a more egalitarian, prosperous, and stable society, has lost most of its popular appeal. It has been all but abandoned even by its erstwhile champions, the Socialist, labor, and workers' parties of Europe. The nationalized enterprised have failed to live up to worker expectations with respect to an increased sense of personal identification with them, and they have done very little to dispel the notion, busily advanced by private industry, that they are inefficient, bureaucratized, and money-losing establishments. In recent years, public opinion in Western Europe has decisively shifted away from state ownership and toward private enterprise.[5] These changes in public attitudes have forced Socialist parties such as the West German SPD since 1959 and even Britain's Labour party, in a somewhat more restrained fashion, to eschew further nationalization as "economically irrelevant." In all these cases of Left-wing parties operating under democratic conditions, the failure to respond to changes in public attitudes would spell an indefinite retirement from power.

Another consequence of the concern with public opinion backed by the recourse devices of a democracy is reflected in the treatment of employees by employers. Historically, the extension of suffrage and the increase in the total relevant political public has had repercussions on economic management in all countries in the direction of a welfare-oriented humanitarianism. Even if the immediate result of improved safety devices, control over health hazards, decreased hours,

[4] See Richard W. Gable, "NAM: Influential Lobby or Kiss of Death," *Journal of Politics*, Vol. 15, No. 2 (May 1953), pp. 254–273, for an account of the activities of the National Association of Manufacturers to reeducate the American public about the virtues of private enterprise in 1933 in the aftermath of the depression. "The overwhelming loss of public support during the New Deal period threatened organized industry." Cited in H. A. Turner (ed.), *Politics in the United States* (New York: McGraw-Hill, 1955), p. 165.

[5] Among many sources, see, for example, Mark Abrams, "State Industry and the Public," in *The Lessons of Public Enterprise*, M. Shanks (ed.) (London: Jonathan Cape, 1963), pp. 207–215; R. Kelf-Cohen, *Nationalization in Britain: The End of a Dogma* (New York: St. Martin's Press, 1958), Ch. XV, pp. 262–263.

and the like dampened the profitability of business, such measures became indispensable in the light of public demands voiced through legislative bodies, the press, the political parties, and, of course, the trade unions. Nineteenth-century concessions to employee welfare were not merely reflexes of gradually more enlightened entrepreneurial opinion; they were significant also as survival measures. Without them, private enterprise could not have withstood the more extreme socialist challenges of expropriation.

If political democracy has such important consequences for the economy, we might well expect that comparably developed economies under democratic systems should have much in common whether they call themselves socialist or capitalist. The two charts comparing Britain under Labour with the United States, and two Scandinavian nations with Canada, the United States, and Britain in the 1960s are illustrative of the relatively narrow range of differences in at least two important areas of economic policy. (See Tables 4 and 5.)[6]

Table 4
Percentage Allocation of Gross National Product to Various Types of Expenditure, Selected Countries, 1964

Country	Private Consumption Expenditure	Government Purchase of Goods & Services: Military	Government Purchase of Goods & Services: Civilian	Fixed Capital Investment	Other*
Norway	57%	3%	12%	29%	−1%
Sweden	57	4	14	23	1
United Kingdom	65	6	11	18	1
United States	63	8	10	17	2
Canada	63	4	11	23	†

* Includes inventory changes, net surplus or deficit in international trade balance and international investments, and (in the case of Canada) statistical discrepancy. Percentages do not add to 100 because of rounding.

† Less than −0.5 per cent.

Calculated from Organization for Economic Cooperation and Development, *National Accounts Statistics, 1955-1964* (March, 1966), *passim.*

The responsiveness of economic mechanisms to shifts in the demands of public opinion may perhaps be regarded as a mixed blessing. Can the sacrifice of immediate consumer gratifications on behalf of some worthy, long-term developments ever be realistically ex-

[6] These tables are reproduced from Nathaniel Preston, *Politics, Economics and Power* (New York: Macmillan, 1967), pp. 133 and 141, respectively. The implications of the close resemblance are analogous to the findings of Dye, *op. cit.* (See footnote 4 in Chapter 1.)

pected in the context of a democracy? The conviction that a democratic political system is always likely to pamper the consumer and may be incapable of sustained long-term sacrifices required for industrial growth and modernization has encouraged the rejection of the democratic way among some of the newly emergent Afro-Asian nations.

Table 5
Effect of Taxation and Benefits on Income Distribution, United States and United Kingdom Compared

Country	Income Distribution Before Taxes and Benefits		Income Distribution After Taxes and Benefits	
	% Within Range*	% Outside Range*	% Within Range*	% Outside Range*
United States (1946-47)	62.6	37.4	74.7	25.3
United Kingdom (1948-49)	62.1	37.9	87.4	12.6

* Range is fixed such that the lowest income is no less than half the average family income, and the highest not more than five times the average. Per cent is of total *number* of incomes reported.

Adapted from Allan Murray Cartter, *The Redistribution of Income in Postwar Britain: A Study of the Effects of the Central Government Fiscal Program in 1948-49* (New Haven, Conn.: Yale University Press, 1955), Table 38, p. 90. Copyright 1955 by Yale University Press. Reprinted by permission.

The question whether democracy is compatible with policies of "steel instead of bread" and "guns instead of butter" must be referred to empirical evidence. Democracies are incapable of imposing long-term plans and controls where the force of public opinion rejects such plans; they can rarely, if ever, impose controls that do not involve the public participation of those interests that may be adversely affected by such controls. Barring these qualifications, democracies as diverse as Switzerland, Britain, and the United States have implemented economic plans and controls that subjected the consumers to long-term sacrifices in behalf of guns and steel rather than bread and butter. There is no doubt that it can be done *sometimes*.

The historic determination of the people of Switzerland to remain free and independent has given rise to traditionally heavy expenditure, and taxation, for the maintenance of a relatively large and technologically advanced armed forces. In the 1940s, the self-imposed economic sacrifices of the Swiss people set a high, and probably prohibitive, price on Nazi aspirations to the control of Switzerland. During World War II, the people of Britain responded to Winston Churchill's pleas for sacrifice at a time when Nazi U-boats were on the

Table 6
Some Comparisons in Resource Allocation Between the USSR and the USA (1958) Capital and Consumer Goods

	Coal (million tons)	Machine Tools (000's)	Steel (million tons)
USSR	496	138	54.9
USA	382	32	77.2
	Passenger Autos (million units)	**Washers (million units)**	**Refrigerators (million units)**
USSR	0.12	0.54	0.36
USA	4.26	3.67	3.05

verge of disrupting Britain's lifeline across the Atlantic. For the British, then, the alternatives to measured underconsumption were either ultimate starvation or surrender. But the resolve of British public opinion was so unmistakable that Winston Churchill did not need any vast, specialized, and, above all, compulsive bureaucratic apparatus to enforce the policy of rationing. (Perhaps for this reason alone, he was entitled to think that Britain's darkest hours were also her finest.)

As the British experience *since* 1945 seems to indicate, however, the capacity of public opinion to support policies of sacrifice is not constant. Conceivably, as some politicians in Britain today argue, the people have not been sufficiently aroused to forego the featherbedded amenities of a welfare state that cut down on British productivity and increase the costs of British exports to the point where they often can no longer successfully compete in the world's market. Conceivably, the people are not capable of *voluntarily* extending the period of self-sacrifice into years and decades, particularly on the heels of the hardships and deprivations of the past.

Do the economic successes of democracy depend on generally fortuitous circumstances that obviate the need for harsh discipline of producers and consumers? To be sure, the decline of Britain has been more than offset by the advances of various other democracies since 1945. But most stable democracies have been among the wealthiest nations with mature, industrial economies. Their outputs have been fairly evenly balanced between consumer and producer goods. Today's modernizers of the non-Western world are more often interested in technological self-sufficiency and in industrial expansion than simply in raising the level of current, often single-crop, single-export commodity, economies. They wish to maximize the output of producer goods.

Obviously, some conditions for economic expansion, in any direction, are beyond the control of political organization. These may involve the presence, or lack, of natural resources, climate, geographic location—the state of the world's economy imposing certain supply-demand limitations—and, at any point in time, also a number of inherited cultural given factors with respect to the technological-economic capabilities of the population. These qualifications notwithstanding, autocracies can and frequently do implement economic policies that would be unthinkable in the democracies.

Judging by the past experience of such effective democracies as the Scandinavian nations, Ireland, the low countries, Switzerland, the United States, Britain, Uruguay, and several Commonwealth countries, there are certain limits to the democratic capability in capital investment. During the present century, a time when these states could be actually classified as "effective democracies," none of them remotely approached the peacetime, and relatively long-term ratio of resource investment in the capital goods sector that has characterized, for example, the Soviet economy.

Not even developing democracies such as Japan, Israel, Lebanon or India have matched the peak industrial commitment of the Soviet Union under Stalin, when heavy industry received about 83 per cent of the total investment by the state from 1934 to 1938 as compared with only about 17 per cent going to the consumer goods industries.[7]

The rationale of this difference is as much political as economic in nature. Just as in the case of taxation, democratic participation makes it virtually impossible to secure long-term agreement on a policy of sacrificing present satisfactions to the vistas of the future on a scale so lopsided that starvation or malnutrition, exposure to the elements through lack of clothing and shelter, or the sacrifice of privacy and of the basic amenities of life (to name some of the implications) should be voluntarily accepted by the people on a large scale.

Extreme policies of underconsumption in favor of massive armaments in peacetime, or in favor of industrial development, have been pursued over relatively long spans of time only by autocratic regimes, not by the democracies.[8] On the other end of the scale, we find traditional autocratic regimes that, amidst widespread poverty, enable

[7] Harry Schwartz, *Russia's Soviet Economy* (New York: Prentice-Hall, Second Edition, 1954), p. 220.

[8] See John H. Kautsky, *Political Change in Underdeveloped Countries* (New York: John Wiley & Sons, 1967), pp. 38–113, for a discussion of communism as a blueprint for social change implemented by nationalist intellectuals in the countries of Asia, Africa, and Latin America. The blueprint involves the rejection of the old colonial masters, destruction of indigenous aristocracy, and industrialization under the leadership of the radical (party) intellectuals.

Table 7
USA/USSR Output Figures of Selected Products at the End of 1966

	USA	USSR	
Coal	492	585	(million tons)
Steel	146	96.9	
Crude petroleum	409.1	265.0	
Cement	67.1	79.9	
Electric energy	1,157,000	480,000	(million kwt hrs)
Aluminum	2,692	1,300	
Bauxite	1,824	4,800	
Asbestos	114.2	840	
Pig iron	85.2	70.3	
Copper	1,296.5	800	
Lead	399.8	370	
Zinc	929.9	470	
Magnesium	72.4	33	
Manganese	18,175	8,000	
Mercury	22	40	
Nickel	12	90	
Tin		12	
Tungsten	8.09	11.5	
ICBMS	1,054	724	(no. of missiles)
Long range bombers	600	200	
Submarines	130	400	
IRBMS	?	900	
Medium range bombers	?	1,200	

relatively small segments of upper- and middle-class elements to enjoy all sorts of consumer luxuries. With large numbers of peasants and slum dwellers living precariously in mud hovels without the benefits of sanitation, electricity, modern transportation or communication, schools, and playgrounds or other recreational facilities, the urban middle class and the landlords enjoy living standards obtainable in the most advanced industrial societies.

These systems provide *fewer* public goods and services to the people at large than *either* the democracies or the Communist regimes. Allowing for their total economic capability, however, they supply far more luxurious housing, automobiles, television sets, appliances, and many other consumable amenities than do the Left-wing innovative-mobilizational regimes.

Thus, nations such as the Union of South Africa, Saudi Arabia, Brazil, Portugal, or Iran are all *relatively* backward—vis-à-vis the Communist states—in per capita provision of health care, schools, welfare benefits to workers, newsprint, electric power, public transportation, and mass consumption theaters, museums, and libraries. But this has not been the case with goods of private consumption, which clearly only relatively small segments of the respective populations enjoy.

Illustratively, Saudi Arabia, with an estimated GNP per capita of $170 in 1957, supplied only one physician for 13,000 inhabitants. Red China, with an $85 GNP per capita, ranked lowest among Communist states with one per 8,700! North Korea, with a GNP per capita of $68, provided one physician per 6,700. Saudi Arabia provided one hospital bed per 1,400 inhabitants, whereas Outer Mongolia provided one for 120. The percentage of Saudi population in school attendance in 1968 was only 3.3, whereas Red China ranked lowest among Communist systems with 13.6.

Table 8
Physicians Per Capita (c. 1960)*

A. *Communist Nations*		B. *Democracies*	
Albania	1/2,000	Australia	1/900
Bulgaria	1/610	Canada	1/520
Czechoslovakia	1/506	Ireland	1/950
Cuba	1/1100	New Zealand	1/670
East Germany	1/1050	United Kingdom	1/870
Mongolia	1/903	Switzerland	1/800
Hungary	1/500	Sweden	1/940
North Korea	1/909	Uruguay	1/950
North Vietnam	?	United States	1/667
Poland	1/796	C. *Other Regimes—Random*	
Rumania	1/682	South Vietnam	1/29,000
USSR	1/490	Indonesia	1/43,000
Yugoslavia	1/1330	Burma	1/9,300
China	1/1500 (?)	Turkey	1/2,880
C. *Other Regimes—Random*		Haiti	0.7/10,000
Spain	1/800	Brazil	1/3,500
Portugal	1/1200	Colombia	1/2,400
Argentina	1/850	Guatemala	1/4,500
Peru	1/5,500	Honduras	1/6,000
Venezuela	1/1,300	Pakistan	1/12,000

*Range of maximum differences in (A): GNP per capita 15:1 (East Germany-North Vietnam). Physicians per capita 4:1 (USSR-Albania). Range differences in (B): GNP per capita 8:1 (U.S.-Uruguay). Physicians per capita 3:2 (U.S.-Uruguay). Range of differences in (C): GNP per capita 9:1 (Argentina-Burma). Physicians 50:1 (Argentina-Indonesia).

But Saudi Arabia possessed some 300,000 television sets in 1968, whereas Red China had only about 100,000. In fact, allowing for the size of her population (6.9 million) and her wealth, this was a very remarkable indulgence in Saudi Arabia. So was the figure of 101,000 motor vehicles that gave Saudi Arabia an average of one vehicle per 68 inhabitants. Among fourteen Communist states, only three—the USSR, East Germany, and Czechoslovakia, all relatively wealthy states —significantly exceeded this average!

Ethiopia, one of the world's economically most backward nations, with 27,000 automobiles for a population of 23.4 million, exceeds in *per capita* terms six of the 14 Communist states, including Bulgaria whose *per capita* GNP is nearly nine times higher than Ethiopia's!

Outlays on housing construction provide similar illustrations of lopsided resource allocations. Here we can consider the capability that the Soviet Union and the East European regimes have developed for supplying housing to the population; how these capabilities compare with those of various non-Communist states; and, finally, how the actual supply of housing vis-à-vis the capability compares in each of these cases.

If we measured national capability for supplying *any* good to the consumer by the GNP per capita, or by the national income per capita, several of the Communist states could be said to have ranked among world leaders since the early 1960s. There is little doubt that on either of these scales the Soviet Union, Czechoslovakia, East Germany, Hungary, Poland, Rumania, and even Bulgaria rank among the top two-fifths of the world's economies.[9]

A more specific index of ability to supply dwelling space could be inferred from certain industrial indices. Thus, we find that, as of 1967, the Soviet Union produced 2,499 kwh of electric energy per person; Czechoslovakia produced 2,699; East Germany produced 3,489; Hungary produced 1,222; Poland produced 1,605; Rumania produced 1,284; and Bulgaria produced 1,636.

The capability of East Germany was surpassed by only six nations: Australia, Canada, Great Britain, Norway, the United States, and Sweden. In total output of energy resources per person (coal, gas, and oil, and so on) only the United States and Canada excelled the USSR, Czechoslovakia, East Germany, and Poland. In per capita steel production, Czechoslovakia considerably exceeded the United States and was second only to Belgium; the USSR and Poland ranked among world's leaders. In the output of cement, the Soviets ranked ahead of the United States (360 to 341 kg per capita); so did Czechoslovakia, Poland, and Bulgaria, with Rumania only slightly behind (329 to 341

[9] See, for example, Preston, *op. cit.*, p. 75, for a listing of 72 nation-states in order of their estimated per capita national income. Czechoslovakia, the USSR, and East Germany are listed eleventh, twelfth, and fourteenth, respectively, as of 1962; and Hungary, Poland, Rumania, and Bulgaria, nineteenth, twenty-second, twenty-fifth, and twenty-sixth, respectively.

kg). In all these areas, the Communist states had very significant capabilities as compared with the 100-odd members of the world community of states. Yet, these political systems have lagged behind many technologically backward and primitive economies in supplying certain types of housing to the population.

As of 1966, for example, available data indicated that in Yugoslavia only 0.7 per cent of all urban apartments were in the large seven-room plus category; in Poland it was 0.4 per cent; in Czechoslovakia 0.3 per cent; and in Bulgaria 1.1 per cent. In Hungary, apartments in two categories, five to six rooms and seven rooms or more, both accounted for 1.2 per cent of all urban dwelling units. Data for other Communist states were not available.

In contrast, however, among the relatively poor, technologically backward Latin American states, we find that these largest apartments represented 7.2 per cent of the urban total in Guatemala; 5.9 per cent in the Dominican Republic; 5.4 per cent in Honduras; 14.7 per cent in Brazil; 24.2 per cent in Colombia; 5.5 per cent in Ecuador; and 5.1 per cent in Peru. Argentina, in the two categories, five to six and seven plus, had 17.2 per cent of its dwellings. In Europe, relatively poor and backward Portugal counted 10.9 per cent of its urban dwelling units in the largest category.

A comparison between some output indices of two particular nation-states, Portugal and Poland, illustrates the different priorities of the two types of regimes: traditional and Communist autocracies.

For many decades Portugal has been the poorest European nation next to Albania. In the 1950s and 1960s, Portugal's GNP per capita was only about half as large as Poland's. Not only is it much poorer, in general, but Portugal has not achieved anything like the level of Poland's industrialization. Illustratively, with a population of 9.4 million, Portugal produced 1.8 million tons of cement; 315,000 tons of steel; and 1,468 million volts of electrical energy. With a population of 32 million, Poland produced 11.2 million tons of cement; 10.5 million tons of steel; and 9,672 million volts of electrical energy.

Yet, with all these advantages and capabilities, the average Polish dwelling in 1966 consisted of 2.6 rooms with 4.0 persons per dwelling and 1.5 persons per room. In 1960 in Portugal, the average number of rooms per dwelling was 3.6, with four persons per dwelling and only 1.1 person per room. In 1966, 54.2 per cent of Polish housing units were in the "dwarf" category (one to two rooms). As of 1960, only 23.8 were in the same category in Portugal! On the other end of the scale, only 4.2 per cent of all Polish apartments exceeded five rooms; in Portugal 30 per cent did! According to Polish statisticians, only 67.5 per cent of Polish dwellings had running water in 1966, compared with 82.1 per cent of the Portuguese dwellings in 1960.

Plumbing was provided in only 47.8 per cent of Polish housing and in 84.2 per cent of the Portuguese! Baths were installed in 40 per cent of Polish dwellings, but in 53.1 per cent of the Portuguese. Only in the area of electrification did Poland excel Portugal with 97.8 to 88.5 per cent of the dwellings equipped with electrical current. In 1966, Poland installed 5.6 housing units per 1,000 population, compared with a not too distant 4.9 units per 1,000 population in Portugal.

Admittedly, Poland sustained huge housing losses during World War II. Portugal sustained none. But as of 1960, West German housing had been rebuilt from extensive war damage to an even more impressive superiority over Poland than the Portuguese. In fact, Portugal consistently devoted between 18 and 21 per cent of its capital investment funds to housing construction from 1952 to 1966. The comparable range for Poland was only 12.3 per cent between 1951 and 1955 and less than 17 per cent on the average, hence. In contrast, Portuguese investment in industry ranged between only 33 and 42 per cent of total investment during this period; and Poland ranged between 48 and 44 per cent.

In 1937, Poland and Portugal were approximately equal in the diffusion of telephones among their respective populations. Poland had eight telephones per 1,000 inhabitants, and Portugal had nine. By 1966, the diffusion increased to 62 per 1,000 in Portugal but only to 44 per 1,000 in Poland. (In the USSR there were 19 telephones per 1,000 inhabitants in 1965, and in the United States 502 telephones.)

In 1938, Poland had 8.6 thousand trucks; Portugal—with its much smaller population—had 13,000. By 1960, these ratios were more than reversed, Poland reaching a figure of some 120,000 trucks, and Portugal 50.4 thousand. But more directly relevant to personal consumption have been passenger cars, where the ratios have remained all but unchanged. In 1938, Portugal's automobiles outnumbered Poland's 34.8 to 29.8 thousand. In 1960, Portugal was still ahead 158 to 117 thousand! In 1968, Poland had 275 thousand autos; Portugal had 280,000. On the other hand, Portugal has lagged behind Poland in the diffusion of cultural, educational, and social welfare outputs to the population.

Interestingly enough, in 1938, when their political orientations and levels of industrialization were more alike, the number of students in institutions of higher learning was 14 per 10,000 people in Poland and 11 per 10,000 people in Portugal. In 1967, the comparison became 90 per 10,000 in People's Poland and 35 per 10,000 in Portugal. Polish newspaper circulation averaged 189 copies per 1,000 inhabitants in 1965 to Portugal's mere 68 copies! In 1966, radio sets averaged 176 per 1,000 in Poland and 143 in Portugal.

In 1966, People's Poland provided 13 physicians per each 10,000 of its population; Portugal had 8.3 physicians. Poland averaged 3.7 dentists and Portugal a mere 0.1 per 10,000 people.

In 1966, Portugal provided its people with 3.9 million volumes of books through seventy public libraries; People's Poland supplied nearly forty million volumes through some 7.9 thousand libraries.

At this juncture we could note that concentrating resources on the pattern of the Communist regime of Poland and of the other Communist nations has not always been effective either (1) in terms of the values of the system or (2) the demands of the people. For many reasons, including the dearth of domestic raw materials, lack of labor incentives, and excessive bureaucratization, the expansion of industrial power under communism has often been wasteful and disappointing in relation to resources consumed. On the other hand, the people have not been satisfied to accept years of austerity in terms of consumable items such as food, housing, and appliances in return for those public amenities of welfare and culture that the party regards as instruments of control and molders of a new society. Limiting the responsiveness of the economic system—by political means—creates the opportunity of single-mindedly pursuing unpopular economic objectives. There may be no guarantee that the goals thus pursued, in splendid indifference to popular opinion, are worthwhile or realistic. But the more innovative and even preposterous they may seem, the more *necessary* it becomes to shed political democracy for those who pursue them. Even where the ultimate goals of development, such as the possession of a diversified, industrialized economy in a primitive one- or two-crop agricultural country, are widely shared by the population, democracy may still seem realistically incompatible with their achievement.

The country may require large export earnings to finance development. Assuming that the mobilization of all its resources *could* purchase sufficient foreign capital and equipment to accomplish the desired diversification, would the people be really willing to give up their favorite foreign imports necessary to accumulate the funds? Would they be willing to give up traditional work methods and consumption patterns? Could they be relied on to eat less, pay higher taxes, and accept strange new social disciplines for the ten, fifteen, or twenty years necessary to modernize their economy? To many a nationalist who craves the grandeur of industrial power, the uncertainties implicit in democracy are simply unacceptable.

An African scholar has summed up the situation in these terms:

> Parliamentary democracy is rejected by many Africans bent upon a rapid transformation of their economies because it is seen as diverting popular energies away from the task of national reconstruction. For President Julius K.

Nyerere, the two-party system " . . . is an oversophisticated pastime which we in Africa cannot afford to indulge in; our time is too short and there is too much serious work to be done."

The fundamental need for a sound infrastructure, capital investment in agriculture and industry and the growth of savings clashes with the mass desire to consume. . . . Governments must act in an unpopular manner.[10]

Analogous doubts about the economic suitability of democracy may be expected to arise in mature, wealthy, industrialized economies during periods of prolonged and severe depressions. One source of difficulty in effecting a desirable recovery is invariably found in the clash of self-serving economic solutions that may prolong the crisis instead of ending it. Agricultural interests may ask for tariffs to boost the prices of their products in the home markets. Exporters may oppose them for fear of foreign reprisals that would adversely affect their interests. Labor and business are likely to expect that "the other fellow" will shoulder the costs of recovery. The former may oppose cost-cutting by business and government as a threat to the social gains and advantages won in more prosperous times. Business may fear that a solution of the crisis imposed by the electorate may embody radical expropriation. Suspicions conducive to the acceptance of Communist and Fascist solutions are thus likely to be stimulated by employer-employee confrontations under circumstances of great and widespread adversity.

It would go beyond the introductory character of our survey of the economic consequences of politics to span the whole range of economic policies characteristic of different regimes. In the main, such research remains to be done. It may suffice to indicate here, however, that many economic phenomena rarely thought of as political devices are, in fact, such; and that the causes of these phenomena may often and in large measure—if not *always* and *completely*—be political.

An illustration of this is inflation. Inflation has been a worldwide phenomenon no less than deflation or depression. But granted its universality, inflation has been unequally serious and unequally treated in politically different, even if economically comparable, situations.

Government fiscal policy, including taxation, control of interest rates, foreign trade, and public spending, is among the means that rulers can use to regulate inflationary trends in the economy. In times of maximum employment and high pressure of demand on the available supply of goods and services, the government may ease the resultant inflationary spiral by siphoning off excess purchasing power through heavier taxation or diminishing the demand by increased interest rates.

Anti-inflationary policies may not always be popular with workers or

[10] Donald Rothchild, "Progress and the One-Party State," *Transition*, Vol. III, No. 10 (September 1963), pp. 32–33.

businessmen, and in turn with all interests that are loath to pay higher taxes and to see their own particular spending plans frustrated by acts of political intervention. On the other hand, chronic and acute inflation poses dangers to most economic interests in society. Above all, it undermines the position of those who live on fixed incomes and those who cannot freely raise the prices of their products or services to compensate for the depreciation in the real value of the currency. Such persons, chiefly employees and unorganized workers rather than entrepreneurs and property owners, are the most vulnerable victims of inflation.

If our view of the influence of politics on economics holds true, we should find that regimes that are politically weak, because of chronic division and stalemate among their policy makers, or because they cannot assure themselves effective physical control over the system they claim to rule, are least effective in holding the line against inflationary pressures in their economies. We should also expect that those oligarchical and quasi-oligarchical regimes that conspicuously exclude the lower classes from political power might occasionally resort to inflation deliberately as a substitute for and as a supplement to other policies.[11]

Thus, inflation could be used to wipe out wage increases secured by employees and by workers from the State and from private firms. It could serve to nullify the value of pensions, grants, and other welfare benefits paid either out of taxation by the State or directly by private entrepreneurs. The effect of such inflation might be not merely to halt any progress in the direction of a more egalitarian distribution of the national income but to effectively, even if indirectly, reverse it.

A manufacturer who promises to retire his workers at the age of 65 at 50 per cent of their lifetime average earnings may be happy to find the real value of that sum growing more insignificant each year, provided, of course, that he continues to receive profits on his products at rates that keep up with the inflationary spiral. Under such circumstances, both the entrepreneur and the government behind him may appear at once usefully "benevolent" and "progressive," while being in fact neither of these.

In systems where taxation is heavily pegged to consumption, inflation may be used to increase the burdens of some interests or groups to the relative advantage of certain others. If prices rise faster than wages, the burdens of every consumption tax to the average workingman are thereby increased. A 2 per cent tax on a loaf of bread takes a bigger bite out of his income, if the price of bread has gone up and

[11] See Carroll Hawkins, "Reflections on Labor's Relation to Government and Politics in Latin America," *Western Political Quarterly*, Vol. XX, No. 4 (December 1967), pp. 930–40. *Cf.* John P. Powelson, *Latin America: Today's Economic and Social Revolution* (New York: McGraw-Hill, 1964), on Latin America's ideologies of inflation, p. 191.

his particular wage has remained the same, or at least failed to rise correspondingly to new costs. The general regressiveness of consumption taxes is thereby also increased. The average worker will now spend more of his income on taxes than he did under a lower price level and the same wages. His ability to save and to purchase a greater variety of products and services for his family will be lessened.

The person whose income does keep up with increasing prices will pay proportionately no more in consumption taxes than he did before. In some cases, inflation may lessen tax burdens, as in the case of landlords, whose taxes can be paid on outdated real estate assessments. Thus, the richest individuals may often wind up paying next to nothing at all for the costs of government.

The deliberate character of a particular inflation, however, notwithstanding all these fairly obvious effects, may be impossible to prove. Government foot dragging, a financially lackadaisical attitude, may be all that is necessary under some circumstances to maintain inflation. It may require mere acquiescence. Hence, the effect felt may be of things not being done, rather than of specific actions decided and taken.[12]

An innovative-mobilized regime of Left-wing tendencies might use inflation to mobilize resources for intensive industrialization—thereby exploiting the workingman of today for the presumed advantages of the workingman of tomorrow.[13] Worthless wages were a guarantee of underconsumption, until the Soviets modernized their economy and the administrative apparatus to the point where effective tax collection could replace the device of inflation. While inflation kept down the purchasing power of workers, the regime destroyed the peasant proprietors whose land and produce it needed to finance industrialization. In 1926, 78 per cent of the population was peasant. Neither the extreme of inflation nor of forced collectivization would have been feasible to Soviet economic innovators on a basis of political democracy. By the beginning of the 1940s, the Soviet government slowed down the acute phase of its inflationary policy, and after 1947 it brought it under a complete *de facto* control.[14]

[12] See Albert Weisbord, *Latin American Actuality* (New York: The Citadel Press, 1964), for a discussion of some relevant policies of the oligarchies. *Cf.* Aldo Ferrer, *The Argentine Economy* (Berkeley: University of California Press, 1967), for a discussion of the political propagation mechanisms of inflation, pp. 194–205.

[13] See W. A. Lewis, *Economic Survey 1919–1939* (London: Allen and Unwin, 1965), pp. 128–135. "In any society that uses money, whether it be capitalist or socialist, there will be inflation if the sums being spent on producing investment goods exceed the sums that people are willing to save, unless the difference is either lent by foreigners or absorbed by a budget surplus." P. 126.

[14] See F. D. Holzman, "Soviet Inflationary Pressures 1928–1957; Causes and Cures," *Quarterly Journal of Economics*, Vol. 74, No. 2 (May 1960), pp. 167–188. In this au-

The favored treatment of specific economic interests can readily take insidious forms in autocracies, inasmuch as all the economic agents do not enjoy the same political rights and recourse as others. Favoritism accorded to specific interests can be kept a quasi-private affair between the regime and the interest. The exploitation of workers by employers in Tsarist Russia or of peasants by Junker landlords in Royal Prussia, far from being regarded officially as scandalous, was accepted as proper and reasonable.[15] Certain public sanctions were available to those particular interests that figured as the semiofficial adjuncts, allies, and supporters of the oligarchy; but they were not available to the oligarchy's opponents.

Areas of economic policy such as subsidies, government loans, price controls, export-import and exchange quotas, excises, and custom duties all can be effectively *removed* from the public arena by autocratic rule. The relationship and the rationale underlying State support for one segment of industry, or even for one firm rather than another, can be made into matters of private influence and secrecy, no more explainable than the whim of a dictator. In democratic systems such favors and privileges—if on a large scale—are subject to bargaining and negotiation among a variety of impacted interests.

If airlines receive government subsidies this cannot take place without a hearing for the railroads, or the trucking industry, not to mention a still wider range of labor, consumers, and occasionally even a more generalized public. If a case can be made against such "favors" by the State, disappointed competitors are sure to make it. Only by bargaining and the securing of some *quid pro quo* could their silent acquiescence be assured.

Whatever the total resources available for allocation, and whatever the direction of economic policy being followed, the reponsiveness of the political mechanisms in the autocracies tends to be heavily and rigidly weighted. In the Russian and Prussian examples just cited, the

---

thor's view the Soviets could not control inflation before completing collectivization even though they wished to control it. No one, of course, can be sure as to what they really wanted.

[15] See Bernard Pares, *The Fall of the Russian Monarchy* (New York: Alfred A. Knopf, 1939), pp. 39–45, on the authority vested in the land gentry ("service squires") by the Russian state in the nineteenth century. *Cf.* H. Seton-Watson, *The Decline of Imperial Russia, 1855–1914* (London: Methuen, 1952), pp. 122–128, on Tsarist policy toward capital and labor. (See p. 121 on regressive budgets from 1878–1897.) On Germany, see W. H. Dawson, *The Evolution of Modern Germany* (London: T. Fisher Unwin, 1914), "The Rural Labour Problem," pp. 265–293. (Pp. 402–423 on regressive imperial taxation.) See also W. F. Bruck, *Social and Economic History of Germany from William II to Hitler* (New York: Russell and Russell, 1938), pp. 128–129 and pp. 265–272; L. Hamburger, *How Nazi Germany Has Mobilized and Controlled Labor* (Washington, D.C.: The Brookings Institution, 1940).

rights of assembly, free speech, and strike that would enable labor to exact specific demands from industrial and agrarian employers were severely restricted, whereas the position of landlords and manufacturers received the support and the protection of the police, the armed forces, the administration, and the courts. The treatment of employee interests was part of the oligarchy's program for repressing subversion; employer interests were identified by the rulers with their own, hence with the *raison d'état*. In Russia, the former were subjected to violence and Cossack charges, whereas the latter were frequently given sympathetic consideration and paternalistic care.

In the upshot of political inequality, workers who challenge their employers under traditionally autocratic regimes, such as Spain's or Portugal's today, face many more State-imposed handicaps than they do in the democracies. The official forces of law and order well-nigh automatically line up behind the employers. In the innovative autocracies, on the other hand, the advantages between employers and employees may well be reversed.

The Italian liberal-democratic State tolerated the Marxist and the trade union organizer even if it did not love them. Their existence was sanctioned by the rules of the political game—prior to 1922, that is. To Mussolini and the Fascists, however, such elements possessed only the "rights of prey," somewhat analogous to the rights of Jewish workers, artisans, merchants, professionals, scientists, and employers under nazism in Germany. They had but the right of suffering extermination.

Given the wide disparity between the political goals of their ideological system and the economic, physical, and social status quo of their environment, Communist economic policies have tended to be even less responsive to the demands of traditional economic agents than those of the Fascists or Nazis.[16]

Far from dispossessing the old rich upon coming to power, the policies of fascism and nazism seem to have benefited these strata, at

[16] As Professor Nove has said with reference to the ubiquitous influence of the party in the Soviet economic experience: "... party control over policy and over its execution is an essential, if not always visible, fact of Soviet life, and affects not only basic planning decisions or the appointment and behavior of a minister but also the choices between alternatives which a factory director or a *Kolkhoz* chairman may wish to make. This is why, although party organization as such is not a question to be dealt with here, it is necessary to emphasize that it affects all aspects of economic life. It is, so to speak, the board of directors (at the top) and the institutional substitute for the motivating force of free competition, the driving force which tries (with some success) to overcome natural inertia," *The Soviet Economy* (New York: Praeger, 1961), p. 95. This view can be contrasted with the assessment of Nazi practice up to 1940, at least, by Arthur Schweitzer: "Whether in terms of power or functions, the top Nazi leaders were only occasionally able to influence, and could not lay down, the economic ... policies of the regime." *Big Business in the Third Reich* (Bloomington: Indiana University Press, 1964), p. 507.

the expense of the economic have-nots. We have already mentioned in Chapter 4 the shift to a higher incidence of indirect taxation generally more burdensome to wage earners than to those receiving high profits. Such a shift took place in both Italy and Germany under their respective autocracies.

In both countries there was also a strong tendency for corporate profits to stay well ahead of inflation and of wages to fall behind price rises. Thus, in Germany under Nazi rule, average monthly wages reached a level of 111.2 per cent of the 1936 average, but food prices rose by about 4 per cent and manufactured consumer products by almost 20 per cent during the same period. In the main, the German worker's lot under Hitler was improved by virtue of full employment and income from overtime pay, but in comparison with pre-Hitler Germany the purchasing power of the average laborer had actually declined.

On the other hand, corporate profits, after taxes, surged from 6.6 billion marks in 1933 to 12.2 billion in 1936 and 15 billion in 1938. Moreover, these tended to accumulate in generally fewer and bigger firms. Between 1936 and 1939, the number of corporations in Germany declined from 39.2 thousand to 23.5 thousand. The number of firms in the capital range of 20 million Reichsmarks or more increased from 110 to 129, whereas all firms below these capital levels declined. The most severe casualties were among firms with capital assets under 20,000 Reichsmarks, which declined by more than 55 per cent in these three years.

Table 9 shows a list of profits, after taxes, realized by several of Germany's leading firms between 1932 and 1939.[17] With respect to land, both in Italy and Germany, what occurred up until the outbreak of World War II was not the breakup of landed estates and their redistribution, but rather an over-all consolidation of more lands in fewer private hands.

Communist economic policy makers in the USSR have been singularly unresponsive to the demands of their foes—landlords, manufacturers, or merchants. As for their responsiveness to the demands of those regarded as friends or allies—the workers and the landless peasants—Soviet economic policies have at least overtly recognized the

[17] Cf. Otto Nathan, *The Nazi Economic System* (Durham, N.C.: Duke University Press, 1944), on the decline of wages from 56.7 to 53.6 of Germany's national income between 1929 and 1938, p.338. Maxine Y. Woolston, *The Structure of Nazi Economy* (New York: Russell and Russell, 1941), reports an index figure for rising inequality in the distribution of income in Germany from .649 in 1931 to .721 in 1935, pp. 217–218. Cf. David Schoenbaum, *Hitler's Social Revolution* (Garden City, N.Y.: Doubleday and Company, 1968), on the fact that real wages of German workers fell between 1934 and 1940 while business profits went up, p. 156.

Table 9
Profits of Selected Private Firms Under Nazism

	1932	1933	1934	1935	1936	1937	1938	1939
Deutsche Waffen u. Munitionsfabriken A.G.	2.6	3.8	11.9	21.7	29.7	31.7	41.5	44.9
Bayerische Motorenwerke A.G.	10.7	16.1	20.7	22.4	23.6	23.2	29.5	32.5
Orenstein und Koppel A.G.	7.0	7.4	15.5	18.4	21.3	18.6	22.7	25.5
Philipp Holzmann A.G.	9.5	10.8	26.7	39.8	45.8	40.0	61.5	72.8
Fried. Krupp A.G.	116.0	130.0	192.0	246.0	287.8	316.6	331.5	395.0
Illseder Hütte A.G.	9.1	14.5	25.8	32.6	38.5	—	—	46.6
Kali-Chemie	13.5	16.9	17.9	19.3	22.2	20.7	25.9	25.6
Gesel. für Elektrische Unternehmung	6.2	6.3	10.0	12.8	15.6	15.8	15.0	26.2
I.G. Farbenindustrie	470.0	491.3	565.1	611.9	704.6	535.0	698.9	786.3
Mannesmannröhrenwerke	45.4	50.4	64.9	82.6	104.5	121.3	136.1	150.2
Wanderer Werke	8.4	9.5	17.2	23.6	29.75	31.1	34.8	—
Vereinigte Stahlwerke	—	107.8	105.6	141	192.0	193.0	215.0	222.0
A.E.G.	142.1	167.0	141.5	138.8	172.1	226.4	207.5	266.5
Siemens S.	154.2	119.9	168.0	—	—	313.0	278	340.0
Siemens H.	144.0	107.8	138.0	—	—	212.0	191	234.0
Total Siemens	298.2	227.7	306.0	—	—	525.0	469.0	574.0

legitimacy of their interests. But the recognition of worker legitimacy has been coupled with adherence to the practical principle that ultimately only the party can judge what is best for the proletarians.

Communist economic policy, therefore, has been traditionally more *for* the workers than *by* the workers. It has involved as much "therapeutic deprivation" in the name of the goals assumed to be in the final or ultimate interest of the working class as responses to the workers' specific, day-to-day wants and demands. One could argue that in some cases the party gave the workers what they ought to have had and what is good for them in the light of Marxist-Leninist ideology or even other value systems. The party itself has never claimed merely to record and implement rank-and-file-worker claims. This would constitute an ideologically impermissible "economism"!

Trade unions may be formally represented in economic planning and in the decision-making units of the system; but these unions are largely representative of the regime—to a large extent simply additional window dressing for it—and not true representatives of labor's rank and file. Such union participation has a bogus quality about it, deliberately intended to confuse appearance and reality and create useful illusions of participation and consent.

Of course, the claims of the totalitarian Communist party sometimes may be compromised: by its inability to secure effective control of the political system; by the need for coalition rule; and by de-emphasis of the revolutionary aspects of the party's programs in the light of international circumstances. Nor is there any inherent reason why, through changes in the clientele and leadership of the party, its actual objectives could not be eroded away from the militant tenets of *any* given ideology.

The characterization here is applicable only where such militant commitment does, in fact, exist and can be implemented by the party as in the actual example of the Soviet Union between the world wars. As also in the Soviet case, the party's capacity for increased reponsiveness in economic management may rise in proportion to the narrowing gap between—to put it in capsule form—itself and the conditions of its environment. After some fifty years of rule, the Russian ruling party has eliminated most of the initial foes in its domestic environment. In the 1920s, the party's unconcern with the claims of peasant proprietors was equivalent to a serious misrepresentation of the total population, and an even more serious exclusion in terms of the traditional role that these proprietors have played in the Russian economy. Forced collectivization, industrialization, and the assorted arts of political persecution over a prolonged period of time have surgically altered the social anatomy of Russia's population. The cultural impact of the regime's rule, its propaganda, and indoctrination may have served to narrow the gap between what the people want and what the party wants. It was largely on these grounds that Khrushchev renounced the indiscriminate uses of terror and that the Twenty-Second Congress of the CPSU proclaimed a transition from a worker-peasant dictatorship to a so-called People's State. As the goals of political innovation recede in scale or intensity, economic planning and decision making tend to become more responsive to popular demands.

In traditionalist or quasi-democratic regimes, the participant economic agents are likely to possess greater autonomy from direct regime control and greater genuineness of identity. But the process of participation is likely to be subject to many unequal restraints imposed from without by the agencies of the State.[18] In the effective democra-

[18] For a comparison of the Yugoslav planning model, midway between "total" cen-

cies, the genuine identity of the economic participants, their equal rights of participation, and the wider range of interests allowed to participate are the distinguishing features of business life.

The implications of economic responsiveness for investment and planning need not be understood as rendering the application of democracy among the poor nations of the world undesirable. They call instead for a realistic examination of the premises of economic development in each case. Various politically oriented goals—including, for example, national economic self-sufficiency, the development of heavy industry, or the possession of nuclear reactors—may be in themselves quite meaningless. They may also be beyond the realization of any indigenous economic effort and hence wasteful, or, worse yet, self-defeating in terms of the human values to which they might be reasonably related.

The politicians who call for sacrifice on behalf of tomorrow need not be exempted from the burden of explaining their disregard of today's here-and-nows. Their right to predetermine the future, if necessary *against* the wishes of their constituents, is itself a basic issue. Democratic planning and State control, such as they may be, are basically pluralistic and are anchored in the right of the electorate to pass judgment on them. Autocracies minimize pluralism and deny that right. If the elimination of the full impact of public opinion will more readily facilitate drastic rather than piecemeal measures, and the imposition of thorough rather than partial, negotiated compromise solutions, it remains to be demonstrated that the former are really preferable to the latter. They may not appear as neat and clear-cut as totalitarian or autocratic devices, but they may be more humane and more realistic in the long run, nevertheless.

Even though it may be difficult to push democratic economies into sharply innovative, austerity-demanding directions, these economies offer compensating advantages in terms of the relative stability and predictability of policies emanating from government sources.

Outwardly, to be sure, the whim of the electorate may change the political situation overnight and alternate conservative respecters of property with socialist confiscators in less than twenty-four hours. This is a real, ultimate danger of democratic politics, depending on the locale and the circumstances. It may constitute an understandable reason for aversion to, or anxiety about, democracy on the part of various interests.[19]

---

tralized Soviet planning and autonomy of interests manifested in less innovative oligarchies, see N. Spulber, *The Soviet Economy: Structure, Principles, Problems* (New York: W. W. Norton, 1962), pp. 234–239.

[19] As Joseph Schumpeter wrote, one of the essential conditions of a viable democracy is that people do not "attempt to rush the shop." He discussed this under the theme of

In those systems, however, in which historically the democratic process has been maintained for a long period of time, institutionalized representation and participation in the making of government economic policy have rendered it in some ways more stable and predictable than under the autocracies.[20] Democratic institutions make it possible for people to know a great deal about who wants what and why. The claims and the counterclaims of organized groups are a matter of the public record, published in newspapers, given as testimony before legislative committees, executive fact-finding commissions, statutory advisory boards to administrative agencies, and in many other ways (as before the quadrennial convention platform committees of the major American parties, for example). The nature and the relative weight of differing claims cannot be kept a secret. Those who ultimately make the decisions allocating resources are generally constrained by the fact that what is wanted is known. They cannot take refuge in the absence of recorded public positions of interest groups on economic issues leaving *them* to represent what *they* take to be the public's demand. The more open and public stages the process of policy formulation involves, the more difficult it becomes for an official to take measures contrary to an apparent community consensus.

The alternation in office of political parties, however outwardly different, but within the context of a functioning democracy, invariably involves a practical exclusion by them of the most extreme, lopsided policy alternatives. If the object of the political game is to keep winning elections, the policies of those in power must be geared to the expectations of a very inclusive, and varied, electorate. The task of offering an attractive and "different" alternative must always be combined with and balanced by sufficient conciliation and reassurance to the waverers, the lukewarm supporters, and even one's erstwhile opponents, to make a victory at the polls possible. In a society of any complexity, it is usually difficult to constitute an elected government on the basis of a single, radical economic interest, whether of Right or Left tendency, and irrespective of whether in a two-party or multiparty context. The high degree of mutual consideration and public dialogue that characterizes the relationship between government and opposition in a viable democracy, greatly minimizes the possibility of

"Democratic Self-Control," *Capitalism Socialism and Democracy*, 3rd. ed. (New York: Harper & Row), pp. 294–295.

[20] The economic pendulum swing represented by British nationalization measures after 1945 is a classic illustration of change that in its timing and details was neither sweeping, sudden, or traumatic as sometimes is perceived from abroad. See, for example, W. N. Loucks, *Comparative Economic Systems*, 6th ed. (New York: Harper & Row, 1961), pp. 279-285.

all-or-nothing oscillations in the field of economic policy. Such oscillations would be too risky in terms of a government's maintaining rule by consent rather than coercion—that is, too risky for the democratic system itself.

Finally, if the election does not result in the overthrow of the democratic system itself (as, say, the 1933 election did in Germany), the interplay of group politics will inevitably balance the election results. Victorious conservatives will need to negotiate with trade union leaders; triumphant socialists will need to deal with bankers and industrialists. The continuity of interest group politics from before-elections to after-elections is generally likely to moderate the actual, *de facto*, oscillation in power.

In autocratic regimes, the knowledge of who wants what and why is not as readily available. The pulse of the public as a whole may not be periodically taken through the device of elections; or the electoral process may be completely inadequate if it does exist. The autocratic oligarchy, not required to consult publicly with relevant economic interests, and essentially independent of the outcome of elections, could suddenly change course in almost any field of economic activity without any prior warning to the public at large. In some areas of policy such changes could be lopsided reversals of course, and so long as the process of decision making remained shielded, they could be made on grounds no more convincing than a mental lapse of the ruler.

The more autocratic the system (that is, the closer to the *de facto* rule of one person), regardless of its tendency or persuasion, the more the likelihood that public policy is made in a virtually private fashion by the executive, be he Stalin, Nkrumah, or Franco. The problem of private decision making—unpublicized, and involving only a few sometimes quite obscure advisors of an autocrat—involves much more than economic policy. But it has a special significance in the field of economics.

Unlike the management of foreign affairs and of national defense, economic decision making does not generally require an inherent element of secrecy; rarely, if ever, does it call for instant response to a mortal danger. Naturally, consultative processes, if not eliminated, may be at least seriously minimized by the needs for secrecy and immediacy of response. Thus, it would not be surprising for the general public of a democratic *or* an autocratic regime to be occasionally taken aback by an announcement of official policy or troop deployment and accept it as more or less justified depending—in the democracies at least—on the reasons officially offered *post facto*. An illustration of such crisis action occurred in 1962 with President Kennedy's response to the Soviet-Cuban missile buildup.

On the other hand, there would be much less likelihood of this type of action in, say, drastically raising the interest rate, or in undertaking a brand new $20 billion spending program. In these economic areas of policy, not only would there be different expectations with respect to the procedure of governmental action, excluding sudden cataclysmic moves, but there would be the need for the policy maker (the President in this case) to involve many other public agencies in disposing of what he may have proposed. In practice, therefore, major economic policies in all effective democracies would rarely emanate analogously to a magician's rabbit out of a hat. Few democratic prime ministers or presidents would risk such moves, and generally speaking the formative stage of economic policy making would not be either sudden or secret but at least in some measure public, deliberative, and consultative. Furthermore, the enactment of policy into law and practice would generally require sanctions that, with or without explicit legislative approval, would entail extensive debate and the consent of public bodies outside the executive.

The impact of procedural openness on the economy is analogous to the values that are conferred upon it by law and order. It gives to economic transactions the security of fairly predictable, reasonably calculable governmental action. And this, no less than enforceability of contracts, is—other things being equal—a significant aid to business operations. The possibilities of sudden, cataclysmic, capricious changes for the whole economy or a segment of it are significantly lessened. The chances of an overnight, as it were, abolition or initiation of major government economic programs, under the centralized and highly oligarchic leaderships of Soviet Russia, People's China, or for that matter even Franco's Spain, are considerably greater than among the democracies, if history may serve us.

CHAPTER 6
EDUCATION AND CULTURE

OTHER things being equal, political systems differ considerably in their impacts on education and culture. In the democracies traditional values as well as pragmatic popular attitudes generally support high levels of expenditure for educational and cultural objectives.[1] The expenditures in turn, tend to be allocated in rather diverse ways within the democratic systems. For no matter how oppressive the weight of public opinion in the direction of cultural conformity may be, marginal, minoritarian, and simply unpopular intellectual causes always find some legal-political shelter within the framework of the underlying democratic formula.

One index of the democratic commitment to education is the share of national wealth channeled to it from all levels of government. Illustratively, among European democracies, we find that public expenditures

[1] "If a nation expects to be ignorant and free, in a state of civilization, it expects what never was and never will be. The functionaries of every government have propensities to command at will the liberty and property of their constituents. There is no safe deposit for these but with the people themselves; nor can they be safe with them without information. Where the press is free, and every man able to read, all is safe." Cited from a Jefferson letter by A. R. Chandler, *The Clash of Political Ideals*, 3rd ed. (New York: Appleton-Century-Crofts, 1957), p. 64.

for education in 1955 amounted to 2.5 per cent of the GNP in Great Britain; 2.4 in Switzerland; 3.4 in Sweden; and 2.5 in Ireland. The average for all of Western Europe was 2.4 per cent of the GNP. The average per capita GNP in Western Europe was $747 in 1955. The per capita GNP's of three of the established democracies were successively just about the highest in Europe: Switzerland, $1,281; Sweden, $1,201; and Britain, $1,047. (Luxemburg and Belgium outranked Britain with $1,194 and $1,076, respectively.)

Ireland, however, had a per capita GNP of only $515, well below the average for Western Europe as a whole. Ireland spent 12.9 dollars per capita on education whereas the average for Western Europe was 18.0 dollars. This means that she spent 72 per cent of the average European outlay while her wealth, as measured by the GNP was 69 per cent of that average. On the other hand, looking at the stable, traditionalist European autocracies, we find Spain and Portugal devoting 1.4 and 1.2 per cent of their GNP to education. Thus, Spain's per capita GNP at $276 was about 38 per cent of the West European average, but her expenditure for education, at $3 per head, was less than 17 per cent of the average Western European expenditure! Similarly, Portugal's per capita GNP of $207 stood at about 27 per cent of the West European average, but her expenditure of $2.5 per person was less than 14 per cent of that average. Even Greece, poorer than Spain, second only to Portugal in Western Europe at $259 per capita GNP, was outspending the Iberian nations with an even 20 per cent of the average Western European public expenditure for education.[2] The discrepancy in spending between them has been remarkably consistent since before World War II[3] until at least the present decade.

Although we have no figures to account for private spending on education in all three countries, every available index of performance puts the total Irish effort well ahead of the Spanish and Portuguese, with all due allowance for different levels of economic development in each case.[4]

In the area of primary education, for example, pupils between the ages of 5 and 14 enrolled in school represented only 56.7 per cent of the total 5 to 14 age group in Portugal and 72.7 per cent in Spain, according to official information. In Ireland they were 89.4 per cent of the age group; even poor and war-torn Greece had achieved an enrollment of 70.3 per cent of this age group.[5]

[2] See J. F. Dewhurst, et. al., *Europe's Needs and Resources* (New York: Twentieth Century Fund, 1961), pp. 125 and 313.

[3] *Ibid.*, p. 336.

[4] *Ibid.*, p. 342.

[5] Figures are for about 1955. *Ibid.*, Table 10–2, p. 315.

Although data, so far as primary school attendance goes, are not readily comparable for all European nations (for example, the Scandinavian countries, the Netherlands, and Switzerland require pupil attendance only from 6 or 7 years of age), data relating to secondary schools and higher education corroborates the trend to ascendancy of the democratic nations in Western Europe. In the age groups between 15 and 19, those in attendance in secondary institutions averaged 15.9 per cent of the total age group in Western Europe. In Ireland the figure was 22.7 per cent; in Switzerland 25.0; in Sweden 35.3; and in Britain 16.8. (Britain ranked first in Europe in primary school enrollments and ranked sixth in general secondary schools.) In Spain it was only 6.5 per cent and in Portugal 5.8.

In higher education, one of the highest ratios of university graduates to population at large before World War II was achieved by Ireland in 1937–1938. Even though there is no comparable data for all the Western European nations, the leaders in the university graduates-to-population ratio after the war (in 1950–1951) were Finland, Ireland, Austria, and Britain, in that order.

Admittedly, no single set of figures can give us an over-all index of excellence. Education clearly represents an area where considerations of quantity, even assuming the possession of completely reliable and comparable statistics, cannot be made without regard to quality. The ratio of university graduates to population in Switzerland in 1950–1951, for example, was 186 per one million inhabitants, whereas it was 144 per one million in Portugal. In 1954–1955 the ratio was actually in favor of Spain over Switzerland, 214 to 148! We know that Switzerland still educates a considerable proportion of its young people through an on-the-job, apprenticeship system reflecting traditions going back to medieval times.

On the other hand, even though we do not have comparable data for other nations, we know that Switzerland has provided a university education to as large or a larger share of its population since the turn of the century than France, Germany, the Netherlands, and Sweden during nine of the seventeen years for which such information is available.[6] And we have reason to believe that the quality of that education has been among the highest in the world.[7] Since the war, just under a quarter of the Swiss population has attended universities. No comparable data for the traditional autocratic regimes are available.

So far as quantitative indices go, there is every evidence of a high commitment to education in public spending among all democracies.

[6] *Ibid.*, p. 333.

[7] See H. G. Rickover, *Swiss Schools and Ours* (Boston: Little, Brown and Company, 1962), passim and pp. 31–32 and 59–60, particularly.

Illustratively, we find that in mid-1950s on a scale of per capita GNP's, the nations of Latin America ranked in this order: Venezuela, Uruguay, Argentina, Cuba, Panama, Colombia, Brazil, Nicaragua, El Salvador, Costa Rica, the Dominican Republic, Ecuador, Mexico, Chile, and Guatemala.[8]

These data are, no doubt, sketchy, selective, crude, and probably in some measure unreliable. But if we were to take them at anything like face value, it would appear from them that only Uruguay had consistently matched its economic capability with its educational performance.[9] If there are indications here that an effective, established democracy utilizes its economic assets with a matching generosity for educational purpose, we can find corroborative evidence in the case of Costa Rica. Unlike Uruguay, Costa Rica has experienced dictatorial rule in the past four decades, but during the entire period since World War I it has generally conformed to the criteria of a political democracy. Costa Rica's record of achievement in public education has exceeded, by far, what might be reasonably inferred from its economic endowments. Thus, we find that in the 1950s Costa Rica ranked seventh in per capita GNP; eleventh in degree of urbanization; tenth in the level of nonagricultural population; and eleventh in infant mortality. But Costa Rica ranked fourth in literacy; fourth in primary enrollment; fourth in levels of secondary enrollment; and sixth in higher education.

Although we can not suggest any ideal absolute figure of resource utilization for education, we do think that the democracies tend to

[8] Data in this section are drawn from I. N. Thut and D. Adams (ed.), *Educational Patterns in Contemporary Societies* (New York: McGraw-Hill, 1964), pp. 362–378.

In degree of urbanization (percentage of population in cities of over 50,000 persons) Argentina ranked first, followed by Chile, Cuba, Venezuela, Mexico, Colombia, Panama, Brazil, Bolivia, Ecuador, Costa Rica, Paraguay, Nicaragua, Peru, and El Salvador. Data for Uruguay were not available. In degree of "least proportion of population engaged in agriculture," Argentina was followed by Chile, Uruguay, Venezuela, Cuba, Ecuador, Colombia, Nicaragua, Costa Rica, Dominican Republic, Brazil, Mexico, Peru, and El Salvador.

As of 1957, Uruguay ranked a close second to Argentina in the rate of literacy of its population, which was officially put at 80–85 per cent in Uruguay, and at between 85–90 per cent in Argentina. Chile and Costa Rica were virtually tied for third place. Venezuela, with all its wealth, however, claimed only 50–55 per cent of the population to be literate and ranked eleventh; Panama with 65–70 per cent and Cuba with a claimed 75–80 per cent literacy matched their per capita GNP rankings. As of 1960, Uruguay ranked first in the proportion of secondary school enrollment followed closely by Argentina; Venezuela ranked sixth. Panama ranked third, but Cuba was in seventh place.

In higher education, Uruguay was in second place in percentage of population enrolled, after Argentina, followed by Panama and by Chile, both at a considerable distance. Venezuela ranked fifth and Cuba seventh.

[9] The Cuban statistics reflect the situation under the Batista regime.

spend more of their resources on education in relation to what they actually possess than members of the international community of states have done generally. And we believe that the reasons for this are intimately linked up with the ideological and institutional concomitants of democracy.

Insofar as autocracies are concerned, their pattern of performance has oscillated much more widely. In Latin America, the dictatorial regime in Paraguay, under General Stroessner, committed considerable resources to education and accomplished more than one might reasonably expect from economic indices. Paraguay ranked eighteenth in per capita GNP, but sixth in level of literacy among twenty Latin American states. It claimed second place in levels of primary school enrollment (that is, as a percentage of children of school age). It ranked tenth in the secondary and eleventh in the higher education enrollments. On the other hand, the Dominican Republic, under Trujilo, was eleventh in per capita GNP, but fourteenth in literacy and nineteenth and thirteenth in secondary and higher school enrollments, respectively.

In terms of *process* or *input* rather than *results*, we can observe that where democratic regimes are replaced by autocracies ideologically hostile to egalitarianism, and in this sense "traditionalist," an education shrinkage usually takes place. Conversely, the replacement of antiegalitarian autocracies by democracies is generally associated with an expansion of educational systems.

There are several European examples of these tendencies. In Germany, for example, the transition from the empire of William II to the democratic Weimar Republic was accompanied by a very substantial increase in the diffusion of university education among the population. Illustratively, the ratio of university students per each 10,000 inhabitants in Germany rose from 11 in 1913 to 18 in 1920, a far more precipitous rise than that recorded in other European countries where no analogous political upheaval took place during, or as a consequence of, the war. Thus, in France the ratio increased from 9 to 10; in the Netherlands from 10 to 13; in Sweden from 11 to 13; and in Switzerland from 15 to 18.

Germany's short-lived democracy (1919–1933) promoted a large expansion of the educational system at all levels of learning, as measured by virtually every conceivable yardstick. In the Great Depression year of 1930, German university enrollments reached their all-time high of 19 students per 10,000 inhabitants. The onset of the Hitler regime reversed this trend dramatically. Between 1930 and 1935, university enrollment ratios dropped from 19 to 11 and then to 8 by 1938, in what was Germany's last peacetime year before the onset of World War II.

It is interesting to note that in each of these instances—Germany's democratic upturn and authoritarian downturn—the changes represented a sharp accentuation of international trends. Just as the expansion of higher education after World War I was a fairly common occurrence, so was the downturn forced by the economic exigencies of the Depression. But under the Nazi regime, the decline was far more precipitous than elsewhere. Dutch enrollment ratios, for example, remained constant from 1930 to 1935 and declined from 15 to 14 per 10,000 inhabitants from 1935 to 1938. Swedish enrollment ratios actually increased from 16 in 1930 to 19 in 1935 and remained at the same level in 1938. France increased her ratio from 14 to 17 by 1935 and declined to a figure of 16 by 1938. Switzerland actually recorded substantial increases: from 15 in 1930 to 19 in 1935 and 23 in 1938.[10]

Under Hitler's rule, the total number of university students in Germany fell from 95,807 in 1931 to a mere 39,236 in 1939. This took place, of course, against the background of a considerably increased total population. The number of students in various higher technical and professional schools fell during the same period from 23,749 to 10,307. Nor were the losses confined to higher education. Under the Nazis, from 1931 to 1940, the number of elementary schools declined from 52,959 to 49,720; the number of full-time teachers from 190,371 to 171,340; and student enrollment was also down from 7,590,466 to 7,327,556.[11]

One of the consequences of the establishment of the democratic Federal Republic in Germany after World War II has been a remarkable reversal of these educational trends of the Nazi era. To take but one comparable figure, German enrollment ratios in institutions of higher learning have climbed to a position of parity or near parity with other economically advanced West European nations. In 1955 and 1956, the German enrollment ratio actually stood slightly ahead of the Swiss, whereas in 1938 Swiss preponderance over Nazi Germany was just about 3 to 1.

Quantitative indices of education in Italy disclose a tendency to stagnation and decline under Fascist rule (1922–1944) following a parliamentary democratic regime, and, conversely, a remarkable revival when fascism, in turn, was replaced by a parliamentary democracy.

In the field of higher education, the largest actual number of students attending universities in Italy prior to the end of World War II was in 1921, the last year before Mussolini's seizure of power! At that

[10] Figures in this section are drawn from Dewhurst, *op. cit.*, p. 333.

[11] R. H. Samuel and R. H. Thomas, *Education and Society in Modern Germany* (London: Routledge and Kegan Paul, 1949), pp. 38, 50, 112, and 132–133. *Cf.* H. W. Schneider and S. B. Clough, *Making Fascists* (Chicago: 1929).

time 43,865 attended universities and other institutions of higher learning. In 1929, the figure was only 27,013. In the 1930s the average attendance was about 37,000 per year. In view of Italy's population expansion between 1921 and 1939, the years of fascism were years of both absolute and relative decline for Italian higher education.[12]

Political democratization revived Italian education. In 1936–1937, Fascist Italy maintained 2,359 public secondary schools with 541,301 students, of whom 191,454 were girls. In 1946–47, the Italian democracy, under extremely adverse postwar conditions, operated 3,242 schools with 678,881 students, of whom 260,645 were girls. Taking into account private and public schools, we find that between 1936 and 1937 and 1950 and 1951, Italy increased the number of its secondary schools from 3,636 to 6,064; the number of students from 674,546 to 1,101,330; and the number of girls receiving secondary education rose from 254,058 to 426,030.[13]

In Spain, the overthrow of the autocratic regime of General Primo de Rivera and the establishment of a parliamentary democratic Republic in 1931 gave rise to a historically unprecedented effort in behalf of educational expansion. The Republic embarked on a large-scale school construction program, modernization, expansion, and secularization of the whole educational system.

Despite the lack of material resources, conflict with the educationally powerful and entrenched Catholic Church, and the abysmally low levels of literacy among the population at large (over 50 per cent were illiterate), the Republic made great headway. In one year, from 1931 to 1932, the percentage of children attending schools was increased from 40 to 55. The number of schools, elementary and secondary, grew from 7,000 in 1931 to 13,570 in 1933. By 1933, the Republic had actually doubled the number of secondary schools it had inherited from the de Rivera dictatorship.[14]

On the other hand, the autocratic regime of General Franco, which took over from the Republic in 1939 at the conclusion of the civil war, inaugurated very different policies. Autocratic Spain gave very low priority to the expansion of its educational plant. After four years of civil war, the educational needs of Spain, quite apart from the nature or content of instruction, had become obviously even greater than they had been in 1931. But the Franco regime did not choose to regard them as such. Whereas under the republican regime Spain

[12] See H. R. Marraro, *The New Education in Italy* (New York: S. F. Vanni, 1936), pp. 249, 255, and 432.

[13] Ministero Della Publica Instruzione, *La Scuola Italiana* (Rome: 1953), p. 10.

[14] See Ramos Oliveira, *Politics, Economics and Men of Modern Spain* (London: Victor Gollancz, 1946), p. 453.

built 6,570 new schools in only two years, from 1931 to 1933, under Franco it took six years, from 1940 to 1945, to build 4,067 schools. The regime devoted relatively more effort to education after the conclusion of World War II (in which Spain was not a belligerent). Still, as late as 1948, the number of secondary and primary teachers in Spain was 56,121, as compared with 47,674 in 1935.[15] The regime did somewhat better in the area of higher education, where the number of students at universities increased from 29.2 thousand in 1935–1936 to 33.7 thousand in 1940–1941.

Such progress in over-all numbers of students, teachers, and schools as has actually taken place conceals a relatively slow process of development. In 1945, only 1.5 per cent of Spanish youth who had received primary education went on to higher education; this figure increased to a mere 2.0 per cent in 1960. In 1945, 19 per cent of Spanish university students were women; this figure actually declined to 17 per cent in 1960. In autocratic Portugal, numerical increases have similarly obscured an underlying stagnation and closeness of the educational system. Where in 1946 2.0 per cent of the graduates of primary schools went on to the universities, the figure was still only 2.3 per cent in 1961.

These discrepancies of development within and among nation-states far more closely reflect political rather than economic factors. Just as we can use examples of *transitions* from one type of political system to another—from autocracy to democracy or vice versa—analogous tendencies can be correlated to less drastic political changes *within* on-going political systems.

In all of our effective democracies the expansion of the educational apparatus and its increasing availability to wider strata of the population have been closely linked to increasing democratization. The cycle of educational reform has generally reflected the extension of suffrage and of access to decision-making organs to an ever-widening range of popular interests. Examples of this are provided by the most stable and effective democracies as well as by the more recently democratized systems.

In Britain, public education was one of the neglected social causes until the extension of suffrage during the nineteenth century began to build increasing momentum for change. The Reform Act of 1832, which still enfranchised relatively few middle-class elements, was followed by an 1833 act increasing public subsidies to schools. On the heels of the much more comprehensive Reform Act of 1867 came the

[15] See Richard Pattee, *This Is Spain* (Milwaukee, Wis.: Bruce Publishing Company, 1951), p. 419. In 1946, the Spanish budget still allocated nearly 60 per cent of government spending to the armed forces and police, but only 7 per cent to the Ministry of Education.

Education Act of 1870, which became the basis for the development of English public mass education—universal and compulsory—until the even more comprehensive act of 1902. We may note parenthetically that it was not until 1884 that Britain achieved universal male suffrage. The extension of suffrage to women came in two stages in 1918 and 1928, and not until 1948 was the privilege of a double vote for university graduates and business proprietors abolished. The gradual extension of suffrage in the nineteenth and twentieth centuries coincided with increasingly effective demands for more, better, and cheaper education for the people as a whole, through Parliament, government and the political parties.

In Japan, considerable educational progress had actually been made under the autocratic regimes of the nineteenth and twentieth centuries. The basic reason for this expansion was the desire of Japan's ruling elites to compete economically and politically with the great powers of the West. But even in the case of Japan, the most striking progress in her educational system coincided with the democratization of her political life. In the forty-year period between 1877 and 1917, the number of students at Japanese universities increased from 235 to 7,291; the number of teachers from 91 to 924; and the numbers of institutions from one to four.

The first great quantitative expansion took place following what might be termed the first democratization of Japanese life—the extension of universal male suffrage in 1925. By 1927, the number of university students in Japan had risen to 34.6 thousand; teachers to 4.6 thousand; and institutions of learning to 37. The second enormous leap forward came on the heels of Japan's second democratization under the auspices of Allied Occupation. By 1952, Japan had some 400,000 university students; 37,000 teachers; and 220 institutions of higher learning. By the early 1960s, only the United States and the Soviet Union possessed higher ratios of university students in relation to total population than did Japan.[16]

The fate of German education under Hitler, Italian education under Mussolini, or Spanish education under Franco was in each case far more significantly predetermined by the attitudes of the power holders than by any underlying economic exigencies. If anything, the economies of Germany, Italy, and Spain under autocratic regimes could all have supported even higher actual expenditures for education than those maintained by their democratic predecessors. And, considering the destruction wrought by war in Germany and Italy, Hitler and Mussolini could have spent more than their democratic

[16] See Herbert Passin, "Japan," in James S. Coleman (ed.), *Educational and Political Development* (Princeton, N. J.: Princeton University Press, 1965), pp. 277–312.

successors, at least in the immediate post-World War II period. What actually *did* happen to education would be incomprehensible without some appreciation of basic Fascist and Nazi attitudes and the institutional implementations of them.

Both Hitler and Mussolini despised "intellectualism" as expressive of decadence and chaos. Moreover, their ideologies can be said to have embodied at once hatred and fear of the egalitarian rationalism underlying the various strands of democratic thought. That men in general could attain an objective and, therefore, common and equal understanding of their environment was vehemently denied by the Nazis and Fascists. Both of these ideologies were openly elitist, trusting to the superior insights and abilities of a few, and ultimately even of one, with little more than contempt for the many, the "mob." Instinct and force, not reason and persuasion, were the characteristic sources of social and political conduct for the Nazis and the Fascists. The ultimate appeal was only to the will, and thereby to the right of the stronger.

The central value-orientations of fascism and nazism were toward expansionism, conquest, and militarism, not toward cooperative, contemplative, or materially productive endeavors. Men were to be made into good soldiers, above all else. The motto of the Fascist man was: "Believe, Obey, Fight." Both Hitler and Mussolini regarded rationalism, the cultivation of the intellect and of the individual's private judgment, as subversive, confusing, and therefore highly dangerous.

Fascism and nazism shared certain orientations and attitudes with various conservative elites, political and economic; all or most of these orientations found institutional expression in their regimes and have had their parallels under Franco, Salazar, and other autocrats of modern times. The belief that "woman's place is in the home" is one illustration of it. In 1933, Hitler decreed a 10 per cent quota limit on the number of women who could be admitted to German universities. Doctrinally, Hitler had prepared the ground for such measures in *Mein Kampf* and elsewhere by asserting frankly reactionary ideological and propagandistic positions toward the rights and opportunities of women. Various less militant and more respectably conservative regimes have shared his biases.

The view that universal, intensive education is bound to cause trouble in the shape of "impossible" claims and demands on the political system has long characterized traditional authoritarian regimes as well as the total, mobilized ones of the Nazi and Fascist variety. As one minister of education under Russia's Tsar Alexander I put it: "To teach the mass of people, or even the majority of them, how to read will bring more harm than good. Education should be proportionate to the prosperity of those who are being educated."[17]

In this century, a Spanish official and university professor put it in these terms: "All the misfortunes of Spain come from the stupid desire to teach Spaniards how to read. To teach a man how to read merely obliges him to assume a position that will cause ill fortune to himself and his fatherland."[18]

In examining the performance of educational systems in different political contexts, we must take into account those pressures from the domestic and international environment that force rulers to modify their policies. Whatever misgivings an autocratic ruler may feel about diffusion of knowledge among people from whom he wishes unquestionable blind obedience, the need of effective competition in foreign markets or adequate defense at home may and must force concessions. To the extent that political systems cannot really secede from the world at large, the autocrats may be forced increasingly to sacrifice preferred policies to possible or viable ones. But, whatever the trends of the future may be, the tendency of antiegalitarian autocratic regimes, whether traditionalist or innovative-mobilized, has been to limit and to inhibit the growth of education, not to accelerate or maximize it.

Mussolini and Hitler did not commit themselves to leveling out socioeconomic differences among the inhabitants of Italy or Germany. In fact, they denied the very possibility of such a process. Thus, more pervasive State controls were coupled *not* with an expansion but actually with a shrinkage of mass education. There were no generous schemes of scholarship support for the poor. Women were encouraged to cultivate the roles of mothers and housewives and to stay out of professional schools. In Germany, learning was permeated with the official racialism of the Nazi party. There was no place for Jews in the German schools or universities, not on grounds of their religion or culture, but because of racial extraction or, simply enough, Jewish parentage.

The incidence of actual punishments and rewards meted out under the auspices of the Nazi and Fascist states depended on the political links between the interests involved and the ruling regimes. Educational institutions with a markedly Leftist tinge, or under Leftist auspices such as trade union institutes or Socialist and Communist adult education schools, were simply suppressed. Representatives of these political tendencies in public educational institutions were among the

[17] Cited by L. B. Pousson, *The Totalitarian Philosophy of Education* (Washington, D. C.: The Catholic University of America Press, 1944), p. 65.

[18] Cited by Laurence Fernsworth, *Spain's Struggle for Freedom* (Boston: Beacon Press, 1957), p. 262.

first to be fired from their jobs. On the other hand, representatives of political tendencies that were regarded as friendly or at least neutral toward the new regimes fared somewhat better. Under fascism in Italy and nazism in Germany, private schools operated by the churches did not disappear. They were submitted, to be sure, to political curricula controls by the new regimes, but in each case there was a continuing and significant attempt to achieve a *modus vivendi.*

In the upshot, the political systems of nazism and particularly fascism never achieved the monopoly of secular education realized in Soviet Russia and in virtually all of the Communist states. But then, of course, neither fascism nor nazism ever publicly associated itself with the position that religion, per se, was a spiritual "opium of the people," and that the ultimate goal of social policy should be its extinction.

Thus, it was much easier for various ultraconservative, nationalist, and reactionary professors and teachers to remain in their posts under Hitler and Mussolini and to continue to express their views, in more or less pristine form, than was the case with their more liberal or Socialist colleagues. Obviously the beliefs and affiliations of the former were both more congenial and more innocuous so far as the autocratic Nazi and Fascist masters were concerned. A catalog of repression, censorship, and regimentation must in each of these cases be placed in the context of wider social, economic, and cultural orientations of the regimes in power.

At the opposite end of the autocratic spectrum, we find that regimes committed to a militant egalitarianism, frankly avowed programs of social upheaval directed against socioeconomic elites of the *status quo ante*, have in fact pursued educationally expansionist policies on an even larger scale than the democracies. The tendency among the Communist political systems has been a virtual reverse of the Nazi-Fascist models in quantitative terms. (See Tables 10, 11, and 12.)

Certain aspects of Communist educational policy, in the USSR and elsewhere, stem from the underlying Marxian emphasis on class struggle as the most salient single feature of man's social development. Ultimately, an "objective" human understanding of one's self and one's environment depends, above all, on the liquidation of class oppression and class differences among men and the realization of the fullest equality in a Communist society. Until the attainment of this goal, all culture, science, philosophy, religion, and indeed all thought are regarded by the Marxians as class oriented and thus substantially "non-neutral." As Marx himself saw it, the dominant culture of every society is the culture of its ruling class.[19] From this basic assumption, all Marxian regimes have

[19] See his 1848 *Manifesto* for this "reproach" to the bourgeoisie:

"Your very ideas are but the outgrowth of the conditions of your bourgeois production and bourgeois property, just as your jurisprudence is but the will of your class made into a

Table 10*
Communist States (c. 1967)

	Population	School Enrollments	% of Population in School Attendance	GNP Per Capita
Albania	1,914,000	417,000	21.8	$ 290
Bulgaria	8,226,564	1,541,313	18.8	480
China	750,000,000	100,800,000	13.5	85
Cuba	7,833,000	1,432,303	18.3	330
Czechoslovakia	14,159,000	2,805,512	19.8	900
East Germany	17,011,931	2,847,334	16.7	1,260
Hungary	10,164,000	1,761,646	17.3	870
North Korea	12,100,000	2,570,000	21.2	190
Mongolia	1,120,000	188,300	16.6	90
Poland	31,551,000	7,100,000	22.5	790
Rumania	19,105,056	3,441,660	18.0	440
USSR	235,000,000	52,100,000	22.1	1,000
North Vietnam	19,000,000	2,728,600	14.3	90
Yugoslavia	19,742,000	3,671,601	18.6	470

*GNP per capita figures from the *Los Angeles Times*, January 21, 1968.
Widest GNP contrasts = 15:1. Widest enrollment contrasts = 1.5:1.

been driven to the conclusion that so far as culture and education are concerned, simply "more" and "better" could never be enough.

A proletarian Marxian State could not hope to maintain itself unless it could successfully combat the cultural influences of its enemies and supplant the reactionary, subversive, debilitating cultural currents with its own revolutionary and progressive ones. Thus, ideologically, and ultimately institutionally, too, communism has identified itself with a policy of pervasive cultural purge. It has demanded much more than token, outward conformity to its sociopolitical ideals. It has denied any sanctuary of political neutrality or objectivity even to art, music, literature, and the sciences. It has everywhere sought to ferret out bourgeois influences and has everywhere waged a struggle for the propagation of a Communist art, Communist science, and Communist literature.

---

law for all, a will whose essential character and direction are determined by the economic conditions of existence of your class.

"The selfish misconception that induces you to transform into eternal laws of nature and reason the social forms springing from your present mode of production and form of property—historical relations that rise and disappear in the progress of production—this misconception you share with every ruling class." Cited by Carl Cohen (ed.), *Communism, Fascism, and Democracy* (New York: Random House, 1962), pp. 104–105.

Table 11
Democracies (c. 1967)

	Population	School Enrollments	% of Population in School Attendance	GNP Per Capita
*Australia	11,479,000	2,536,905	22.9	$2,805
Austria	7,255,000	1,102,211	15.2	1,466
Belgium	9,499,234	1,902,904	20.0	2,039
*Canada	19,919,000	5,041,810	25.3	2,805
Denmark	4,758,000	884,246	18.9	2,497
Finland	4,631,000	958,999	27.3	1,874
West Germany	59,313,000	8,882,717	15.0	2,021
*Great Britain	54,436,000	10,657,427	19.6	1,977
Iceland	192,000	41,231	21.5	2,720
*Ireland	2,855,000	673,609	23.6	1,067
Italy	51,494,000	7,304,597	14.2	1,279
Japan	98,870,000	22,237,922	22.5	1,155
Lebanon	2,280,000	376,673	16.5	450
Luxembourg	333,000	46,158	14.0	2,155
Netherlands	12,387,000	2,574,998	20.8	1,804
*New Zealand	2,676,919	682,672	25.5	2,001
Norway	3,723,000	671,670	18.0	2,199
Philippines	33,470,000	6,151,315	18.3	278
*Sweden	7,773,000	1,276,895	16.4	3,041
*Switzerland	5,945,000	921,229	15.5	2,597
*USA	196,580	56,572,685	28.3	4,037
*Uruguay	2,780,000	450,000	16.2	613

*Nine established democracies (marked by asterisks) and several more recent Democracies. Widest GNP contrasts = 14:1. Widest enrollment contrasts = 1.8:1.

Under the slogan of "Socialist realism" for example, the ruling Communist parties have demanded that their writers, artists, and composers create works that would inspire and promote the construction of Communist societies and that would increase public support, esteem, and affection for Communist rule. The bureaucratic apparatus in each of the Communist states has sought to maximize a "carrot-and-stick" policy rewarding those writers, historians, artists, and scientists whose contributions meet party standards while punishing the others. The State's monopoly of all employment and publication media has made it all the more feasible to render such Communist manipulation and discrimination effective. The alternatives to cooperation with the party for the rebellious intellectuals have been generally limited to starvation, imprisonment, or exile.

Table 12
Other States (c. 1967)

	Population	Total School Enrollments	% of Population in School Attendance	G.N.P. Per Capita
Afghanistan	15,227,000	348,000	2.3	$ 65
Algeria	11,290,000	1,339,000	11.9	225
Argentina	22,691,000	3,895,275	17.0	633
Bolivia	3,748,000	587,370	15.8	189
Brazil	83,890,000	10,697,924	12.7	333
Burma	24,732,000	1,913,012	7.9	70
Cambodia	6,250,000	697,917	11.1	146
Cameroon	5,210,000	606,580	11.6	110
Taiwan	12,716,000	2,861,000	22.5	274
Ethiopia	22,590,000	358,755	1.6	55
Haiti	4,660,000	257,133	5.5	84
Indonesia	105,300,000	10,592,370	10.6	104
Iran	23,428,000	2,524,070	10.8	283
Iraq	7,160,000	1,094,106	15.3	262
Jordan	1,976,000	339,688	17.2	268
Kenya	9,365,000	931,143	9.9	85
Libya	1,677,000	205,083	12.2	490
Mali	4,576,000	126,817	2.7	60
Mexico	44,045,000	7,392,273	16.7	528
Morocco	13,323,000	1,180,262	8.8	174
Nepal	10,100,000	397,548	3.9	102
Nicaragua	1,685,000	212,917	12.7	359
Nigeria	57,500,000	3,153,103	5.5	80
Pakistan	105,044,000	8,542,713	8.5	125
Paraguay	2,094,000	356,266	17.0	224
Peru	12,012,000	2,248,694	18.7	283
Portugal	9,199,000	1,205,376	13.0	489
Saudi Arabia	6,750,000	224,194	3.3	320
South Africa	17,867,000	2,758,797	14.3	618
Syria	5,634,000	790,783	14.0	234
Thailand	30,591,000	4,711,918	15.4	155
Tunisia	4,675,000	837,587	17.9	214
Turkey	31,391,207	4,424,730	14.0	353
UAR	30,053,861	3,985,686	13.2	181
South Vietnam	16,124,000	1,416,700	8.8	126
South Korea	29,086,000	5,954,073	20.5	162
Liberia	1,083,000	76,389	7.0	180
Colombia	18,068,000	2,471,802	13.7	313
Dominican Republic	3,750,000	550,443	14.6	275
Ecuador	5,238,000	805,568	15.3	231
Ghana	7,740,000	1,196,400	15.4	230

Widest GNP contrasts = 11.5:1. Widest enrollment contrasts = 14:1.

Imbued with the concept of class struggle, Communist cultural policies have been heavily permeated with suspicion of subversion. Leninist doctrine anticipated an all-out assault on the Marxian State by those class elements that it had dispossessed and replaced in power. Thus, the vigilance of the party against sabotage, treason, and espionage has had a historic counterpart in the close surveillance and policing of the cultural-intellectual life of society, ever on the lookout for "bourgeois wreckers and saboteurs."

These orientations have led Communist regimes to indoctrination and censorship schemes of historically unprecedented scope and intensity. The sheer volume of cultural regimentation in the Communist states has greatly exceeded the Nazi and Fascist prototypes.

An illustration of this is the ideological training administered to the armed forces. In Russia and China, for example, the ruling parties have literally made Marxism-Leninism a compulsory lifelong subject of study for military personnel from the rank of recruit to that of general or admiral. With some regard to the scale of effort involved, nothing quite like it was ever imposed on the total armed forces of Germany under Hitler or Italy under Mussolini.

On the other hand, certain other aspects of Communist educational systems—notably the stimulus to rapid quantitative expansion, the achievement of universal literacy, and the emphasis on technical, scientific, and professional training—are rooted in that portion of Communist ideology that can be called its economic development aspect.

The expropriation of capitalists and landlords is but the first step in the Marxian ideology toward the ultimate goal of a classless society. Among the steps on the way to it, skilled and dedicated personnel to replace the vanquished minions of the capitalist-bourgeois order are needed. New personnel are required partly from a political point of view: to prevent the restoration of capitalist rule and the overthrow of the party. But the ultimate realization of communism is predicated not simply on the expropriation of property owners and the maintenance of party rule; above all, it rests on an enormous expansion of the economic potential of society. In the final analysis, Communist doctrine sees the grand formula—from each according to his ability, to each according to his need—in the context of a historically unprecedented abundance. Such abundance could only be realized by massive, and preferably rapid, industrialization—the precondition of which would be, above all, scientific and technological cadres; only skilled personnel could bring about this material advance. Thus, the training of the cadres is one of the first objectives of Communist policy in virtually all cases where the party seizes power.

Empirically, the values of Communist ideology can everywhere be correlated with a high rate of investment in popular education. This is reflected in some spectacular quantitative results. In the Soviet prototype of communism, for example, in the period between 1917 and 1939, regular primary and secondary school enrollments increased from 7.9 to 34.6 million. Between 1940 and 1959, Soviet university enrollments rose from 76.6 to 213.0 thousand.[20] Increases of this magnitude have easily outstripped what might be regarded as normal adjustments to population growth. They have been particularly impressive—and significant—in view of the economic primitivism in which much of this growth took place. Similar results are equally, and perhaps even more, striking in political systems whose economic foundations have been even more meager than the Russians' in 1917.

The circumstances of educational development in the Communist systems—in Russia, China, and in all of east-central Europe—highlight the importance of the "political factor." In every case, that development took place within the context of extensive war damage to the economy (generally not merely analogous to but in some cases—like Russia's in 1921, or Poland's in 1945, or China's in 1949—even greater than, say, Spain's in 1939). It took place in countries where, with the possible exception of Czechoslovakia, the levels of economic development and past commitment to educational expansion could not be reasonably regarded as logical forerunners of the rapid expansion policies followed by the Communists after their seizure of power.

A case in point is Albania. Prior to the establishment of Communist rule in 1945, Albania was probably *the* poorest of European nations. Her prewar per capita national income and GNP were believed to be well below those of Portugal and Spain. In 1938, it was estimated that Albania's illiteracy rate was approximately 80 per cent of the adult population. There were no institutions of higher learning in the country before 1945. Under Communist rule, the ratio of literate to illiterate population appears to have been reversed within a decade of 1945. By 1950, Albania was in possession of professional schools of medicine, finance, agriculture, engineering, and education.

In the Yugoslav case, we find that in 1938–1939, with a population of about 16 million, there were 1,471,000 students in 9,190 primary schools staffed by approximately 35,000 teachers. By 1958–1959, with a population of about 18 million, there were 2.5 million students in some 15,000 primary schools taught by 80,000 teachers. Between 1938 and 1958, secondary and technical education in Yugoslavia was literally doubled in the number of schools, students, and teachers. Even more spectacular, but characteristic of all Communist systems, has been the enormous expansion of university education.

[20] See Nicholas de Witt, *Education and Professional Employment in the U.S.S.R.* (Washington, D.C.: G.P.O., 1961), pp. 133 and 210.

In Yugoslavia, in 1938, 26 institutions of higher learning taught some 17,000 students with instructional staffs of 1,200 persons. In 1958, there were nearly five times as many such institutions (126); enrollments in them grew to 97,000 and the instructional personnel to about 8,000. In the years between 1919 and 1941 some 30,000 Yugoslavs were graduated from institutions of higher learning. Between 1946 and 1958, 67,000 graduates were turned out—more than twice as many in half the period!

All these trends have been substantially replicated elsewhere among the Communist systems. One result of this expansion has been the attainment of higher educational objectives by poorer Communist states than by a number of wealthier, non-Communist ones.

The political propensity of communism to promote literacy and technical and scientific education has, naturally enough, yielded the most spectacular results in countries that were relatively most backward, or underdeveloped, at the time of the Communist seizure of power. Obviously, in a society in which only a very few people can read, it is not particularly difficult to double or treble the literacy rate within a fairly short time. On the other hand, results of this magnitude cannot be achieved in societies in which education has been traditionally well developed and well diffused. This does mean that the Communist propensity to achievement in learning is certain to be differently deployed and unequally expressed under different conditions. It certainly does *not* mean, however, that the propensity is either merely propaganda, or that it constitutes some sort of an economically natural compensation for underdevelopment, which one might expect under any regime in the same economic circumstances.

Communist rule has resulted in rapid and large-scale educational expansion in Czechoslovakia and East Germany, neither of which could be regarded as underdeveloped areas prior to 1945. And just as the rate of development of educational and cultural media in Albania since World War II has exceeded the efforts of Spain, Portugal, or Greece, the "developed" Communist countries have also done much better as compared with economically analogous, even wealthier, non-Communist ones (Italy, France, and Britain, among others). (See Tables 13, 14, and 15.)

At the end of the decade, the United States led all the world's states with 28.3 per cent of its population enrolled in schools. The average for all nine established democracies was 22.6 per cent. The fourteen Communist states had average enrollments of just over 19 per cent. It must be remembered, however, that the gulf in respective per capita national incomes between these groups of states was still very wide. Eight of the fourteen Communist systems—Albania, Bulgaria, China, Cuba, Mongolia, North Korea, North Vietnam and Yugoslavia—were

Table 13*

1956 Comparison of Public Libraries, Their Holdings and Their Annual Circulations. Some Communist Bloc States and Selected Countries

	No. Public Libraries	Volumes (in 000's)	Annual Circulation
Czechoslovakia (1950)	14,650	10,750	20,853
Hungary (1954)	10,892	7,263	21,556
Poland (1954)	4,585	21,198	50,198
Rumania (1954)	18,978	23,471	no data
Yugoslavia (1954)	4,138	3,441	no data
Brazil (1953)	363	2,387	728
Cuba (1955)	102	1,450	612
Finland (1953)	3,364	3,878	8,173
Ireland (1953)	2,261	1,828	no data
Portugal (1954)	156	4,219	1,531
Spain (1954)	683	1,170	5,530
Sweden (1954)	3,507	10,757	23,334
Turkey (1954)	63	495	no data
United Kingdom (1954)	618	59,540	369,355
Union of South Africa (1952)	340	4,157	13,580
Venezuela (1954)	95	152	336

* Based on *Basic Facts and Figures International Statistics Relating to Education, Culture and Mass Communication*, UNESCO (1956).

significantly poorer than Uruguay, the poorest of the established democracies. Uruguay's enrollment ratio was 16.2 per cent.

The lowest enrollment figure among Communist states was China's, at 13.5 per cent of the population. Twenty-six states in the world community lagged behind China, several of them richer, some poorer. No state of comparable per capita income, however, exceeded the Chinese effort. (See Tables 10, 11, and 12.) North Vietnam and China were the only Communist states with enrollment ratios lower than those of Uruguay.

In the late '60's, among the 14 Communist states, the range of enrollments has been a high of 22.1 per cent for the USSR and a low of 13.5 per cent for Red China; four states have been above the 20 per cent mark (Albania, North Korea, Poland, and the USSR); and five over the 18 per cent figure (Bulgaria, Cuba, Czechoslovakia, Rumania, and Yugoslavia). Characteristically, enrollment ratios in East Germany exceed those in West Germany and those in North Korea exceed those of South Korea, contrary to the implications of economic capability comparisons.

Table 14A
1965 Library Comparisons

	No. Public Libraries	Volumes (in 000's)
Communist States		
Albania	22	414
Bulgaria	6,273	21,631
Czechoslovakia	20,669	32,897
Germany (GDR)	12,703	15,723
Hungary	9,572	16,142
Poland	7,914	39,539
Rumania	11,456	41,790
Yugoslavia	2,154	8,570
USSR (1961)	135,721	845,183
Cuba (1962)	43	449
Some Others		
Brazil	1,465	6,894
Finland	4,100	6,500
Portugal	70	4,903
Spain	1,290	3,412
Sweden	2,217	17,485
Turkey	97	1,210
Union of South Africa (1958)	368	4,933
United Kingdom	562	77,200
Venezuela	22	128

Unesco: Statistical Yearbook, 1965 (Paris: 1966). Based on 1964 reports from Tables 24-26.

The variations within the Communist and democratic groups are much less than among the others—that is, among the assorted unstable and autocratic regimes other than those that are Communist. The widest enrollment difference among Communist nations is at about 1.5 to 1 ratio. Among the democracies, the disparity between the United States and Uruguay is also about 1.5 to 1. Yet, the range of economic differences within these two clusters of states is much wider. In per capita GNP, the difference between East Germany and Red China is approximately 15 to 1. The analogous difference between the United States and Uruguay is probably about 8 to 1.

Disregarding political differences, we would expect Kuwait, with a $3,240 per capita national income in 1966, to lead the world in school enrollments. In fact, its ratio was 14.2 per cent; only one of the 14 relatively poor Communist states (China) ranked behind Kuwait. Albania, among world leaders in enrollments, had an estimated per

Table 14B
1965 Museum Comparisons

	No. Museums	No. Rep's Visitors	Visitors (in 000's)
Communist States			
Albania	27	14	261
Bulgaria	132	132	7,445
Czechoslovakia	415	415	14,393
Hungary	144	142	5,596
Mongolia	26	26	236
Poland	263	263	14,260
Rumania	215	215	8,527
USSR	937	937	56,000
Yugoslavia	265	265	5,927
Some Others			
Argentina	174	174	2,139
Belgium	219	90	3,889
Brazil	174	174	2,139
Canada	385		
Portugal	123	123	1,984
Spain	354	162	7,028
Sweden	141	138	5,554
Switzerland	346		
Turkey	67	67	2,748
Union of South Africa	21	19	1,758
United Arab Republic	25	25	856
United Kingdom	964	11	5,943
USA	3,443	1,946	187,767

Unesco: Statistical Yearbook, 1965 (Paris: 1966). Based on 1964 reports. (Data from Table 27.)

capita national income of less than $300 and economically ranked fortieth, just behind Nicaragua (12.7) in a recent worldwide economic ranking of 72 states.[21]

Among the other states, the differences are immense. Within the traditional autocracies are found the world's lowest ratios of school enrollments during the past decade: Afghanistan 2.3 per cent; Ethiopia 1.6; Haiti 5.5; Nepal 3.9; Saudi Arabia 3.3; for Yemen figures

[21] See Nathaniel Preston, *Politics, Economics and Power Ideology and Practice Under Capitalism, Socialism, Communism and Fascism* (New York: Macmillan, 1967), Table 2, p. 75.

Table 15
Newspaper Circulation per 1,000 Inhabitants—
Figures for the Communist States and Other Selected States*

Country		Country	
Albania	43	Japan	439
Bulgaria	164	Mauritius	116
Cuba	n.d.	Mexico	112
Czechoslovakia	284	Nicaragua	49
East Germany	n.d.	Rhodesia	15
Hungary	175	Saudi Arabia	8
Mongolia	n.d.	South Africa	n.d.
Poland	154	Syria	21
Rumania	171	U.S.A.	337
USSR	229	Venezuela	71
Yugoslavia	89		
		Belgium	n.d.
Canada	223	Denmark	344
Ceylon	37	Finland	n.d.
Chile	118	Iceland	434
Costa Rica	77	Ireland	244
Ghana	32	Netherlands	284
Hong Kong	339	New Zealand	399
India	12	Norway	387
Israel	n.d.	Sweden	505
Italy	111	Switzerland	365
		United Kingdom	523
		Uruguay	n.d.

* *Unesco: Statistical Yearbook, 1965* (Paris: 1966). Based on 1964 reports. (Data from Table 38.)

were unknown; South Vietnam 8.8; Iran 10.8; Pakistan 8.5; and Indonesia 10.6.

The enrollment-ratio difference between Taiwan and Afghanistan was 10:1, or 22.5 per cent versus 2.3 per cent of the respective populations in schools. With comparable national incomes per capita, Taiwan was ahead of Iran in school enrollments by virtually 2 to 1. In the same region of the world, and with virtually identical per capita incomes, Iraq ($218) and Iran ($216), under two differently oriented regimes, maintained 15.3 and 10.8 per cent enrollment ratios, respectively!

King Hussein achieved vastly higher enrollments in Jordan in 1966 (17.2 per cent) on a lower per capita income ($214) than his more traditional colleague, King Ibn Saud (3.3 per cent) on a per capita income of $288! The developmental discrepancies, between Communist Albania and royal Saudi Arabia, represented by a 6 to 1 enrollment difference, are not to be found among viable democracies.

Figures on public library holdings, circulation, and museum attendance all attest to the remarkably greater diffusion of popular culture under economically poorer Communist regimes than under other equally or even more affluent regimes. Venezuela ($911), Argentina ($633), Spain ($822), and South Africa ($618), in that order, are ahead in per capita GNP of such Communist states as Albania ($290), Rumania ($440), Yugoslavia ($470), Bulgaria ($480), and in the case of Venezuela even Poland ($790). Judged by the indices of Tables 13 and 14, and allowing for population differences, all these states are nevertheless substantially, even drastically, backward compared with the Communist regimes. Equivalent performances are to be found only among some of the world's wealthiest states with democratic political systems (for example, Sweden, Iceland, and Denmark).

The widest and most striking discrepancy is between Venezuela and Albania. With a population of about 1.9 million and per capita GNP of $290, Albania claimed 414,000 volumes in public library collections; Venezuela with more than nine million people and $911 *per capita* GNP had only 128,000! In Albania, 261,000 persons visited museums in 1964, obviously few of them tourists; there were no figures for Venezuela in 1964. In 1947, the Venezuelan attendance was only 132,000!

If democracies are somewhat less generous in support of education than Communist regimes, they are also much more diversified and open in their offerings than the Communist systems. Indeed, on the score of openness and diversity of educational curricula, the democracies differ from all types of authoritarian regimes.

In the public institutions, ideological indoctrination of the student body and the degree of censorship or control tend to be low, first in terms of time allotted to such subjects as civic training; secondly in the number of subjects or areas included within the purview of political controls of the curriculum; and, thirdly, in the intensity or seriousness with which such political-orientation training and controls are implemented.

To be sure, there are no political systems that do not sanction *some* degree of control in their educational systems, more or less subtly. Instruction in the general areas of social sciences, humanities, and particularly in courses dealing with history and political institutions can rarely, if ever, be entirely value free. Policies relating to teacher training and recruitment and the selection of textbooks and courses can all compensate to some extent for formal censorship and outward political controls. Even these latter may be present in the effective democracies to some extent as, for instance, in the disqualification of Communist teachers and others as subversive in recent American experience. But these restrictions and controls are, all in all. verv much less extensive and very much less serious in the democracies than they are in the autocracies, traditionalist or innovative.

In addition, the citizens of the democracies have access to diversified sources of private education and privately endowed cultural activities, subject to even fewer overt or covert political controls. Among autocratic regimes, private education is much more limited. It ranges from the virtually nonexistent, as in the innovative Communist states, where a few theological seminaries, and part-time religious instruction to the young, are what pass for private education. Private education is admittedly represented in some traditionalist, antiegalitarian autocracies in large numbers, but it simultaneously tends to be narrowly confined to those interests that the regime recognizes as legitimate and that are, in fact, its acknowledged supporters. Such education also tends to be more closely supervised politically.

Spain under Franco is an illustration of the latter type of regime. One of the effects of the Franco victory in the Spanish Civil War was to restore the role of the Church as a prime educator of the people. In fact, since 1939, education has become something of a joint State-Church enterprise in Spain. In 1959, some two and one-half million students attended public primary schools, and more than 800,000 attended private schools. There were 182,000 students in the public secondary schools and 172,000 in private ones run mainly by the Catholic Church. In both State and Church schools, overtly political instruction has been provided by the Falangists. Religion, philosophy, and ethics have been consigned to clerics. So far as the supervision of the whole educational system goes, it has been formally centralized in the hands of the Ministry of Education. However, the policies of that ministry have been both formally and informally subjected to far-reaching Church control. Spanish education must conform, according to a 1938 Franco decree, to the dogma and to the ethical and legal principles of the Spanish Catholic Church. As one author summed it up:

> The law on education recognized that the Church has the right to watch over and inspect all teaching in both public and private institutions and that the bishops . . . [to that end] may require all books, publications and teaching materials contrary to Catholic dogma and ethics to be withdrawn or forbidden.[22]

We may note in passing that religious instruction required in all the primary and secondary schools in Spain has been based for many

[22] L. Fernsworth, *op. cit.*, p. 264.

years now on a catechism text that declares the following to be the thirteen principal errors condemned by the Church:[23]

Materialism	Protestantism
Darwinism	Socialism
Atheism	Communism
Pantheism	Syndicalism
Deism	Liberalism
Rationalism	Modernism
Masonry	

Informally, the Church's influence has been maintained through its numerous advisors to and officials in the Ministry of Education, all helping to shape government policy.

A significant role for private schools has also characterized other traditionalist autocratic regimes, allied with and protective of particular vested interests. In Portugal, for example, the enrollments in public and private elementary schools during the 1930s were virtually equal. In secondary institutions, public instruction accounted for about three out of four students. The maintenance of private education has been a significant link between the Fascist and Nazi totalitarian regimes and other traditionalist but antiegalitarian autocracies. In Italy and Germany it was maintained insofar as the interests and policies of the private schools and of the State were recognized as mutually complementary. In Italy in 1936–1937 some 133,000 students attended private secondary schools, as compared with 541,000 in the public schools. This ratio was about the same as that maintained in the first decade of the democratic republican regime that followed after World War II.[24]

The decisive differences between democracies and autocracies relate not to *numbers* but to kinds of private schools available. Only those private interests that are political "insiders" could maintain (legally) institutions of education under these antiegalitarian autocracies. The prerogatives of the Catholic Church in Franco's Spain or Mussolini's Italy never extended to various other nongovernmental associations: to political parties, to trade unions, to dissident religious organizations, to smaller private groups, or simply to individuals promoting unorthodox philosophic, social, or political doctrines.

Few contrasts are more instructive than that between the treatment accorded non-Catholic education in predominantly Catholic but

[23] See John Hughes, *Report from Spain* (New York: Henry Hall, 1947), p. 77.

[24] F. W. Roman, *The New Education in Europe* (New York: E. P. Dutton, 1930), p. 215.

democratic Ireland as opposed to the predominantly Catholic but also autocratic Spain. What is free and open to all under one system has been proscribed and persecuted under the other.

In education, as in other areas, politics does not always decide everything. The political objectives of rulers may be compromised by paramount economic necessities, even if it is apparent that such compromises may be politically costly and dangerous. But even where the needs of commerce or national survival dictate the massive upsurge in certain kinds of training, political considerations shape the new adaptive policies. If more persons must be trained in new skills, this could readily present danger to an autocratic ruler whose power has hitherto rested on the parochial ignorance, dependency, and noninvolvement of his subjects. To some extent this danger may be offset by discriminatory policies in the admission of students and teachers to educational institutions.

Traditionalist autocracies can seek a measure of safety in providing education largely to those who can pay for it. This assures a preponderance of skills to social strata representing *status quo* power. For the Communist regimes, the concern with safety or invulnerability of their power has dictated precisely the opposite policy. To educate the children of the upper and middle classes on whom the Communists had declared total war would be clearly dangerous and foolhardy. In consequence, Communist policies with respect to school admissions particularly at the higher, more select, and sensitive levels of education have been as openly and brazenly discriminatory as any in modern history.

One consequence of the establishment of Communist power in Russia, China, Eastern Europe, and parts of Asia has been a truly unprecedented extension of educational opportunity to the sons and daughters of peasants and workers. Those who—by and large—were effectively excluded from the benefits of education under the previous regimes found a gateway to professional and personal development—through public education—under communism. This has been even more striking in secondary and technical than in primary schools, and more striking still in the field of university training. But all these accomplishments have been accompanied by the most flagrant denials of opportunity to certain politically persecuted minority groups.

Thus, the Soviet Union, legally and officially, closed the doors of its universities not merely to nobles, bourgeois, clerics, kulaks, Army officers, and officials of the pre-1917 regime. It legislated also against the admission of the sons and daughters of these strata, and made the exclusions all the more catastrophic for the outcasts by virtue of the State's monopoly of education. For these people, as for Jews in Germany, there could be no reprieve and no recourse. Banned from public institutions, they could not turn elsewhere. In contrast, we find no effective democracy in which educational disabilities have ever been imposed on a whole segment of the population on the basis of a second-generation or, strictly speaking, hereditary link to those regarded as politically undesirable or dangerous. Nor have the democracies ever countenanced government monopoly of educational institutions.

Let us consider why different results are likely to be produced under different systems. In terms of *structure*, we find that the loci of decision making within the democracies are generally diffuse. This is probably most obvious in the United States or Canada where the responsibility for virtually all educational decisions such as the upkeep and costs of schools, curricula, personnel, textbooks, admissions, and ultimately taxes to pay for all this are shared by various authorities: national, state, provincial, municipal, or local. These authorities are made up of popularly elected officials under circumstances of open competition analogous to national legislative or presidential elections.

The structural differences are less obvious where the educational system is centralized under a ministry of the national government, as was the practice in France under the Third Republic and its democratic republican successors. Under the latter circumstance, the functions of local authorities are in a legal sense either simply advisory or delegated—that is, presumably at the discretion of the central ministerial authority. But in practical terms, the decision-making structure of a democracy turns out to be remarkably diffuse and pluralistic under both models.The minister of education in a centralized—but democratic—system owes his office directly or indirectly to election. His activities are supervised and subject to the pleasure of the national legislature with all access guaranteed to the minister's opposition. If, as in the British case, the minister's opponents are unlikely to be able to either vote him out of office—*between* elections—or even cut his appropriations, they can nevertheless mercilessly expose every weakness of his policy and his administration to the voters. And it would be an understatement to say that the minister could hardly remain indifferent to such a fate. Moreover, the structures of the advisory and delegated authorities that make the whole system work, at both national and local levels, are generally reasonably open and diffuse in the democracies. The democratic official listens to a greater variety of interest groups than his autocratic counterpart. Fewer groups can be effectively excluded from his advisory boards and his implementing agencies. If their wishes are disregarded, the *recourse* that is open to them in the legislatures, in the press, and through every medium of communication is much more formidable than in the autocracies.

In consequence of this, a local school board even under a centralized democratic system is quite likely to have its advice frequently rendered into *de facto* policy. Its local autocratic counterpart is less likely to be so effectual; it is more likely to be simply an echo of the "top of the system." In terms of grass-roots sensitivity of the educational establishment—the contrast between nineteenth-century Britain and Germany was an approximate opposite of what might be expected from the unitary-federal difference between these two systems. In Britain, parliamentary laws of 1870 and 1902 confided the management of public education to local bodies with wide discretionary policy-making powers. These local educational authorities, in turn, increasingly reflected the choices of popular suffrage inasmuch as they were elected largely from among county and borough council members.

The ultimate creation in 1944 of a central Ministry of Education was buttressed by the creation of representative advisory bodies with powers of recommending measures to the ministry, without abolishing or curtailing the powers of the local authorities.

In the democracies, popular control and participation in educational decision making can take place with or without the diversity of federalism. Where the controls of the system lie at the central level, the national legislature exercises supervision over the executive agencies in charge of the system. In practice, unitary democracies, such as Britain, frequently delegate authority over educational matters to local agencies representative of the citizenry in the particular localities.

In authoritarian systems, however, the policies and the execution of the policies are invariably controlled by political organs of an ultimately "closed" character—that is, not subject to the participation or scrutiny of public opinion.

This ultimate, closed political authority may be a royal bureaucracy, like that of Ethiopia or, at one time, Prussia. It may be more concerned in its activities with the maintenance of traditional patterns of education—or even noneducation, as the case may be—than with the zealous promotion of any new concrete political programs and beliefs. Such authority may be functionally constituted as simply a watchdog against subversion, not a promoter of new faiths or new programs. This type of limited authority is likely to be exercised in traditionalist regimes, oriented to the maintenance of a given sociopolitical *status quo.* Controls may also serve in militant, activist policies of persuasion, and change, under the auspices of a political movement—such as the Communist movement—dedicated to a restructuring of its environment.

A basic difference between democratic and autocratic regimes in general can be expressed in terms of the degree of openness in the policy-control mechanisms. Who ultimately decides such questions as the relative allocation of resources to education, the nature of the curricula, the standards of instruction, the criteria for admission, and the promotion within the system for students and teachers alike? In the autocracies the ultimate decision makers are generally fewer and politically more homogeneous in their loyalties than they are within the democracies. However, the functions performed by these decision makers among the autocracies vary from simply exercising veto power over the pursuit of historically well-established patterns to innovating and changing the whole educational environment around them.

In traditionalist Prussia and other German states in the nineteenth century, local school authorities had narrow powers and their membership was closely controlled by the autocratic executive in each case. In Prussia, itself, public education was under the control of so-called Provincial Boards of Education. Each such board was made up of several inspectors, between three and five usually, all appointed by the Minister of Education and confirmed by the King. We may note that the minister was not responsible or removable by parliament but was a royal appointee responsible ultimately only to the monarch himself. This board controlled virtually all phases of education, including "... building plans, school ordinances, examinations, textbooks, and inspection of all schools that gave admittance to the University. The appointment and dismissal of all teachers except the director were in its hands...." Such elective local school boards as did exist were made up of a few individuals in each case, not very representative politically; in rural areas they were in fact largely appointed from among "leading citizens"; their functions were actually not those of policy makers or even advisors but of executors of certain functions ranging from supervising the construction of buildings, payment of taxes, enforcement of attendance, and disbursement of teachers' salaries.[25]

In our discussion of the relationship between politics and education, we have necessarily limited ourselves to a few points and illustrations. The linkage between types of political systems and types of educational-cultural outputs, or policies, is one that clearly deserves a much more extensive treatment.

To the question whether the adoption of a particular political regime will produce a determinable effect on the individual in terms of his schooling and his cultural and professional opportunities, all other things being equal, one can offer an affirmative reply. Effective democracies tend to spend generously on educational and cultural goods. Democracy also implies a great diversity of educational-cultural offerings to the people, many choices and relatively few compulsions.

[25] *Ibid.*, pp. 215–217.

It is relatively tolerant toward those kinds of education that embody causes frowned on by the rulers (or a majority of the whole population as the case may be).

Among autocratic regimes, education tends to be more regimented and narrowed down in its content, particularly insofar as it is perceived as politically "sensitive" and "explosive." The degree and intensity of such regimentation depends in large measure on whether the particular autocracy is oriented to maintaining a traditional status quo or changing it. So far as the material commitment to education is concerned, autocratic regimes of the first type (but also including the Nazi-Fascist systems) generally fall behind the democracies. Communist innovators tend to keep abreast of them.

CHAPTER 7
SOCIAL WELFARE

THE performance of the world's well-established democracies in the field of welfare has fluctuated with changes in the character of their electorates and in the circumstances of the times. In some respects many democracies still continue to be more frugal in welfare disbursements to the population than several authoritarian regimes, notably the Communist ones.[1]

This pattern of relative welfare restraint derives from a rationale analogous to that which underlies the democracies' tax and spending policies. The popular appetite for what critics call handouts is always to some extent opposed and offset by a concern with the costs and the burdens of public largesse. In the American experience:

> Public social welfare has not developed without engendering some major conflicts in values. Subjects of some of these conflicts have been: deep disap-

[1] In 1958, for example, the expenditures for all social purposes according to a UN survey, by various levels of government, showed the Soviet Union spending 20 per cent of the State's net material product on social services. The United States total government expenditure accounted for 9.4 per cent. The balance of private expenditure in the case of the United States, although probably very large, was unknown. See United Nations, Department of Economic and Social Affairs, *Report on the World Social Situation* (New York: 1961), Section IV, pp. 71 and 74.

proval of dependency and a glorification of self-reliance; distrust of government as a source of personal aid; disapproval of the growing tax burden; distrust of the official agency in dealing with anything so directly personal as family welfare.[2]

The character of the electorate, its social and economic characteristics, and its self-perceived needs and aspirations, have all played a part in shaping political pressures for very divergent social welfare policies in each of the democratic polities.

In a comparative study dealing with social legislation in Canada, Australia, and the United States, A. H. Birch calls attention to the diversity of environmental circumstances that created an earlier demand for welfare services in Australia than in the countries of North America:

> ... The fundamental reason for the difference ... was the absence of an expanding frontier in Australia. There was a great deal of land to the West, but it was nearly desert, and the periodic gold rushes are not analogous to the steady opening up of the western territories that took place in the United States and Canada. In the North American countries it was mainly this constant expansion, and the individual opportunities afforded by the possibility of migration, which held back both the development of a national party of labour and the growth of a demand for social security. In Australia the limitation of this kind of opportunity led to the development of social and political attitudes very different from those of North America, and in the early years of the century all the political parties favored the idea of old-age pensions.[3]

Similarly, we could expect the electorates' attitudes to fluctuate in time—with increased concern for welfare measures in response to widely experienced privations of unemployment or natural calamity, for example, and considerably lessened anxieties about such measures in times of general prosperity and a widely experienced sense of well-being.

It is for these reasons that most of the states that in the nineteenth century led the world in terms of the degree of suffrage extended to the population, and in the genuinely open and representative character of their elections, did *not* lead it in terms of welfare programs. Nineteenth-century United States and Great Britain lagged far behind

[2] Wayne Vasey, *Government and Social Welfare* (New York: Holt, Rinehart and Winston, 1963), p. 42.

[3] A. H. Birch, *Federalism, Finance and Social Legislation in Canada, Australia and the United States* (London: Oxford University Press, 1955), p. 205. The author recalls that in 1928 the Republican party's platform predicted that the "unchecked progress of private enterprise" would soon abolish poverty. "In the boom atmosphere of the 1920's only a small minority urged insurance against a slump which most people were confident would not arrive.... " P. 27.

the authoritarian Bismarckian Reich in the generosity of their welfare policies. Even the Scandinavian democracies did not match it in some respects until after the turn of the century.[4] Public opinion in the democracies was not yet mobilized on behalf of welfare objectives in the context of the economic and social conditions of the nineteenth century. The several Socialist parties had not yet won much support for the claims of their working-class followers, outside their own ranks. Bismarckian programs, on the other hand, represented a remarkable authoritarian initiative: a bold attempt to win the industrial workers over to the Kaiser Reich from under the banners of the Marxian German Social Democracy, and to do so well in advance of any general consensus of middle-class and agrarian groups as to the merits and desirability of such measures.

Only in the twentieth century has there been a general development of large-scale, publicly financed welfare programs among *all* the world's democracies in response to such factors as increasing industrialization, the increasing role of the professional and salaried elements among the middle-class electorates, the increasingly severe challenges of economic depressions, and ultimately, the increasing acceptance by all segments of public opinion of many humanitarian and economic demands that were once advanced almost solely by labor, socialist, and trade union interests.

Among autocracies, there has been a marked tendency to devote resources for welfare purposes in rough proportion to the innovative-mobilizational character of the regime—that is, as a major instrument of reshaping society. The changes brought about under communism in Russia, China, and in Eastern Europe are illustrative of the furthest extreme among the innovative regimes.

In the United States, up until the period of the Great Depression, the Federal Government did not engage in *any* activity that might be described as relief to the needy, except (1) to a certain extent under the services of the Indian Bureau and (2) in times of disaster by occasional appropriations. Aiding the indigent was widely regarded as a local responsibility, and the aid rendered by states was, on the whole—that is, by present-day expectations—quite meager, even if we allow for the fact that welfare needs before the Depression were not as great as they became afterward.

Pre-Depression public attitudes in the United States encouraged and sanctioned apathy toward the problems of the poor on the part of politicians and administrators. In the words of Josephine C. Brown:

[4] See George R. Nelson (ed.), *Freedom and Welfare: Social Patterns in the Northern Countries*, The Ministries of Social Affairs of Denmark, Finland, Iceland, Norway, Sweden (1953), Ch. II.

Studies of the methods which were in use in local poor relief offices between 1911 and 1932 reveal practices and attitudes which had evidently changed but little in two or three hundred years.

One fundamental fault in the haphazard methods of administering relief was the quality, character and training of the men and women who did the job. Public officials who were responsible for the administration of relief were often elected or appointed to discharge some other function and handled relief merely as a part-time extra duty. . . . Among a majority of these early officials the characteristic attitude was indifference. They took paupers for granted. Their general objective appeared to be to conserve the public funds by keeping relief expenditures to the lowest possible figure. They made little attempt to secure any accurate information about the circumstances of the applicant. . . . They put much emphasis upon the difference between the "worthy" and the "unworthy" poor, but to both the ineradicable stigma of dependency was attached as soon as they were given even emergency or temporary relief, however small the amount might be. To be "on the town" or "on the county" was the lowest state outside prison to which a member of the community could descend.[5]

Similar attitudes, unsympathetic to the plight of the poor, were characteristic of nineteenth-century England, until the extension of suffrage, political agitation, and social change all combined to create a more compassionate public. For most of the century:

To the well-to-do "the poor" were a race apart, inevitable but unpleasant like sin or death, to be tolerated and pitied, or to be despised if they fell into the hideous category of "paupers." Pauperism meant more than misfortune, it implied moral failing. Those who accepted parochial aid were legally assumed to be guilty of sin, of laziness and improvidence.[6]

Although the Depression can be regarded as the universal welfare-state threshold for the democracies of the world, no absolute standard or benchmark for post-1928 activities can be posited. In the United States, the enormous expansion in welfare programs on all levels of government has not kept up with all the demands and expectations of all the segments of the public.

If our objective is a fuller life for all, then we cannot be satisfied with the programs of today. . . . The deficiencies in social insurance, public assistance, child welfare, and other services are [still] formidable.[7]

The American welfare state certainly is not yet a complete fabric for individual well-being and security. People are still provided retire-

[5] Josephine C. Brown, *Public Relief 1929–1939* (New York: Henry Holt and Company, 1940), pp. 13–14 and 15.

[6] Bentley G. Gilbert, *The Evolution of National Insurance in Great Britain: The Origins of the Welfare State* (London: Michael Joseph, 1966), p. 21.

[7] *Cf.* Vasey, *op. cit.*, p. 500.

ment pension coverage under the Social Security program *only* by virtue of their contributions—not yet simply by virtue of need. Families are frequently denied various forms of public assistance by means of eligibility requirements so stringent that if *one* person in the family is classified as "employable," the family cannot obtain state help, *even* if that one person cannot find work. As late as 1934, fourteen American states denied the right to vote and to hold office to recipients of relief.[8]

By some estimates, there were at least thirty million people in the 1960s in the category of dire economic poverty. It is estimated that only seven million of these are being assisted from public funds.[9] About half a million migrant farm workers in the United States were ineligible for any social insurance aid in the 1960s. Poverty still carries with it a public stigma; it incurs an officially sanctioned rebuke, and the thresholds of qualification for assistance (the "means test" in many states) are widely regarded as unjust and unrealistically high.[10] Even among the Scandinavian states, there is widespread public recognition that at least some public welfare programs are still inadequate to meet the needs that they are designed to serve.[11]

Nevertheless, some basic principles of public welfare, organized and financed by the State, have become widely accepted throughout the world, at least in the second half of the twentieth century.

These principles embrace such policies as the provision of unemployment insurance to workers and employees; the payment of pensions to those unable to work through injury or ill health; the granting of subsidies to families and individuals to maintain "minimally satisfactory" standards of nutrition and health; and also, broadly, the payment of subsidies to public institutions, governmental or private (such as schools, hospitals, and recreation centers) for the promotion of the material, physical, and spiritual or cultural well-being of persons served by them.[12]

There has been a worldwide diffusion or acceptance of relatively new welfare concepts as compared with the prevailing approaches of the nineteenth century and earlier periods. The responsibility for the fate of the unemployed, the indigent, and the disabled is

[8] See Elizabeth Wickenden and Winifred Bell, *Public Welfare: Time for a Change* (Project on Public Services for Families and Children. New York, 1961, pp. 24–29; *Cf* Brown, *op. cit.*, p. 10.

[9] See Lenore Epstein, "Unmet Need in a Land of Abundance," *Social Security Bulletin*, Vol. 26, No. 5 (May 1963), pp. 10–11.

[10] See Jules H. Berman, "The Means Test: Welfare Provisions of the 1965 Social Security Amendments," *Social Service Review*, Vol. 40, No. 2 (June 1966), p. 169.

[11] See, for example, Nelson, *op. cit.*, pp. 504-506.

[12] UN Report, *op. cit.*, pp. 79–80.

no longer generally assumed to be that of the individual himself, his family, and the charity of privately organized groups.

The consummation of social welfare reforms in the democracies of the nineteenth and twentieth centuries has always heavily depended on the nature of the decision-making public—not only in terms of *who* was in it, but also in terms of the calculations of political advantage, risk and/or danger, on the part of the professional brokers of these publics, the politicians. The close relationship between politics and welfare is illustrated for the British case in the study by Bentley G. Gilbert, who concludes thus on the enactment of three different welfare programs (the feeding of school children, school medical service, and old-age pensions):

> These measures had long been under discussion if not by the public at large at least among a considerable group of enthusiasts. Their political story repeats the familiar history of such nineteenth century reforms as Penny Postage, repeal of the corn laws, or free education: extra-parliamentary discussion, petition, lobby delegations, waiting upon ministers and M.P.'s, until one party or the other became convinced of political profit to be garnered from the measure in question. Only when this occurred did the proposal become political in the technical sense.[13]

On the other three programs (the establishment of labor exchanges, unemployment insurance, and health insurance) the author concludes that they "owed more to Germany than to any British model. The impulse behind this second phase of reform activity could hardly be described as philanthropic. National insurance was the Liberal response to the threat of socialism."[14]

Ultimately, Gilbert notes, "since the days of the Roman republic, politicians have discovered that State measures for popular welfare are difficult to oppose."[15] But, as is clear from this and many other similar studies, the need to appease popular wishes is related to the character of popular participation in politics. A democratic politician simply cannot afford to adhere to the proposition that "the voters be damned": not unless the electoral process is somehow vitiated through popular indifference, fraud, intimidation, and like causes. And as the electorates have tended to become more inclusive of populations, the slogan of "let the public be damned" has also tended to become untenable for the professional politician.

Within the institutional context of an autocracy, however, whether innovative or traditional, the politician generally possesses much more

[13] *The Evolution of National Insurance in Great Britain: The Origins of the Welfare State* (London: Michael Joseph, 1966), p. 448.

[14] *Ibid.*

[15] *Ibid.*, p. 449.

leeway or discretion in catering to popular wants. To some extent, these wants may not be manifested as openly and clearly within the politician's environment as they would in a democracy. By obstructing or reducing, not to say eliminating, the articulation of popular demands, the autocrat can make sure that there can be no generally known consensus on desirable measures. The effect of a "known consensus" would be clearly one of moral and political pressure on him and his regime.

Nor does he need to respond to popular demands as if they were conditions of remaining in office—that is, with the same immediacy or urgency that would confront him under periodic and open elections. Yet, the democratic politician who cannot openly flout the popular demands for welfare is rarely, if ever, the creature and spokesman of the whole electorate that ultimately passes judgment on him. Subject to his specific needs for election and reelection, a democratic representative or executive may be really much more concerned with the costs and the administrative burdens of welfare to his particular constituents or allies than with its benefits to others. The conservative, cost-oriented opponent of welfare may seek to limit and "balance" the application of what he publicly alleges to be a sound and worthwhile principle to particular cases, or otherwise fight a "rear-guard action," reconciling the perceived attitudes of the public with his own and his particular supporters' misgivings.

Opposition in principle to certain measures in the context of democratic politics does occasionally become untenable. In Britain, the struggle against social welfare legislation since the nineteenth century has been generally carried on "through the back door," sometimes in fact by attempts so "to extend coverage and benefits [as] to make the [welfare] proposal[s] ruinously expensive."[16]

Economic differences continue to be important in determining the quantity and types of assistance that are both actually and potentially available to people in different societies. Unemployment rates, pegged to the scale of American wages, are higher today in the United States than in any other polity. Obviously the *amounts* of funds available for welfare programs can be increased among the more wealthy nations far beyond the physical optimum available to the poorest. Absolute limits are imposed on social expenditure by the scarcity of resources in any polity.

But over and beyond economic differences, there are also great political differences among regimes that determine how much and what kinds of welfare are available to each member of society.

The salient features of the democratic response to an increased

[16] *Ibid.*, p. 451.

public demand for welfare have been (1) pluralism of organization, (2) the development of extensive procedural safeguards for individuals affected by welfare programs, and (3) the establishment of bureaucracies that are relatively autonomous and distinct from the administrative organs of government and dedicated to a humanitarian, rehabilitational approach in the welfare field somewhat analogous to the doctor-patient relationship of the medical profession.

In their 1961 study, *American Welfare* (New York: New York University Press) Alfred de Grazia and Ted Gurr have illustrated the remarkable degree to which private groups and agencies have participated in the well-nigh revolutionary upsurge in American welfare activity in recent times. A 1960 survey showed that 337 voluntary national organizations were active in the social welfare field at the beginning of the decade. The magnitude of their combined effort was underscored by the fact that as of 1959, 41 leaders among these organizations collected just under $300 million for a variety of welfare and welfare-related projects. Among these organizations were the American National Red Cross; National Association for Mental Health; American Foundation for the Blind; National League for Nursing; and many other highly diversified and specialized associations.[17]

In this characteristic of welfare pluralism, the American democracy is typical of all the world's democracies: in Europe, Latin America, and among the Commonwealth countries. Such pluralism, reflecting mixed State-private voluntary efforts, has been traditionally characteristic of the Scandinavian nations. In this respect, the democracies differ from the innovative-mobilizational autocracies, where the State assumes either a complete monopoly of welfare functions or very nearly approaches it.

The distinction between traditional status quo autocracies and the democracies is not nearly so clear. Pluralism and mixed State-private efforts are common enough among these autocracies. The principal differences relate to the generally narrower range of autocratic pluralism and the more frequent tendency to fiscal parsimony from government sources, regardless of structural arrangements.

The second feature—institutionalized avenues of appeal and redress for recipients—are highly developed among all the democracies. This involves both legal and political means. In the United States, in the 1930s, for example,

> The Federal Relief Administration and later the Works Progress Administration recognized the right of clients to organize and openly encouraged the movement. They recognized their right to complain and to appeal to the highest authority.

[17] De Grazia and Gurr, pp. 82 and 84.

> ... pressures exerted by organized client groups not only succeeded in correcting numerous local deficiencies in the administration or emergency relief but were potent in securing larger appropriations of funds from local, state and Federal governments.[18]

The provision of such remedial techniques for appeal and redress, legal and political, is least developed among the innovative-mobilizational autocracies. It is somewhat more developed by the status quo-oriented authoritarian regimes. In the political aspect of the appeal-and-redress machinery, even such highly legalistic autocracies as the Second Reich did not match the recourse available in the democracies, not only because the federal government placed the political activity of suspect groups under all sorts of legal and administrative disabilities, but also because the relationship between petitioners and voters in Germany and the political executive was never one of genuine interdependence.

No German chancellor was subject to dismissal from office by an adverse vote either of the parliament or of the electorate. Such action was, practically speaking, in the hands of the Kaiser alone. And no German bureaucrat seriously needed to worry that political public pressure (as distinguished from a conviction in a court of law) might result either in his removal from office or even in a diminution of the prerogatives of that office.

Finally, we have specificied the development of professional social welfare personnel in the democratic states. The existence of a body of professional persons who participate in the implementation of welfare programs on behalf of the State or other institutionalized interests is a highly significant aspect of democratic welfare in its broadest sense. Even though the technical competence of those who counsel and give guidance to people with respect to such diverse problems as mental health, employment, family and child welfare, criminal rehabilitation, recreation, or youth work may be quite variable, its *orientation* toward the person as the principal client, as the chief measure of value and service rendered, has a capital importance for the recipients of such services and the society as a whole.

We might add that even in democratic political contexts, the orientations of professional welfare workers clash with those that identify themselves as representive of the "whole community," national or local. This is probably most salient in the work of probation-parole agencies, where the client orientation of the counsellor frequently conflicts with the punitive and community-protective orientations of other administrative, police, and judicial personnel.

For those persons who, because of a variety of possible needs and

[18] Brown, *op. cit.*, p. 265.

circumstances, come in contact with the social worker, this disposition toward them as individuals represents a safeguard of a truly personal service. The professional attitudes of a politician, a judge, a police officer, or a government administrator are generally pegged to at least several other major, community-bound considerations. Even though the professional social welfare worker is not, and indeed cannot be, oblivious to larger community interests, his focus is such that even in his work with criminals he "... feels that the only genuine guarantee of community protection lies in the client's personal adjustment since external conformity will only be temporary and in the long run may make a successful adjustment more difficult."[19]

By and large, the social-worker orientation to the whole cluster of problems of welfare is one that autocratic regimes do not and cannot afford.[20] In the innovative regimes, such an orientation would be an intolerable stumbling block to the realization of far-reaching reforms. The social worker whose major focus of concern is the individual before him would be at best a dangerous imponderable in the execution of policies among the population, something of a virus of unknown potential; at worst the social worker would be regarded as an outright sabouteur: one who subordinated the "important" interests of the party or movement to the "ephemeral" ones of the individual.

Even the more traditionally oriented autocracies prefer to entrust the care of bellies and souls to institutional agencies that they think they can trust because of their well-established, predictably safe status quo orientations. An autonomous social service profession is compatible only with an open, pluralistic society whose "ends" and "goals" are not rigidly defined by an autocratic elite.

Cross-national statistical comparisons are extremely difficult, because we cannot readily standardize the impacts of welfare programs in countries whose living conditions are very different. It is clear, however, from data recently compiled by the U. S. Department of Health, Education, and Welfare that commitment to extensive welfare programs is a universal characteristic of the well-established democracies.[21]

The HEW study divided the programs pursued in the various countries into five basic categories of benefits: (1) old age, invalidity, and

[19] L. E. Ohlin, H. Piven, and D. M. Pappenfort, "Major Dilemmas of the Social Worker in Probation and Parole," in M. N. Zald (ed.), *Social Welfare Institutions* (New York: John Wiley, 1965), p. 528.

[20] See Harold L. Wilensky and Charles N. Lebeaux, *Industrial Society and Social Welfare* (New York: Russell Sage Foundation, 1958), Ch. II ("The Emergence of a Social Work Profession").

[21] *Social Security Programs Throughout the World, 1964* (Washington, D.C.: Social Security Administration, Division of Research and Statistics, 1964).

death; (2) sickness and maternity; (3) work injury; (4) unemployment; and (5) family allowances. The following States provided, as of 1964, *some* coverage under *all* of these categories: Algeria, Argentina, Australia, Austria, Belgium, Canada, Chile, Denmark, Finland, France, West Germany, East Germany, Greece, Hungary, Iceland, Iran, Ireland, Israel, Italy, Japan, Luxembourg, Netherlands, New Zealand, Norway, Spain, Sweden, Switzerland, Great Britain, Uruguay, and Yugoslavia. With the exception of the United States, which does not participate in the family allowance programs, every one of the solidly established democracies is included in this grouping.

A survey of the areas of coverage is, of course, a mere first approximation to the real significance of a given welfare program. In the case of the established democracies—that is, those States that have maintained uninterruptedly their political characteristic since before World War II—there is every evidence that the programs are not simply "statute-book tokenism."[22] We note, however, that of the thirty States possessing the "five-area welfare coverage" in 1964, seven were classifiable in our category of autocracies at the time: Algeria, Argentina, East Germany, Hungary, Iran, Spain, and Yugoslavia. This raises the question of the nexus between economic development and welfare, and about the place of the autocracies on the scale of welfare orientations.

It seems that commitment to welfare, like the commitment to popular education, is as much a function of the political orientation of a regime as of its level of economic development, wealth, urbanization, industrialization, and other similar *objective material* factors. The pattern of autocratic orientations to welfare is one of extremely wide fluctuation. It is, in fact, a zigzag that cannot be explained or inferred simply from the facts of economic development, or some reasonable assessment of literacy and demography.

No economic indices would suffice, to explain the sharp contrasts in welfare programs between Algeria and Saudi Arabia, or between the republics of Mali and Ivory Coast, on the one hand, and Ethiopia on the other; between Guinea and Haiti, or between Iran and Portugal, or even the contrast between Iraq and Jordan.

We have in the preceding examples some striking imbalances: relatively well-to-do autocracies spending very little on welfare and relatively poor ones spending a great deal. Discounting for all possible economic factors, no two democracies differed as widely in their social insurance schemes as Algeria did from Saudi Arabia in 1964. On

[22] See *ibid.*, pp. vii–viii on the limitations of the data reported. "There may be cases in which actual practice or implementation is somewhat at variance with the law itself. Where this is true, the charts ordinarily reflect the statutory provisions themselves instead of prevailing practice."

the other hand, Communist regimes underscore the anomalies of autocracy inasmuch as they may be said, collectively, to represent the most extreme welfare commitment. This distinct category of states includes Albania, Bulgaria, Red China, Cuba, Czechoslovakia, East Germany, Hungary, Poland, Rumania, the USSR, North Vietnam, and Yugoslavia.

Even though each of these systems subsumes a wide variety of levels of economic development, as between East Germany and North Vietnam, for example, or between Albania and Czechoslovakia, they all exhibit high welfare commitments. With the exception of the category of unemployment insurance (allegedly unnecessary in their planned, full-employment economies), all these states, excepting Red China with no general family allowance program, provide coverage under each of the remaining four categories of social insurance. Moreover, they do so with a generosity that apparently exceeds the contributions of many non-Communist regimes, whose wealth in terms of per capita GNP is considerably superior to theirs.

As compared with the pre-Communist practices in each case, there has been a massive shift from reliance on private charity, chance, and local communal voluntary organizations to State management and control of welfare programs.[23] There has been a massive increase in the amounts of national income made available to such programs. The range of social welfare services has been enormously increased, both in terms of the kinds of services provided and in the share of the population affected by them. More than this, however, welfare services have become a means for changing the total character of the respective societies and providing the regimes with new, augmented mechanisms of political control.

To the extent that religious, voluntary, cooperative, and family institutions undertook the care of the sick, the aged, the indigent, the orphaned children, the handicapped, and the unemployed, social welfare activities and institutions tended to reflect the pre-Communist societies of which they were a part. They existed within the framework of traditional cultures and subcultures of their societies. Communist regimes have proved universally unwilling to leave these activities in the hands of the old forces of the status quo. They have everywhere attempted to integrate welfare activities into the framework of the Marxian-Leninist revolution in form and content.

Thus, the widespread mobilization of women into the working force

[23] In the USSR all voluntary welfare agencies were eliminated with the termination of the so-called New Economic Policy in 1928. *Cf.* Bernice Madison, "Social Welfare: Soviet Model," *Social Service Review*, Vol. XXXIII, No. 2 (June 1964), p. 201, and "Contributions and Problems of Soviet Welfare Institutions," *Social Problems*, Vol. 7, No. 4 (Spring 1960), p. 301.

has been accompanied by an extensive development of supervised children's centers, homes, playgrounds, and facilities that make it possible for young mothers to hold full-time jobs and that simultaneously, under the leadership of the party, serve as political socialization mechanisms for the young. Through activities and associations maintained publicly away from the home, the party brings up the young in its chosen image of the new Socialist men and women. It weans them away from the traditions and values of the old, prerevolutionary society and inculcates them, overtly and covertly, with the new political orientations of the rulers.

Another illustration of the political aspects of welfare is in the subsidized and controlled uses of leisure time. The provision of paid vacations and holidays has been coupled with the development of State-supported resorts, sanatoria, "retreats," and recreational and cultural programs. Almost all of these are organized in such a fashion that the vacationing worker's and employee's ostensibly free time is harnessed to the party's propaganda and educational messages. The sense of identification with and loyalty to the regime is assiduously cultivated and reinforced through the political exploitation of leisure time. The uses of leisure time *during* the working day have also provided media for organized exposure to party lectures, discussions, and various kinds of programs, many of them of an ostensibly educational, cultural, and even safety or health-protection character. To a significant extent, the totally manipulated world of George Orwell's *1984* has already been realized through this and other aspects of a massive political invasion of human privacy that has characterized welfare schemes under Communist rule for decades.

Under communism, social welfare measures have reinforced and supported cultural and educational activities aimed at the total absorption and the remaking of the individual in the rulers' vision of a new society.

The care of the sick, the injured, and those confined to the home, for whatever reasons, but dependent for subsistence on cash benefits paid through public institutions, has provided Communist regimes with far-reaching surveillance opportunities over the whole labor force. This surveillance has been generally exercised by the officials of the ruling parties and trade union organizations. Among its objectives have been the elimination of malingering and industrial sabotage among workers, as well as checks upon the political loyalty and therefore the "worthiness" of the recipients of social welfare subsidies.

The absence of genuine organizational autonomy, or separation, as between the party, on the one hand, and the trade unions and the labor courts on the other, has deprived the average employee in the Communist states of any genuine protection or safeguards against the party's views on all such obviously crucial matters as, for example, what precisely constitutes malingering, industrial sabotage, or indeed even the public interest, not to mention political loyalty.

The machineries of labor legislation, labor courts, and the ostensibly nonparty welfare organizations run by the trade unions are all substantially fused under party control. The publicly formulated principles of all these entities are based on a denial of the possibility of genuine conflict between the interests of the employees and their employer—the State. Such conflict is said to be a fundamental characteristic of capitalist, not Communist societies. In the field of labor relations, with all the subsidiary welfare questions subsumed under this head, the party could not possibly be in the wrong. Its interest *is* the interest of the workers.

Welfare activity is therefore seen by regime leaders in the nature of a party tool to help it lead and, as necessary, educate, chastise, and rehabilitate or even punish the occasional recalcitrant workers—parasitic backsliders in the monumental tasks of socialist construction! Individual errors and even crimes are possible and expected; so are misunderstandings and mistakes. Conflicts of interest in which an impartial third party may decide between the claims of the State and the claims of the individual are not legally and theoretically sanctioned by Communist rules.

Communist welfare politics has materially aided certain population groups much more than others. In all Communist states the insurance benefits to those employed in industry have been on the whole much more generous than those available to farm workers and the rural elements. This has been true in Russia as well as China and, so far as existing data tell us, in every Communist-ruled state not excepting such widely divergent entities as Cuba, North Vietnam, and East Germany. Workers are generally guaranteed retirement and disability pay by the State; usually the funds are contributed by the establishments employing them and by the State's central treasury. Exceptionally, in Hungary and East Germany, workers contribute to these funds from their own wages.

On the other hand, farmers are generally expected to rely on the largesse of the local communal economic units in which they have been resident. In the Soviet Union each collective farm is expected to save a part of its current income for the purpose of supporting welfare costs of its sick, disabled, and elderly members. There are no provisions for matching grants or other types of subsidies from the State to insure some minimally acceptable subsistence level for all the disabled or retired farm workers in the USSR. Under such circumstances, welfare benefits vary widely from area to area and from farm to farm and depend heavily on the vicissitudes of the agricultural economy with its good and bad harvests.

Although the benefits paid to industrial workers are, by American or

West European standards, quite low in all the Communist countries, they at least provide a bedrock of security for workers that is not available to the farmers. This discriminatory policy is political in that it reflects the regimes' biases: first toward enhancing the role of the proletariat as an allegedly revolutionary and progressive social force at the expense of the backward property- and tradition-oriented peasantry; and secondly toward the primary task of industrialization over the indiscriminate provision of comforts and amenities to the population on the basis of the given social and technological status quo.

Communist regimes have everywhere singled out for favored treatment those groups in the population that are seen as particularly important in the Communist ideology's blueprint of the future. Industrialization has been everywhere connected with the theme of developing cadres—technological, scientific, and professional. Workers, technicians, and scientists have become objects of extensive social welfare manipulation. The tasks of massive economic *and* social change have also required the Communists to focus attention on the family, the women, and the young. The extensive use of female labor in such widely differing activities as medicine and science and arduous highway or dam construction and street maintenance has had its welfare aspects.

The absorption of women into the labor force has been accompanied by the extension of certain benefits that were generally not available to women under previous regimes while undermining the functional centrality of the home for families. Thus, for example, maternity care benefits and paid leaves that have been made available to women under Communist rule have exceeded in virtually every single case the generosity of analogous public provisions under the former regimes in the entire arc from Cuba to North Vietnam. At the same time, however, the extensive provision of children's playgrounds, day care centers, kindergartens, and the like, has also cut down on the roles of the mother and the family as socializing agencies for the young. It has shifted some of these roles and responsibilities to teachers, supervisors, and administrators of welfare institutions.

The solicitude for the youth has manifested itself most strikingly in the field of subsidized schooling, medical care, and in the provision of new, extensive organizational channels for tapping the interests, energies, and the loyalties—hopefully—of the very young.

On the other end of this scale, those social elements regarded by the Communists as reactionary or unproductive have suffered in the Red version of the welfare state. Suspicion and mistrust of the peasant have been reflected in the meagerness of State support for his disability and old age. The elderly, as a general population category, have not been treated nearly as generously under communism as the young.

The care and support of disabled or indigent persons identified with the old middle and upper classes have been drastically curtailed. Public assistance schemes have been typically designed to exclude so-called antisocial and parasitic elements. On the other hand, the opportunity available to people under other, and previous, regimes to assure themselves against the hazards of accident and illness through voluntary, cooperative, and private insurance schemes has been virtually eliminated under Communist rule. Thus, the only circumstance worse than being poor under communism is the complicating misfortune of being identified with the former rich.

In summary, we can describe Communist social welfare policies as being generous in the sense that they have everywhere entailed much greater public expenditure to the social welfare sector than had been the practice under all their predecessor regimes. They have been discriminatory in the sense that the increased public allocation of welfare funds to certain segments of society has been combined with overtly planned and serious deprivations of other segments according to a pattern substantially corresponding to the revolutionary tenets of Marxism-Leninism and to an overriding concern with industrialization.[24]

As Joyce K. Kallgren concludes in her recent study of Red China's welfare programs:

> The priority of treatment that emerges from [the official] regulations clearly indicates that those centrally involved in the industrial process and likely to return to the industrial process in a reasonably brief period, fare best under the system. The more remote the contribution to industrialization in terms of skill or age, the lower the benefits.[25]

Describing the policies of the Soviet Russian regime, Michael Stewart observes that:

> As compared with the Democracies, the U.S.S.R. devotes more attention to social services aiding the young and those of working age, and less to those which benefit the old.[26]

[24] For exclusion of farmers from social insurance in the USSR, see W. W. Kulski, *The Soviet Regime* (Syracuse, N. Y.: Syracuse University Press, 1963), pp. 350 and 324–332. On China see Chang-tu Hu, *China* (New Haven: Yale University Press, 1960), pp. 393–405; on other Communist states, see Social Security Administration, *Social Security Programs Throughout the World* (Washington, D.C.: 1964), pp. 40–41 and 220–221. *Cf.* Cuban Economic Research Project, *A Study on Cuba* (Miami: University of Miami Press, 1965), p. 696.

[25] Unpublished Paper of the SSRC Conference on Microsocietal Study of China (August 1967), p. 33.

[26] Michael Stewart, *Modern Forms of Government* (London: Allen and Unwin, 1961), p. 243. *Cf.* Carl H. Farman and Daniel S. Gerig, "Medical Benefits for Old Age Pensioners Under Foreign Social Security Programs," *Social Security Bulletin*, Vol. 26, No. 1

Finally, these policies and their administration have been *revolutionary* in the sense that they have emphasized (1) the changing roles for the family, the individual, and the State; (2) the extinction or subordination of welfare roles of voluntary and communal associations through State and party control; (3) and concomitantly the development of welfare programs and agencies into instruments of far-reaching political-ideological control and indoctrination of the individual. These are frequently destructive of individual and family privacy.

As Kallgren points out with respect to Red China:

> In order to receive [income supplement aid, the worker] is subject to a "means test," that is, an appraisal of resources available to him. This examination goes beyond income and savings and involves an intimate judgment about his possessions. A trade union activist makes a home visit, consults with the neighbors, and investigates the tangible aspects of life, food, and furniture, clothing, etc. as well as political enthusiasm. Upon receipt of aid . . . the family's actions would be [generally] subject to scrutiny and the possibility of neighbor criticism.[27]

The test of political reliability, which is implicit in all Communist welfare programs, goes hand in hand with political discrimination and preferential treatment for those deemed particularly valuable by the party. One scholar recently noted that:

> While access to a resort or a sanatorium does not depend on one's political standing, members of a Party elite and their families have at their disposal special governmental clinics and resorts that are much superior to those available to the common man.[28]

Thus, the party provides the means to physical survival and wellbeing for its supporters while denying these means to its opponents and to those whom it regards as indifferent or unimportant insofar as its own survival is concerned.

This description of Communist welfare policies is most salient—in its discriminatory, revolutionary, and politically manipulative aspects—when projected to those regimes and those periods in history where the gap between the overtly articulated aspirations of the party and the conditions of the status quo represented the widest discrepancy. Thus, in the USSR the manipulative and political aspects of the welfare programs would probably seem more clearly such to the average

---

(January 1963), pp. 21–27.

[27] Kallgren, *op. cit.*, pp. 20 and 21. See also her "Social Welfare and China's Industrial Workers," A. Doak Barnett (ed.), *Chinese Communist Politics in Action* (Seattle: University of Washington Press, 1969), pp. 540–573.

[28] Stephen Fischer-Galati, *East Europe in the Sixties* (New York: Praeger, 1963), p. 11. *Cf.* Chang-tu Hu, *op. cit.*, p. 394.

citizen during Stalin's collectivization, when the party was waging a ruthless campaign of social reconstruction with no holds barred, than during the 1921–1928 quiescent period. It was probably less apparent during World War II, when the party emphasized the theme of all Russia's patriotic-national defense against aggression from the outside. It reverted to militancy after 1945 and has again become relatively more apolitical in consequence of the accumulation of reforms, purges, and changes already realized under successive leaderships since Stalin. The changes include, of course, those in party policy toward such objectives as internal security, permissible levels of dissent, and lessened pressures for all-out industrialization regardless of human costs.

The concern with the values of work and of "socialist collectivism" is a significant continuing feature of the Soviet welfare system, spilling over into the fields of psychotherapy, child rearing, education, and law. In the Soviet (and indeed generally Communist) scheme of welfare, the happy and healthy individual is one who has a positive orientation toward his work and toward the community within which he functions. The community is represented on the lowest, most immediate level by one's fellow farm dwellers or fellow occupants in an apartment building. The apex of the community, the embodiment of its most cherished values, is officially, of course, the party. Positive dispositions toward work and the community are axiomatic assumptions of human normalcy so far as the party is concerned. Deviations in these areas are treated as survivals of maladjusted presocialist conditions and characteristically are generally treated by increased, intensified exposure to more of the same: work therapy and community supervision. Individual therapy to the maladjusted based on the psychoanalytic approach is, like privacy, sacrificed to the rigid demands of the system. In Soviet practice, in consequence of this approach:

> . . . the problems, desires, and hopes of every member [of the *Kollektiv*] became the legitimate business of the whole group, and the latter is held responsible for the welfare and the behavior of each member. Privacy, in the sense that what an individual does and experiences is strictly his own business unless he himself wishes to share it with someone else is rejected as unhealthy.[29]

Interestingly enough, in the 1960s, Soviet planning called for the vastly increased construction of boarding schools that would "accommodate the majority of school-age children" perhaps by the mid-1970s.[30] Thus, the tendency to publicly direct communal programs has gone on unabated since the Stalin era.

Soviet unwillingness to recognize welfare needs as significantly per-

[29] Madison, "Social Welfare: Soviet Model," *op. cit.*, p. 200.
[30] *Ibid.*

sonal and individual, apart from the interests of work and community, is closely linked to the refusal to establish a professional social work service. Instead, there has been a trend to administrative and trade union decentralization, under supervision of the Social Welfare Ministry of each Union Republic of the USSR. This decentralization has made possible a more flexible administration of welfare programs by local trade union committees in the last decade (specifically since 1957). But it has not introduced political pluralism into the Soviet welfare system in the sense in which the delegation of any powers from Washington D.C. to state governments almost inevitably would. The party's grip on the trade unions has been in no wise relaxed. It is perhaps a debatable point whether the individual is better served today by the increased discretion of his local party leadership or through the earlier rigid application of party rules prefabricated thousands of miles away in Moscow. The improvements in Soviet welfare programs, noted by Western observers since the 1950s, owe much to the substantially increased allocation of State funds and to the "humanistic," consumer- and welfare-oriented turn in the party's general policy since, at least, the undisputed ascendancy of Khrushchev in 1957.[31]

Outside the Communist systems, welfare policies of autocratic regimes have followed two patterns of development. Those regimes that can be described as innovative, in the sense that the rulers have committed themselves not merely to power but to far-reaching change in structuring popular attitudes and behavior, have all pursued interventionist welfare policies somewhat analogous to the Communist examples. They have tended to redirect public spending on welfare and to augment the kinds and amounts of social services available to the people. They have used welfare programs and agencies for purposes of directly mobilizing political support among the masses and for increasing the means at the rulers' disposal for control over the subjects. They have resorted to manipulation of welfare subverting the inherited social status quo. These regimes are represented by the Sukarno experiment in "guided democracy" in Indonesia; Nasser's Arab Socialism in the UAR; several African states in the 1950s and 1960s (Ghana and Guinea, for example); and also by the Nazi and Fascist regimes in pre-World War II Europe.

It is significant that the ideological orientations of fascism and nazism could not be said to be intrinsically welfare oriented. Compassion for the weak, the poor, and the destitute did not fit into the "iron laws

[31] The Soviet's State social insurance budget increased from 17.2 billion rubles in 1950 to about 70 billion in 1960. See Gaston V. Rimlinger, "Social Security, Incentives and Controls in the U. S. and U.S.S.R.," M. N. Zald (ed.), *Social Welfare Institutions* (New York: John Wiley, 1965), fn. p. 103.

Table 16
Temporary and Permanent Injury Benefits (and/or Pensions) to Employees. Communist States (c.1964).

	Temporary Disability	Permanent Disability
Albania	95% earnings payable from 1st day or *until* recovery or certification of permanent disability	Pension: 85% average earnings last year . . . plus other supplements and benefits
Bulgaria	90% earnings, same conditions as above	Pension: 55-85% earnings in inverse proportion to wage class
China	Full wages required from employer	Pension: 60% plus other supplements and benefits
Cuba	70% earnings from 1st day up to 26 weeks or 52 weeks if recovery probable	Pension: 55% of earnings plus 1.1% of salary per each year of employment beyond 25, plus medical benefits
Czechoslovakia	60-90% earnings depending on length of employment	Pension: 65% of earnings plus 1% of earnings for each year of employment over 15 yrs, more for onerous work plus supplement; e.g., constant attendance 50% of pension plus dependent allowance plus medical benefits
East Germany	90% of earnings	Pension: 66 2/3% plus 40 marks a month plus supplements, medical benefits
Hungary	75% from 1st day up to 12 weeks	Pension: 60% earnings plus 1% for each year of employment plus other supplements and benefits
Poland (1 zloty = 25 U.S. cents)	70% up to 26 weeks or 39 weeks maximum	Pension: 80% average monthly earnings plus 20% for category below 1200-2000 zl, plus other supplements and benefits
Rumania	90% paid right away for indefinite period	Pension: 85% of average mo. earnings plus 10-20% depending on scale, length of employment, plus other supplements and benefits

Table 16 (continued)

	Temporary Disability	Permanent Disability
USSR	100%	Pension: 90% plus 10% if disability is total, plus other supplements and benefits
North Vietnam	100%	Pension: 60% up to 90% plus other benefits
Yugoslavia	100%	Pension: 100% if total disability, plus other supplements and benefits

of the jungle"—the imperatives of "kill or be killed," of the inevitable and salutary triumph of the strong over the weak. These "laws" both fascism and nazism professed to esteem. The attitudes toward the underdog in these particular "isms" are thus noticeably different from Marxian messianism toward the poor and the oppressed of this world. They are also noticeably different from most—if not all[32]—strands of the liberal-democratic political tradition that has generally emphasized compassion for and solidarity with the downtrodden elements in society.

Nevertheless, both these regimes pursued interventionist welfare policies, less generous materially than their democratic German and Italian predecessors, and less generous than their Communist counterparts, to be sure, but interventionist still. In both cases, State agencies extended the sphere of their welfare functions at the expense of private voluntary and communal organs. In both cases, there was a tendency to use welfare programs for political mobilization purposes, as agencies of control and diffusion of propaganda.

But, apart from the fact that the content of propaganda and control imposed by the Fascists and Nazis differed from the Communist models, the scale of material commitment was much less in the Fascist and Nazi systems. Where Communist welfare spending has everywhere exceeded the spending by predecessor regimes, the cases of nazism and fascism were the reverse: they spent less in proportion to national income than their predecessors.[33]

The relative niggardliness of fascism and nazism was rooted not

[32] Such as Herbert Spencer's Social Darwinism and the philosophies of those liberals of the laissez-faire school more recently led by Professors Hayek and von Mises.

[33] *Cf.* Maxine Y. Woolston, *The Structure of Nazi Economy* (New York: Russell and Russell, 1941), pp. 217–218.

only in the social philosophy of its leaders but in the social and economic conservatism of many of their backers, allies, and supporters. Their vigorous administrative controls and comprehensive programs in the field of social welfare can be linked to the needs of mobilizing and controlling the masses. These can be appreciated especially in the context of the peculiar "genius" of fascism and nazism: their claim of being far more effective and, in a sense, more sophisticated, antidotes to Marxism than the old bourgeois and conservative parties. The Fascists and the Nazis set out not to exclude the workers or ignore them, but to divert them from their Socialist and Communist organizations, leaders, and orientations. Welfare measures, under close State control, played an essential part in the Fascist and Nazi efforts to "tame and convert" the proletariat. It was autocratic policy on a neo-Bismarckian model, albeit with even closer control and regimentation by the State.[34]

> ... Social policy was neither advanced nor neglected in the Third Reich; rather it was manipulated.... The hitherto autonomous unemployment insurance fund was tapped to finance the *Autobahns*, family allowances, and supplemental old age insurance. Apart from overcoming unemployment... State-directed social policy during the six peacetime years can only be called minimal.

The Nazis did, as a matter of fact, extend compulsory old-age insurance to handicraftsmen. They offered marriage loans and baby bonuses to parents; and benefits were conferred upon large families, all in line with the Nazi "virile" expansionist population policy. Compulsory health insurance was extended to agriculture, a move that reflected Nazism's traditional concern with the racial backbone of the *Volk*—the German peasant-proprietor.[35]But welfare payments to industrial workers in various categories, to the indigent and to the old seriously declined.

A different path in social welfare is generally associated with traditional, quiescent autocracies dedicated not to the remaking of their societies in some chosen image, but simply to the perpetuation of an inherited order and of their own place in it. Among these autocracies, ranging today from the states of the Iberian peninsula in Europe, to Duvalier's Haiti in Latin America, or to Ethiopia in Africa, social welfare is still a relatively neglected public national expenditure and its administration is still traditionally oriented toward the local communities and voluntary associations, churches, religious groups, and the family. It is neither politically mobilizational, socially innovative, nor

[34] David Schoenbaum, *Hitler's Social Revolution* (Garden City, N.Y.: Doubleday and Company, 1968), pp. 98–99.

[35] *Ibid.*, p. 114.

materially generous. In scope and method it is still more reminiscent of the patterns of the nineteenth century than of the twentieth.

At this juncture in our account, let us turn to the welfare policy differences between democracies and autocracies taken as generalized opposites. It is true that for good and sufficient reasons—related to economic conditions, the limited extension of suffrage, and the understandable disposition of public opinion—the democracies of the nineteenth century were by no means models of generosity in welfare policies. By the mid-twentieth century, however, the difference between the democratic and the authoritarian States had developed into a remarkable parallel of the difference in the field of education. *All* the democracies of the post-World War II period are welfare states, with heavy public spending in proportion to national income and with multifaceted programs administered in large measure by government agencies in virtually every conceivable area of social concern: from infant-care foster homes to old-age pensions, or, in the apt expression, from the cradle to the grave.

On the other hand, autocratic regimes oscillate far more widely on both sides of the line of commitment to public welfare. Among the innovational regimes, notably Communist ones, there are some "peaks" of State involvement and commitment that are not matched by *any* democracy. At the other extreme, we find autocracies whose commitment to welfare, either in percentage of the GNP or in proportion of governmental revenue and spending, or all of these, is very much less than even among the poorest democracies. (See Tables 16—19.)

Even though there are considerable differences in amounts of public spending among the democracies, the discrepancies between the least and the most generous spenders are not nearly as great as between the autocratic extremes. As in the area of educational expenditure, these differences of resource commitment are more strikingly correlated to political factors—to the intentions and the policies of the rulers—than to objective economic factors such as per capita GNP and the degree of urbanization and industrialization and so forth. On the basis of economic indices alone, we would have every right to expect Spanish welfare programs to be more generous than the Bulgarian; the Portuguese far more so than the Albanian or even the Yugoslavian; and the Argentinian more so than the Polish or the Rumanian. But, in fact, even though the evidence is still more fragmentary and incomplete than it could be, the opposite clearly appears to be the case.

There are also certain qualitative differences between welfare policies and programs whose impact makes a great deal of difference to the man in the street: the ultimate consumer of the services and ben-

Table 17
Temporary and Permanent Injury Benefits (and/or Pensions) to Employees
Some Other States (c. 1964)

	Temporary Disability	Permanent Disability
Argentina	100% of average earnings last 12 mos., payable after 5-day waiting period for up to 12 mos.	Lump sum payment of 3 yrs.' pay plus medical benefits
Belgium	80% for 1st 28 days of incapacity, 90% afterward indefinite	Pension: 100% of earnings if totally disabled plus constant (50%) attendance supplement plus medical benefits
Brazil	100% average earnings after 2 days, up to 12 mos.	Lump sum (4 years' earnings)
Ceylon	15-60% of wages in inverse proportion payable after 7-day waiting period—until recovery or permanent disability	Lump sum: from 1 1/3 to 3 1/2 yrs.' wages varying inversely with scale of wages if disability total
Chile	75% of earnings payable from 1st day up to 1 yr.	Pension: 60% of earnings if totally disabled, 20% constant attendance supplement plus medical benefits
Taiwan	70% of earnings from 1st 6 mos., 50% thereafter payable after 3-day period for up to 1 yr.	Lump sum: 60 mos.' earnings, medical benefits for only up to 6 mos.
Colombia	100% of earnings for up to 6 mos. For employees in smaller firms only 66 2/3% up to 6 mos. and 66 2/3% up to 3 mos.	Lump sum: 30 mos.' earnings (if employer's capital below 50,000 no benefit paid) plus medical benefits for up to 2 yrs.; or none depending on capital of employer's firm
Costa Rica	50% earnings up to 1 yr.	Pension: 66 2/3% of earnings if totally disabled plus medical benefits
Ethiopia	50% required of individual employers up to 6 mos.	Lump sum: 6 yrs.' earnings

Table 17 (continued)

	Temporary Disability	Permanent Disability
Finland	60% of earnings plus 20% supplement for 1 or more dependents payable from 1st day for up to 12 mos.	Pension: 60% of earnings if total, dependent supplement 30% for one; 100% with 2 dependent plus constant attendance and medical benefits
Greece (1 dr. = 3.3 U.S. cents)	50% of earnings plus 10% for up to 2 dependents. Maximum: 60 drachmas a day, paid from after 3-day waiting period indefinitely to recovery or permanent disability	Pension: from 60-90% of average earnings in last 2 yrs. of work plus medical benefits
India	50% of earnings paid on 3rd day of disability indefinitely	Pension: "about" 50% plus some medical benefits (. . . varies from state to state)
Indonesia	100% for 1st 4 mos. 50% thereafter indefinitely	Pension: 50% of earnings plus 20% constant attendance supplement plus medical benefits
Iran	66 2/3% of earnings after 12 mos., 40% for single workers; 50% for married ones; paid indefinitely	Pension: minimum of 50% of earnings for single, 70% for married workers, plus medical benefits
Israel (1 pound = 33.3 U.S. cents)	75% of earnings up to 9 pounds/day payable after 2 days for up to 26 weeks	Pension: 75% of earnings up to 270 pounds maximum, plus medical benefits
Japan	60% of earnings payable up to 3 yrs. (after 7-day waiting period at 100% rate)	Pension: 66 2/3% of earnings for 6 yrs., plus medical benefits (up to 6 yrs.)
South Korea	60% of earnings up to 12 mos.	Lump sum: less than 3 yrs.' (1,000 days') earnings plus "necessary medical expenses"
Portugal	33 1/3% of earnings for 1st 3 days; 66 2/3% thereafter paid indefinitely	Pension: 66 2/3% of earnings plus 13 1/3 constant attendance supplement plus medical benefits
Saudi Arabia (1 riyal = 22.2 U.S. cents)	100% of earnings for 1st week of disability; 75% thereafter for up to 12 mos.	Lump sum: variable—12,000 riyal minimum and 27,000 riyal maximum

Table 17 (continued)

	Temporary Disability	Permanent Disability
South Africa (1 rand = .719 U.S. dollar)	75% of earnings up to 40 rands plus 60% of income between 41-100 rands for up to 12 mos. paid to non-natives after 3-day waiting period. Natives paid only if disability exceeds 6 days	Pension: Non-natives 75% of salary up to 40 rands, 60% between 41-100 rands. Natives: Lump sum of 36 mos.' earnings up to 40 rands/mo. and 20 mos. between 41 and 100 rands
Spain	75% of earnings payable from day of injury for up to 18 mos.	Pension: 75-100% of earnings if totally disabled; if only for usual work 55% of earnings. Plus 50% constant attendance supplement plus medical benefits
Switzerland (1 franc = 23.4 U.S. cents)	80% of earnings; maximum benefit 32 francs/day after 2-day waiting period; paid indefinitely to recovery or certification of permanent disability	Pension: 70% of earnings if totally disabled; maximum: 700 francs/mo. constant attendance supplement—30%, plus medical benefits
United States	60-66 2/3% of earnings in most states. About 1/3 of states provide supplements for dependents. Maximum benefits $30-150/wk according to state. $50 maximum in about 1/2 of the states	Pension: 60-66 2/3% of earnings in most states if totally disabled. Maximum pension $30-150/week according to state. Payable for life in only 3/5 of states; rest for only 330-550 weeks or up to $10,000-30,000; in remaining 3/4 of states medical benefits given too
Uruguay (1 peso = 5.8 U.S. cents)	50% of earnings for 1st 30 days; 66 2/3% thereafter, minimum benefit 3 pesos/day, payable from 1st day indefinitely	Pension: 85% of earnings if totally disabled. Plus medical benefits
Venezuela (1 bolivar = 22 U.S. cents)	66 2/3% of average earnings in last 10 weeks according to 9 wage classes, payable after 3-day waiting period for up to 52 weeks	Pension: approximately 66 2/3% average earnings in case of total incapacity, constant attendance supplement 50% of pension. Minimum = 600 bol. Maximum = 2,400 bol.
South Vietnam	50% of earnings payable after 3-day waiting period for duration of medical treatment	Lump sum: 1 yrs.' earnings if totally disabled

Table 18
States That Did Not Pay Life Pensions for Permanent Disability to Employees (c. 1964)*

Afghanistan	Kenya
Argentina	South Korea
Brazil	Liberia
Cambodia	Malaysia
Ceylon	Nigeria
Taiwan	Peru (at employer's option)
Colombia	Saudi Arabia
Cyprus	Sierra Leone
Ethiopia	South Africa (for "Natives")
Ghana	Sudan
Guatemala	Tanganyika
Iraq	Trinidad and Tobago
Jamaica	Uganda
Japan	South Vietnam
Jordan	

**Note:* None of the established democracies or Communist States are on this list.

efits provided by the State. The democracies generally maintain certain values in their welfare programs that are frequently absent or neglected under autocratic regimes. These values may be subsumed under categories analogous to the values of their educational and legal systems. However variable in their generosity, all democratic welfare policies are characterized by significant qualities of diversity, openness, and a quasi-judicial concern for the rights of the individual: the "neutral" or objective treatment of each person and respect for the sanctity and privacy of the individual, the family, and of existent social institutions.

These qualitative aspects might be described in large measure as procedural—that is, they pertain to the question of *how* the individual benefits by the largesse of the public treasury. What protections and recourse are available to the recipients of such benefits in the process of allocation and disbursement? In part, these aspects are also related to the pluralism of democratic political regimes. However far reaching public assistance and welfare programs are, there is always some recourse to agencies outside the State: private, cooperative, and voluntary groups can and do provide services and benefits to individuals that are analogous to those offered by the State or under State auspices. Frequently, cooperative and private agencies are used in the implementation of government-supported programs.

Table 19
States Which Paid Temporary and Permanent Disability Pensions to Employees at Rates of 70% of Earnings and Up in Both Categories with Allowance for Cash Supplements (c. 1964)*

Albania	Hungary	Rumania
Australia	Ireland	Spain
Bulgaria	Israel	Sweden
Canada	Luxembourg	Switzerland
Czechoslovakia	Mexico	U.S.S.R.
Finland	Netherlands	North Vietnam
West Germany	New Zealand	Yugoslavia
East Germany	Poland	

**Note:* Only Cuba and Red China fell below the range maintained by these 23 states; Mongolia was not included in the survey. Ten Communist states were represented with per capita GNP's ranging from $85 to $1,260. Among the well-established democracies, the United States, Britain, Norway, Denmark, and Uruguay all fell below these standards although all possessed highly advanced welfare systems. Spain was the only seemingly anomalous entry among the twenty-three inasmuch as it represented a traditional autocracy. Tables 16-19 are based on *Social Security Programs Throughout the World*, U.S. Department of Health, Education and Welfare (Washington, D.C., 1964).

To the extent that such cooperative and private associations are *not* dominated by a single political purpose of a totalitarian party or other monolithically dominant political interest, the man in the street need not feel wholly at the mercy of the rulers. There are various choices and options open to him. Analogously to his position vis-à-vis "the law," the man in the street need not feel that in the area of welfare policy the disbursing agencies are at once judge, jury, and prosecutor all wrapped up in one framework.

All of the established democratic systems provide for two basic kinds of appeal and redress from the decisions of their welfare agencies: through the administrative and ordinary courts. A disqualification or penalty imposed on an individual under the Canadian, Swedish, or Dutch social security programs always can be appealed to an administrative tribunal that is separate and independent of the disbursing agency. Under certain conditions, and within certain legal limits, the individual can appeal alleged mistreatment to judicial tribunals wholly independent of the welfare system. Even structurally—that is, in terms of the kinds and numbers of bodies and procedures available for appeal—most democracies exceed by far the available institutional recourse of most autocracies. But beyond the mere letter of the law, there is always the far greater likelihood of the *de facto* capacity of review tribunals, administrative and judicial, to defend individual interests against State encroachment where the reviewers can be reasonably sure that they are not jeopardizing the lives and fortunes of their families and themselves in the process. On this point, there is very considerable evidence for the presumption of such a difference between welfare referees in the United States and, say, People's China or the Hitler Reich.

Another area of policy difference that has a significant impact on the interests of every man relates to the leverage of publicity. The existence of autonomous groups and communication media in the democracies makes feasible public recourse against corruption and wrongdoing; such recourse is either wholly lacking or not nearly as readily available under autocratic regimes. Thus, if an individual or group feels wronged by the distribution of public welfare funds and services, it may not only appeal to administrative and judicial tribunals with reasonable hope of redress, but ultimately to public opinion. It can expose and accuse the bureaucracy, public or private, professional or not; and it can work for a change in any rules that are regarded as unfair. The opportunities for such action are generally more limited in the autocracies, and most strikingly so under the innovative-mobilizational regimes.

American legislation, in the Social Security Act of 1933, compels all states that participate under the act to provide a fair hearing and appeal to all individuals covered by the programs pursuant to it. Each state maintains for this purpose an Office of Hearings and Appeals, independent of the field administrators of any specific social security program. Further appeals may be lodged with an Appeals Council in each state.[36]

In Great Britain, the work of appeal tribunals, scattered in all the different social welfare programs, was brought under the supervision of a Council of Tribunals in 1958. This body provides a central avenue of appeal and redress against bureaucratic mistreatment to the ordinary citizen. In addition to the field tribunals, and the council, there has existed also, since 1939, the Citizens' Advice Bureau (CAB), whose task is to make available information to every interested person on how to get and use State welfare services. The bureau informs people of their rights and of the recourse open to them. It has thus helped to channel complaints against welfare administration as well as provide factual information to the public. Among the democracies that have in recent years imitated the example of Britain by setting up their own equivalents of CAB are Australia, Kenya, and Israel.[37]

Even though these are only some examples, it is certainly accurate to say that *all* the established democracies maintain elaborate review

[36] See John S. Morgan, "Appeals Against Administrative Decisions Under Welfare Legislation," *Canadian Public Administration*, Vol. 4, No. 1 (March 1961), p. 46.

[37] Birch, op. cit., pp. 190–191.

and appeal structures within their welfare programs.[38] This generalization could not be made with respect to the surviving autocracies of our time or, historically, to autocracies generally.

The role of social workers in the democratic states, as professional, independent administrators of welfare programs, finds no parallel in the totalitarian, "ultramobilized" political systems of the twentieth century. The reasons for this are analogous to those that explain the absence of an independent judiciary and an independent bureaucracy. An innovative-mobilizational regime could not bring itself to pass up the opportunity of entrusting the care of the youth, the workers, or, for that matter, any sizeable population group to anyone who, as a professional, would avow *neutrality*, or *indifference*, or even possibly *hostility* toward the State—in behalf of the sick, the aged, and the indigent. Such attitudes would be tantamount to subversion from the totalitarian point of view. To accord them legal and economic recognition, or subsidy, would be a folly and a crime in the context of totalitarian politics. Social welfare administration has thus been welded into the bureaucracy of the State and the regime-run trade unions. Welfare functions have been generally delegated to essentially political, rather than professional, organs and personnel in these states. Social work as a profession meant to serve the individual and the community, separated from any overt political role, can be found today most often and significantly among the well-established democracies.[39]

[38] See, for example, Morgan, *op. cit.*, p. 49. *Cf.* Nelson, *op. cit.*, pp. 495, 450, and 452–454.

[39] For reasons that seem fairly obvious, UN surveys tend to focus as far away from political intersystem differences as possible. One typically discreet statement regarding such data is worth quoting here: "... it seems ... that those countries where considerable discrepancies exist between the economic and social indicators ... are usually countries where the existence of social or economic strains reflecting this disparity are widely recognized; especially where the economic indicators are much higher than the social, political strain and instability are also apt to be quite marked." UN Report, *op. cit.*, Section IV, pp. 63–98 and 61.

CHAPTER 8
POLITICS AND SOCIAL CHANGE

THE significance of political policies with respect to the social organization of a people may be appreciated in terms of many criteria. One of them is the pool of manpower that policies make available for leadership roles, political and otherwise. Among these, apart from the opportunities of government service, are the provision of financial aids to disadvantaged social groups so that they can improve their lot and climb the ladder of social ascent in the professions, trade, industry, and agriculture; the maintenance of access to institutions of technical and higher learning; and the provision of subsidies and scholarships for vocational and academic training. The promotion of indirect aid—such as increased economic capability conceivably resulting from land reform—and the imposition of legal and administrative regulations by the State on the economy and society—such as the legal definition of minors; the obligations of apprenticeship; the rights of residence; the definition of the legal rights of women, in and out of marriage; and the licensing requirements for starting a business, are all political instruments for social change.

In all these categories of activity, what a regime does, or what it does not do, is bound to affect the chances of people under its rule for a better job, a better education, a chance for a business or professional career, or even for the opportunity of moving to a more desirable neighborhood or owning a plot of land. In all of these areas—recruitment, fiscal supports, and regulations—the traditional autocracies tend to be more rigid than the democracies; they reinforce relatively more closed societies, which discourage the upward ascent of the have-nots and inroads on the haves. If such ascent be regarded as progress, it takes place in spite of and against the political system, not with its aid. And the political discount of autocratic controls on the dynamics of social mobility is not merely an important one. Under some circumstances its significance may readily exceed that of virtually all other factors in the society.

Traditionalist autocracies are generally most restrictive in promoting people to leadership roles. This is symbolized in some cases, in the personage of the hereditary monarch whose title and claim to power are purely ascriptive. One is either born to rule or one is not. There are no elections to the position of top political leadership. Merit, skill, and achievement play no role in this. Looking more broadly at the various political and nonpolitical pyramids of power in society, we find traditional autocracies oriented to policies that restrict, if they do not completely eliminate, the inflow of new elements into those pyramids. They may do so overtly and directly by ascriptive recruitment policies such as those which supported the position of the French nobility under the pre-1789 Bourbon monarchy. They may, however, be carried out under formally "modernized" arrangements, where the alleged criterion is each person's capacity for the effective performance of specific functions.

Nevertheless, rigid protection of landed wealth and other types of property; the exclusion of the bulk of the poor from educational opportunities; and legal disabilities imposed on new and potentially dangerous or disruptive social strata are all factors taken together to ensure that the pool of available talent, trained and capable of exercising administrative, economic, and cultural leadership, will invariably emphasize the preponderance of the haves over the have-nots. Direct and indirect methods of recruitment can be readily made to converge. A regime need not practice overt discrimination in choosing its judges, administrators, generals, or diplomats, if it can trust to the natural consequences of inherited wealth. It may justly claim that it hires its servants only from among the best-qualified and the most meritorious persons in the land. But what does it take to become qualified and who has it?

With respect to this indirect control of elite recruitment, there are strikingly wide differences among the autocracies. What all autocracies have in *common* is the great power to promote orthodoxy and repress nonconformity in their elite recruitment practices. In order to ascend to a position of public responsibility in an autocracy, an individual must be, above all, politically conformist. Whether his station be cultural, political, administrative, economic or judicial, central or regional, he can rarely be a person who could even privately say: "Chairman Kosygin and I—or Generalissimo Franco and I—have some basic policy differences between us."

That a diplomat, a jurist, or a military officer should have an opinion that *publicly* contradicts that of the chief executive (made apparent through the medium of a press interview, testimony before a legislative body, or the like) is out of the question in *all* autocratic states.

There may only be nonpolicy and nonpolitical differences. Those who prefer Shakespeare to Pushkin could conceivably rise to General Staff positions in the USSR, even if their preferences were known, those who believe and avow that collectivization of farming was a colossal mistake or that the Arab states initiated the 1967 conflict with Israel could not.

Even though it is granted that in democracies there are also some socially and even legally imposed conformisms, a significant difference between the need to conform to *some* political stands as opposed to virtually *all* political stands distinguishes the career requisites of American and Soviet, Chinese, or Spanish public officials. Thus, in recruitment to official, overtly political positions of leadership, the access routes in the autocracies tend to be narrower and more homogeneous in terms of the ideological and overtly articulated policy orientations of the recruits. In the nonpolitical, or at least outwardly nonpolitical spheres, in the recruitment to scientific, cultural, religious, and economic enterprises under private, cooperative, and nongovernmental management, the pattern corresponds to the differences discussed in Chapter 3. To the extent that the autonomy of such institutions tends to be compromised under autocracy, political constraints and the demand for orthodoxy apply here, too. These constraints and demands are far heavier and more effective among the innovative-mobilized, totalitarian regimes, such as the Communist, than they are among the more traditionally oriented regimes.

Much of the argument about a "New (ruling) Class" and a new system of stratification in place of an old one in the Communist states is irrelevant because it focuses on the continuing fact of inequality without facing up to the distributive change that it entails and the new ways in which it is realized. Although some people are apparently "more equal" than others in all societies, it makes a great deal of difference to everyone as to precisely "who is who." Another "antipolitical" fallacy is represented by the approach that implicitly looks to industrialization and economic change as the major, if not the sole, determinants of this New Class and of upward social mobility, in general.[1]

From the standpoint of the impact of political manipulation on the fortunes of ordinary men and women, the significance of the political can hardly be exaggerated. One can, of course, take a reductionist position ("in the long run we'll all be dead") and argue that a difference of twenty-five or fifty years of social change under alternative routes of political development is historically trivial. But to a peasant or worker, to whom his son and his grandson are concrete and important people, the dimensions of a historical perspective are no trivial matter. Sufficiently numerous and detailed comparative social mobility studies are simply not yet available to sustain conclusive judgments, but if we may refer to such studies as investigations of the "outputs" of different systems, it would require a wholly untenable disregard of some massive "inputs" to justify the antipolitical line of thought.

To take a famous example, Russian industrialization of the 1880s, carried out under a traditionalist autocracy, did result within several decades in some marked changes for Russian society—Tsarism notwithstanding. Illustrative of these was the rapid expansion in school and university enrollments. Whereas in 1880 the proportion of peasants', craftsmen's and workers' children enrolled in universities was only 15.7 per cent of the total, it grew to 38.8 per cent by 1914.[2]

Yet, as one writer has pointed out:

> ... the Ministers of Education under Nicholas I attempted to *restrict* access to higher education and this remained, indeed, a feature of Russian educational policy right up to 1905, even to 1917. Financial obstacles were supplemented by periodic changes in the curriculum of schools designed to make things hard for plebeian children. But these measures were ineffective: they delayed but did not prevent the spread of secondary and university education.[3]

The point is applicable not merely to Russia but elsewhere too. The

[1] This is the position of Seymour Martin Lipset and Reinhard Bendix in *Social Mobility in Industrial Society* (Berkeley: University of California Press, 1960), which abounds in such statements as "the over-all pattern of social mobility appears to be much the same in the industrial societies of various Western nations," p. 13, and "the proposition that the rates of economic expansion and industrialization are more significant in determining the extent of social mobility in a given society than variations in political, economic, or cultural value systems, has recently been forcefully reiterated," p. 281.

[2] See Cyril Black, "The Nature of Imperial Russian Society," *Slavic Review*, Vol. XX, No. 4 (December 1961), p. 579.

[3] Hugh Seton-Watson, in George de Huszar (ed.), *The Intellectuals* (Glencoe, Ill.: Free Press, 1960), pp. 42–43.

intervention of political power can significantly affect the *rate* of change—progress or decline—in social mobility, even if it obviously does not totally manipulate the whole environment.

Among the traditional autocracies, the political order has played the role of a *brake*, if not a barrier, to the social pressures emanating from the lower rungs of its own social pyramid and from the international environment. These attempts are not equally evident in all spheres of social activity and, above all, it must be remembered that they are not always successful. But such attempts are nevertheless serious, institutionalized features of any traditional autocracy with tangible consequences. They are manifested initially in those activities under the direct control of the State—that is, in the selection of personnel into the government service.

Within the framework of a conservative authoritarian political order, autocracies tend to exclude from important government jobs the representatives or scions of peasants and manual workers; women; the young; and members of ethnic, religious, and political groups that may be described as deviant from the identifications of the ruling autocrats.

Thus, whether we want to look at the membership of the cabinets, the principal administrative chiefs, the leaders of the armed forces, the police, the judiciary, or the diplomatic corps, we will find the pattern repeated in such diverse past and present autocracies as the Russia of Nicholas II, the Germany of William II, the Spain of Franco, and the Portugal of Salazar. Even though technological, economic, and military needs have forced these and other autocratic regimes to recruit government personnel from *outside* the "optimum" social categories in each case—notably from among the middle classes—some barriers have never been crossed.

In due course, it is conceivable that the progress of the industrial revolution in Bismarckian Germany might well have brought about a fundamental change in the social position of women. Perhaps it was equally inevitable, from the standpoint of a contemporary observer looking back on Germany in, say, 1870 or 1880, that the sons of workers and of coal miners would some day—within a century—become the managers of the economic, social, and political life of the country.

But in 1870 and 1880 the ruling autocracy did *not* sanction or encourage such developments. These social strata were beyond the pale of Germany's unofficial constitution in the sense that their share in the ruling apparatus of the country was virtually nil; it continued so until the revolution of November 1918, which toppled the monarchy. The official values of the Kaiserreich identified the place of the woman in the home, not in the professional, let alone the political, sphere. These values gave no sanction to the egalitarian acceptance of working-class elements in positions of political and administrative responsibility. The government of William II was prepared to accept wealth as a supplement to noble birth in the higher offices of state. It was not prepared to accept merit and ability apart from the criteria of class and status, and it was not prepared to encourage the sharing of power with the lower classes or other potentially revolutionary and outcast elements.

Another example of politically restricting the mobility of people was evidenced by traditional Tsarist policies toward Jews from the eighteenth until the twentieth centuries. In 1791, Catherine the Great restricted Jews to residence within a so-called Pale of Settlement, an area largely made up of newly acquired western territories. The Pale excluded such "prime areas" as Moscow and Petrograd and most of the territory east and north of Kiev. Jewish merchants within the Pale were subjected to a rate of taxation twice that applied to non-Jewish merchants. In 1859, the richest Jewish merchants were finally allowed residence outside the Pale, and through successive decrees of 1861, 1865, and 1879 a small percentage of the richest and best-educated Jews were permitted to escape from the ghettoes of the Pale. This liberalization, however, was coupled with the imposition of other restrictions on Jews including, for example, quotas on the employment of educated Jews by government services; power vested in the Minister of Justice to exclude Jewish lawyers from practice in the courts; and in 1887 a quota system was officially promulgated restricting the admission of Jews to the universities. Within the Pale Jews could constitute no more than 10 per cent of a university's total student body; outside it only 5 per cent; and in Moscow and Petrograd no more than 3 per cent.[4]

The attitude toward the social, economic, and political rights of women is one of the distinguishing features of different regimes. Traditional autocracies and the mobilized Fascist and Nazi systems have been characterized by their hostility to these rights. The hallmark of their social policy has been male supremacy. The well-worn phrase "woman's place is in the home," or in the old German version "*Kinder, Kuche und Kirche*," sums up the legitimate concerns of women in the official views of these States. Communist regimes, on the other hand, have followed feminist social policies of extending women's rights and in encouraging women to assume active roles in virtually all spheres of political, economic, and social activity. Democracies similarly have been generally feminist in their policy orientations.

The political orientation of a regime is frequently more important in

[4] See Jesse D. Clarkson, *A History of Russia* (New York: Random House, 1961), pp. 252 and 333.

determining the woman's place in her society than is economic development. Japan, under the rule of the militarists, and Germany, under the rule of the Nazis, provide striking examples of social systems in which high levels of industrialization and modernization were combined with the relegation of women to inferior status. In both countries, the autocracies managed to *reverse* previous trends, under parliamentary regimes in the 1920s, and reverse them *despite* the continuing, even accelerated, progress of economic development, industrialization, and urbanization. When the autocracies were abolished in both Germany and Japan at the conclusion of World War II, the democratic successor regimes not only resumed, but extended, the progress in women's rights.

During the 1920s, under parliamentary government, there was an organized feminist movement in Japan. After the election of 1925, as one author notes:

> The movement to secure woman's suffrage was . . . pursued vigorously for a decade by its leaders. However, the movement came to an unexpected end. As early as 1937, Japan was already organizing her effort to become a war state, and the government took steps to suppress [it].[5]

To be sure, the massive progress of industrialization, in the semifeudal Japanese society of the nineteenth and early twentieth centuries, did bring new economic roles and new responsibilities to women. By the turn of the century, women had become the principal work force of Japan's textile industry and the backbone of other manufactures; but notwithstanding the many deep economic, physical, cultural, and social changes, "from the end of the Tokugawa feudalism to the end of World War II, a span of 80 years . . . the social position of the women of Japan [had] comparatively speaking, changed little."[6]

What impeded the process of change to equality and opportunity for women?

> . . . attempts to solve these problems were defeated time after time by the overwhelming opposition of the conservative elements of Japanese society who were successful in manipulating events leading to national crises. The strength of such conservative forces could not be successfully overridden by a gradual process of social evolution. In so far as the change in the position of women was brought about directly by the new law and the new constitution and by the democratization of the educational system, the liberation of Japanese women can be attributed in large measure to compulsion from without.[7]

Like the Tsarist autocracy in Russia, the predemocratic, pre-1946

[5] Takaski Koyama, *The Changing Social Position of Women in Japan* (Geneva: UNESCO, 1961), p. 12.

[6] *Ibid.*, p. 14.

[7] *Ibid.*, pp. 15–16.

Japanese regime disadvantaged women by legal disabilities in such fields as marriage, inheritance and employment, and the right to an education comparable to that of men. It was not until 1899 that the need of women for education beyond the primary level was even recognized by the autocracy. The objective, however, was still "not to provide girls with education comparable to that of boys [but] to make good wives and wise mothers for people of middle and upper-class families."[8] As late as 1920, the proportion of women to men receiving secondary education was about 1:2; 63 per cent of the students were men; 37 per cent were women. By 1940, the ratio had risen to 55:45. In consequence of the post-1945 democratic revolution, amidst a general expansion of Japanese enrollments, women have progressed faster than ever before. The most striking results can be seen in the field of higher education. In 1950, there were some 360,000 male students and still only 40,000 females in Japanese colleges and universities. By 1957, the number of males increased by 44.3 per cent, but the number of females by 184.7 per cent. The imbalance between men and women dropped from a ratio of 9:1 to less than 5:1 in a period of only seven years.[9]

Educational advances for women have resulted in far-reaching occupational-employment changes. The number of professional, scientific, and cultural employees among women has risen. As Koyama notes: "In former days, the women who entered the arena of gainful occupation were predominantly . . . either factory workers or in service."[10] The new influx of professionally educated women into Japanese society is now likely to further enhance the social position of women.

In pre-1917 Russia, women were more prominent in the revolutionary movement than in virtually any organized professional field of endeavor. The laws and regulations of the Tsarist regime were so flagrantly discriminatory and oppressive that the change inaugurated by the Bolshevik Revolution represented, from the feminist standpoint, a 180-degree turn for the lot of Russian women.[11] Changes brought about by the Soviet regime in (1) women's access to schools and (2) access to professional and nonmanual jobs, as compared with

[8] *Ibid.*, p. 22.

[9] See Table 5, *ibid.*, p. 30.

[10] *Ibid.*, p. 31.

[11] See Fannina W. Halle, *Woman in Soviet Russia* (London: Routledge, 1933). The author writes that under the reign of Tsar Alexander III (1881–1894) "Jewish women students were forbidden to live in St. Petersburg and had to purchase the right to study by entering their names in the register of prostitutes, for these were granted the right of residence." Pp. 74–75. On the contrast between the marriage laws of the two regimes (with the implicit Tsarist principle that the wife was part of her husband's property), see pp. 126–128.

pre-1917 Russia, were well-nigh spectacular within a very short period of the Communist assumption of power; moreover, these politically induced changes *preceded* rather than *followed* massive industrial-economic changes in the Russian society.

The social positions achieved by Soviet women in the 1920s owed much less to economic than to political impulses; the striking comparison between the upward mobility of Soviet and Japanese women in the 1930s—or German women, for that matter—has very little to do with industrialization and economic change.

Even as early as 1928 Jessica Smith noted that:

> As opposed to the discrimination against women in some quarters [the Soviet] tendency [was] to push women into all kinds of work irrespective of whether they are fitted for that type of work or not.[12] . . . there is no kind of work in Russia today which one is surprised to find a woman doing. There are women plumbers, locksmiths, lathemen, draughtsmen, electricians, seamen, soldiers, architects, engineers, Red Army officers, and even captains of ships.[13]

Already in 1926, women constituted 6.4 per cent of top Soviet trade union leadership; 12.6 per cent of union professional organizers; 13.1 per cent of party members; and about 20 per cent of the deputies to the various Soviets. Among Russia's then 240,000 journalists, more than 30,000 were women. Thus, long before the great Soviet industrialization of the 1930s began, Russian women were making considerable inroads on what used to be an exclusive man's world.

Communist industrialization admittedly brought many more women into arduous factory and construction work, but, unlike Nazi Germany and Imperial Japan, it also brought them into many leading professional and managerial positions. Perhaps the fact that in 1954, 69 per cent of Soviet metal drillers and 70 per cent of the turret lathe operators were women is neither remarkable nor laudable. But along with these increases came others: among employees with higher education women numbered 53 per cent; among economists, statisticians, and planners they numbered 69 per cent; among physicians, 76 per cent; among lawyers, 31 per cent; among teachers, 70 per cent; and among librarians and miscellaneously classified cultural employees, 72 per cent.[14] In Germany and Japan, on the other hand, transitions from

[12] *Women in Soviet Russia* (New York: Vanguard Press, 1928), pp. 23–24.

[13] *Ibid.*, p. 25. *Cf.* Alice W. Field, *Protection of Women and Children in Soviet Russia* (New York: E. P. Dutton, 1932), for a discussion of Soviet advances over pre-1917 health and welfare protection.

[14] See *Equality of Women in the U.S.S.R.; Materials of International Seminar*, Moscow, September 15–October 1, 1956 (Moscow: Foreign Languages Publishing House, 1947), p. 104. For the successive impacts of democratic and Communist revolutions in China, see Helen F. Snow, *Women in Modern China* (The Hague: Mouton, 1967), pp. 62–67 and *passim*.

democratic to oligarchic regimes had precisely opposite effects on women's social ascent, *despite* augmented industrialization.

In Japan, with mounting industrial output during the 1930s, hundreds of thousands of women worked in light and heavy industry and even in mining but, illustratively, only one woman in all Japan was admitted to the practice of law in 1937; one woman worked as a patent attorney; only four women held degrees of doctor of science; and in 1938 only fourteen women were believed to be physicians in private practice.[15]

The lack of vocational opportunities for women was coupled with, and reinforced by, their subservient legal status within the family, in some respects as virtual chattels of the husbands,[16] and by the neglect of social and legal protections against the discrimination, exploitation, and abuse of women employees.

In Germany, where Hitler shared the antifeminist orientation of the Japanese militarist oligarchy, his war preparations also entailed substantial economic expansion that could not be accomplished without the employment of millions of women. But here, too, the regime blocked their paths to a variety of leadership positions.

Although the Nazi law of April 25, 1933, which had set a 10 per cent enrollment quota for women in the universities, was formally rescinded in February 1935, the proportion of women attending universities continued to decline steadily relative to the pre-1933 levels.

Moreover, for many of those graduated, there were simply no jobs because of the regime's antifeminist hiring policies. One example was the January 10, 1936, order of the Nazi Ministry of Justice prohibiting the continued employment of women by the State in legal capacity. In consequence, even those women who had been Nazi party members, and experienced and skilled professionals, were fired from their jobs as judges and government attorneys. In the field of education, even in schools for girls, the Nazis decreased the number of women teachers from 11.3 thousand in 1932–1933 to 9.9 thousand in 1934–1935. Only in the field of medicine—and even here not without bitter conflict—did women maintain their approximate pre-1933 positions into the later 1930s. In the political arena, the impact of Hitler's revolution was illustrated by the figures on Germany's parliamentary (Reichstag) representation. In 1932, 38 women were serving in the

[15] Tetsu Katayama, *Women's Movement in Japan* (New York: Kenkyusha Press, 1938), pp. 15–17 and 26–27. Only in mid-1940, in fact, did the first Japanese women attorneys, three of them, appear in court. See H. V. Straellen, *The Japanese Woman Looking Forward* (Tokyo: Kyo Bun Kwan, 1940), p. 103. *Cf.* Harold Wakefield, *New Paths for Japan* (New York: Oxford University Press, 1948), Ch. IX.

[16] *Cf.* Waka Yamada, *The Social Status of Japanese Women* (Tokyo: Kokusai Bunka Shinokai, 1937).

Reichstag of the Weimar Republic; in the fateful balloting of March 1933, which preceded Hitler's consolidation of power, 30 were still elected. In November 1933, with the Nazis in undisputed possession of the State, not one woman sat in the all-Nazi Reichstag—not even in its new, purely ceremonial character. No woman held cabinet-rank government or party office or any other remotely equivalent position of political power and prestige. Leadership roles for women were strictly confined, both in theory and in practice, to those tasks that were "in accordance with womanly nature"—of course, as the Nazis saw it.[17] Their tasks included, according to official sources, nursing, domestic science, and work with youth. In the upshot, as Clifford Kirkpatrick wrote in 1938, "women of smaller stature [were] now standing in smaller shoes"[18] in Nazi-ruled Germany.

Illustratively "politics" imposed drastic checks upon "economy" in Germany even when the Nazi industrial machine had reared up to its maximum to sustain Hitler's war effort.

As A. S. Milward notes:

> The local shortages of unskilled labour which occurred from time to time [during World War II] could have been avoided by employing more women. But the Party was the victim of its own subservience to, and propaganda for, the idea that the place of the woman was in the home. Hitler held quite decided views that the employment of women would not only make industrial relations more difficult . . . but would also be biologically harmful to the race . . . between Summer 1939 and Spring 1942 [the employment of women] decreased by about 40,000.[19]

In terms of its antifeminism, Nazi Germany and Fascist Italy were more similar to traditional, status quo-oriented oligarchies than to other innovative-mobilizational regimes. In different cultural-economic contexts, the link has been the use of political power to repress the aspirations of women. Among the more recent and currently surviving traditional oligarchies, there are many illustrations of these parallels of policy.

Antifeminist practices had been sanctioned by autocratic rule in Afghanistan since the eighteenth century.

Until 1959, women were virtual outcasts in terms of their educational and professional employment opportunities. Traditionally, Afghan wives had been regarded as their husbands' property, and until 1959 women in the urban areas, at least, were legally required to wear

[17] See Clifford Kirkpatrick, *Nazi Germany: Its Women and Family Life* (Indianapolis, Ind: Bobbs-Merrill, 1938), p. 251, and Ch. 9, pp. 230–253, *passim*.

[18] *Ibid*., p. 252.

[19] *The German Economy at War* (London: Athlone Press, 1965), p. 46. Cf. his Table, p. 47.

veils (*chadhuri*). In 1959 and 1964, these seemingly immutable cultural aspects of Afghan society were undermined by the decrees of the very autocracy that had nourished and protected them for some 200 years. Through royal initiative—embodied in the Constitution of October 1964—Afghanistan gave women legal equality with men all at once. In 1965, four women were elected to the 215-member Afghani Parliament, and in 1966 the King named a woman to the post of Minister of Health.[20]

Admittedly, one could argue that assorted pressures for modernization, from within and without the country, exercised a compelling influence on the autocracy. Yet, how can we account for the fact that relatively backward and poor Afghanistan could no longer "afford" antifeminist policies circa 1960, while the very advanced and technologically ambitious Germany and Italy of the 1930s and 1940s could? Moreover, we find that, other present-day autocracies of traditionalist orientation continue the practices that Afghanistan has begun to abandon.

Saudi Arabia is a case in point. The status of women in virtually all spheres of life there has been that of abject subordination to men. As one author put it:

> [Saudi] Arabia is a man's world. There is no question of equality of sexes—manhood reigns supreme. The male is looked upon as the aggressive and responsible actor in the society, which it is tacitly assumed would disintegrate if men were not present to give direction and enforce order.[21]

With oil royalties pouring in at a rate of some $400 million per year since 1959—and available to the Saudi monarchy in varying amounts since 1933—not only has public education been generally neglected (about 5 per cent of the population was believed to be literate in 1956 among the approximately seven million Saudis), but women have been legally and officially excluded from it. In the late 1950s the first regularly conducted schools for girls were established under private auspices. Thus, the traditionalist monarchy of Saudi Arabia has acted as a brake on the social emancipation of women where the Afghan monarchy has been its accelerator.

Until relatively recent times, traditional autocracy supported antifeminist policies in Iran but here, forty years before the changes in Afghanistan, the personal orientation of the ruler promoted significant innovations. Reza Khan, who became the Shah of Iran in 1926, began an egalitarian modernization at a time when most royal oligarchs of the Near East, Asia, and Africa stood for rigid traditionalism.

[20] See John C. Griffiths, *Afghanistan* (London: Pall Mall Press, 1967), pp. 76–87 and 90–108.

[21] George A. Lipsky, *Saudi Arabia* (New Haven, Conn.: Hraf Press, 1959), p. 297.

Even before experimenting with a mass movement of political supporters in 1939 (two years before his abdication), which distinguished the innovative autocracies of Mustafa Kemal in Turkey or Juan Peron in Argentina, Reza Shah managed to effectuate basic reforms within the framework of a traditional monarchy. Thus:

> For the first time in history, women were considered to be a worthy element in the social structure. Not only did the ruler tear off their veils and introduce them to Western clothing and the facilities for education, but he insisted that they had both rights in and responsibilities to society.[22]

In the industrially advanced countries of Italy and Germany—under democratic regimes—antifeminism was on the decline before Mussolini and Hitler seized power. In the technologically more primitive autocracies of Asia, it was an established traditional value before the onset of innovative policies by the oligarchs of Iran and Afghanistan—although one could argue that it was being undermined by economic, social, and cultural changes within these countries and by pressures from without. In Saudi Arabia, however, with similar traditional values, the political response to such changes and pressures has been as yet almost nil.

In terms of our discussion thus far it seems clear that "political power" can produce dramatically tangible effects on individuals' social status; that it certainly does not simply issue seals of approval to slowly nurturing processes within any given society. It seems reasonably clear that as a causative agent of social change, political power embodied in the idiosyncratic personality and entourage of a ruler may weigh on either side of economic and cultural change. Thus, granted the power of all the environmental influences, the importance of this factor can be underrated only if we are willing to say, "What do fifty or one hundred years matter in the life of a nation?"

In addition, the examples of reform in both Iran and Afghanistan illustrate the oligarchical potential for policy oscillations. In neither case was far-reaching reform originally embedded in any program of an ideologically structured, committed organization or a response to an electors' mandate. So far as the world could judge, the reforms came out of the bounty of monarchical decree power backed by the idiosyncratic personal orientation and determination of the ruler. In both cases, the reforms represented a sharp break with past practice and traditional culture.[23]

[22] Donald N. Wilber, *Contemporary Iran* (New York: Praeger, 1963), p. 75. Reza Khan's son, the current Shah of Iran, has been so innovative in his orientation that some regard him as a self-destructive liquidator of a monarchy that has traditionally rested on a sharply pyramidal social structure. See also, E. A. Bayne, *Four Ways of Politics: State and Nation in Italy, Somalia, Israel, Iran* (New York: American Field Universities Staff, 1965), p. 310.

[23] On social change in earlier autocracies and different interpretations of the experi-

Current differences in the respective positions of women as professionals, educators, and political leaders between, say, Spain and Yugoslavia, cannot be accounted for by any reasonable reading of economic indices. A comparison between Spain and Yugoslavia as of 1939, when both were traditionally oriented autocracies, shows basic similarities in antifeminist orientations; a comparison of Spain between 1931 and 1936 under the Republic to the then Yugoslav monarchy discloses dissimilar feminist orientations.

In all these cases, only the differentiated exercise of political power, not cultural or economic factors can explain divergent feminist orientations (or indeed the differences between Portuguese or Haitian educational systems and, let us say, Bulgarian or Albanian).

The classic mobility patterns of fascism and nazism were substantially, if not wholly, congruent with those of the traditional autocracies. Under both Hitler and Mussolini, land-reform projects came to a virtual halt. Taxation policies became more regressive and discriminatory against have-not elements. Above all, educational access for the broad strata of population was severely curtailed by governmental decrees and by the regimes' deliberate nonsupport of mass education. Antifeminism became an official, *de facto* policy under each regime. Such upward mobility for persons from lower-class, worker and peasant backgrounds as did occur can be more readily attributed to causes beyond the control of the Nazis and Fascists than to any measures that they themselves sponsored or espoused.

The other extreme of political impact on mobility is evidenced by the arch-innovative autocracies: the Communist regimes. Their recruitment, fiscal, and regulative policies have maximized the degree of social upheaval. In a number of concrete historical experiences, Communist regimes have promoted the destruction of status quo social elites on a larger scale and at a more rapid pace than in any other instances in modern history, while promoting the aspirations of persons drawn from the lowest social strata.

---

ence of ancient China, see Wolfram Eberhard, *Social Mobility in Traditional China* (Seiden: E. J. Brill, 1962), and Ping-ti Ho, *The Ladder of Success in Imperial China* (New York: Columbia University Press, 1962). Ho concludes that, "While it is true that in no period of Chinese history did the Confucian ideal fully materialize, the institutionalization of a competive examination system as the main avenue of sociobureaucratic mobility and the existence of a large number of state and private schools are probably without parallel in major societies prior to the coming of the Industrial Revolution and national compulsory education." P. 256. Eberhard concludes that, "ability" was only one factor of importance in promoting mobility in ancient China and that, "Law assigned to each family a definite position and generally tried to prevent changes of status. Where the law permitted change of status, as in the examination system, it limited the number of those who could qualify . . . " p. 264.

One way of changing the distribution of statuses in a society is obviously by bringing the top down—that is, by depriving those who at a particular juncture constitute the upper strata of those perquisites and attributes that differentiate them from those below.

Illustrative of such social changes are agrarian reforms carried out under Communist auspices in Asia and Europe. In every instance, these reforms have featured the principle of outright expropriation of land—that is, confiscation of it without *any* remuneration or compensation to the former owners. Most of these programs have also been characterized by a significant measure of violence and arbitrary, *ad hoc* decision making by administrative authorities acting under the aegis of the party. Violence and the forcible seizure of land were sometimes "allowed to happen" through situations in which the "wrath of the peasantry" was simply allowed to manifest itself freely against rural oppressors, while the party paralyzed the possibilities of any defense against it. Looting and destruction in the countryside were also often informally encouraged by party propaganda.

In other instances, often simultaneously, as classically both in China and the Soviet Union, violence and arbitrariness became the official actions of the State. Certain party decrees sanctioned expropriation and even, more or less euphemistically, the "elimination" or "liquidation" of landlords. The authority for administering such measures was vested in local bodies, under party control, that were given complete and final discretion over the fate of the landlords. They were made judge, jury, and executioner all in one.

Since 1917, all Soviet and Communist land-reform schemes have repeated a familiar pattern of taking over the lands of large, medium, and small holders—in that order—moving, as it were, from the smallest and easiest to the largest and hardest targets: from the expropriation of the great baronial estates to the collectivization of all land. In several cases, the cycle has yet to be completed, although its beginnings still bear the common sequence-of-targets features just described.

One of the persistent characteristics of Communist rural reforms has been the victimization not only of those proprietors who were the official targets of particular expropriation campaigns but also of many who were not. This was hardly avoidable, given the magnitude and the tempo of Communist reforms as well as the loose and arbitrary criteria and procedures by which distinctions among individual cases could be made. Such occasional, even frequent, "injustice"—in terms of the Communists' own standards—have been more or less gleefully tolerated by those eager to realize the grand design of the "reform," whatever the human and material costs to individuals might be.

But even more than a sum of individual tragedies was at issue in the *ad hoc* processes of Communist rural reforms. The party has generally reaped the windfall of the violence, uncertainty, and upheaval that it promoted. As the conflict over collectivization in the Russian countryside increased in the 1930s, recalcitrant peasants frequently slaughtered and burned their livestock and implements rather than surrender them to the Communist collectives. The results for Russian agriculture were disastrous. In livestock breeding, the Soviet economy fell behind the levels achieved under the rule of the Tsar, after more than twenty years of Soviet power and in the face of a considerably larger total population. Whereas in 1916 the total cattle population of Russia (within the borders of today's USSR) was 58.4 million heads, in 1940 it was only 47.8 million; whereas in 1916 there were 23 million pigs, in 1940 there were only 22.5 million.[24]

The comparisons between the beginning of collectivization and its height are even more lopsided. Thus, the actual number of cattle in 1928 was 66.8 million heads; it declined to 33.5 million in 1933. Sheep and goats declined from 114.6 million to 37.3 and pigs from 27.7 to 9.9 million in the same period.[25] Not until 1955 did the Soviet Union get back to the 1928 levels of its cattle population; by that time its human population had just about doubled. All of this has had obvious consequences for human nutrition, precisely for those people in whose interests the Bolshevik Revolution and collectivization presumably took place—the workers and toilers generally.

According to one recent estimate of Russia's agricultural performance under Soviet rule, with the production level achieved in 1928 put at 100 (the last year before collectivization began), it took twelve years to reach an index figure of 114, in 1940. Four years after the beginning of collectivization in 1932, the index stood at 86. This meant that the Soviet regime had fallen behind total output figures that had been achieved under the Tsar in 1913. In that year Russia's agricultural production was estimated at 95 per cent of the 1928 level.[26]

By 1940, on the eve of Soviet entry into World War II, even the advances recorded in arable crops were relatively modest. The production of wheat rose from 26.3 million tons in 1913 to 31.7 million; the output of potatoes from 31.9 million tons to 47.9. Inasmuch as the population of the Soviet Union rose from about 160 million in 1913 to 192 million in 1940, the per capita increases were nil in the case of wheat and only about 25 per cent in the case of potatoes.

[24] Lord Walston, *Agriculture Under Communism* (London: The Bodley Head, 1962), p. 35.

[25] Kenneth R. Whiting, *The Soviet Union Today* (New York: Praeger, 1962), p. 175.

[26] Peter Wiles, "The Pursuit of Affluence: The Economic Record," in Samuel Hendel and Randolph Braham (eds.), *The U.S.S.R. After 50 Years: Promise and Reality* (New York: Alfred A. Knopf, 1967), p. 96, Table 2.

Given this performance of Russia's agriculture, it is clear that the Soviet regime could have improved the diet of the average citizen, if at all, only through the more equitable and effective distribution of agricultural products. Even the latter assumption would require us to believe that (1) the Soviet regime was *not* diverting huge amounts of foodstuffs and agricultural products from the domestic market in order to finance industrialization through purchases abroad and that (2) it had managed to solve the technological bottlenecks of adequate transportation, storage, and distribution facilities that were traditionally inadequate before the victory of the revolution. In fact, both these additional assumptions are false.

The difficulties of guessing the real distribution of goods hidden behind gross production figures in a society obsessed by secrecy are formidable. The most optimistic but reasonable claim about the performance of Soviet agriculture is that if the diet of some categories of employees (in the particularly crucial segments of the industrial complex, for example) was notably improved over the Tsarist period, the diet of many other humble people, peasants and city dwellers, must have been actually worse. And if this was the case, the beneficial impact of the agrarian reforms must be sought elsewhere. Were they worth the sacrifice of some ten million peasant lives?

The Chinese Communists, on the eve of their final victory over Chiang Kai-shek's forces in the mainland, provide us with another excellent illustration in the technique of bringing the top down with a heavy suddenness. The party's Basic Program for Agriculture promulgated on October 10, 1947, declared the "Abolition of landownership rights of all landowners, ancestral shrines, temples, monasteries, schools, and other institutions and organizations [and] cancellation of all debts incurred in the countryside prior to the land reform."[27] The redistribution scheme that followed this declaration of expropriation made no provision for the compensation of former owners, although it allowed them an equal share in "[the] distribution with the rest of the population."[28] Even the latter proviso was undermined by the qualification that "national traitors, collaborators and civil war criminals"[29] were excluded from such redistribution.

In 1949, having already defeated Chiang on the mainland, the Communists undertook a policy of so-called New Democracy, which, like the Russian NEP of 1921–1928, was intended as a breather for the war-torn economy of the country. Expropriation was made more selective: it excluded industrial buildings and properties and certain

[27] Sidney Klein, *The Pattern of Land Tenure Reform in East Asia After World War II* (New York: Bookman Associates, 1958), p. 144.

[28] *Ibid.*, p. 145.

[29] *Ibid.*

kinds of movable assets; and the decree distinguished between landlords and rich peasants offering more lenient treatment to the latter. Significantly, however, the administrative decisions that would determine each specific case were put in the hands of village peasant organizations. They decided "which individuals were landlords or rich peasants, and were to carry out the land reform subject to review by the district or subcounty government."[30] In 1953, the Chinese Communist party reembarked on a tough policy, analogous to the Soviet policy in 1929, eliminating the individual, private cultivation of the soil through the organization of cooperative and collective farms. The peasants, as in the USSR two decades earlier, were drawn into these farms by an assortment of persuasion, incentives, and force.

From the standpoint of its social consequences, the Communist policy succeeded within a period of much less than a decade (1949–1959) in destroying the rural middle and upper classes of China's society. Confiscation and, after redistribution, collectivization not only destroyed any remaining traditional foothold for those classes in the countryside, but made it practically impossible for them to *transfer* resources from one setting or one sector of the economy to another. British mine owners, who were compensated under the nationalization acts of 1945–1951, could maintain their affluence and status by investing elsewhere. For the Chinese middle classes, the Communist reforms represented the end of the road.

These reforms represented a massive and relatively quick change, and from the vantage point of pre-1949 Chinese society, a change toward equality. For whatever could be validly said about the gradual substitution of a new party elite for an old propertied elite, the economic differences among the post-1949 cultivators of the soil were greatly narrowed, and their openly hereditary character was destroyed. The change was probably a source of considerable, although scarcely calculable, psychological gratification to millions of poor peasants throughout China.

On the other hand, it is certain that even for the very poor, and certainly for the peasantry as a whole, the change was in several respects a change for the worse. The sustained drive toward egalitarianism was linked, to borrow a Marxian expression, with a significant immiseration of the rural masses. The material handicaps of communism's rural reforms, not only in China and Russia but in all the Communist states so far, have been sufficiently great to call in question their basic worth.

The land-reform program carried out in North Korea was, if anything, even more arbitrary and violent than the Chinese. Based on an

[30] *Ibid.*, p. 150

agrarian law of March 1946, it provided for the summary expropriation of land and the physical expulsion of the former owners, who ranged from "collaborators with Japanese imperialists" to those who simply "fled from their native places at the time of Korean liberation from Japanese oppression," to all those who did not till the land personally.[31] Unlike the Chinese, the North Korean Communists did not allow expropriated owners to share in the redistribution of land in their home counties. In April 1948, the categories of people who were subject to both expropriation and "evacuation" were more closely defined as:

1. Landlords and property owners;
2. Persons who held high government positions during the rule of the Japanese;
3. Persons who were "intimate with the Japanese while they ruled";
4. Members of the "Democratic Party";
5. Families with members who fled to South Korea;
6. All present and former business men; and
7. All persons suspected of being anti-Communist.[32]

The enormity of the net for wreaking punishment and havoc in the countryside implicit in such a sweeping measure could only be imagined. As Sidney Klein puts it:

> It was apparently the intent of the communists to frighten out of North Korea all persons with wealth or formal education who had not established rapport with the local Peoples Committees. Even if the first six categories had been explained in detail, the seventh was of so "catch-all" a nature that, in practice, hardly a person in North Korea was not liable to "evacuation" or punishment under it.[33]

By every available index the execution of the land reform in China, North Korea, and other Communist states was followed by a period of substantial decline in the productivity of agriculture. Even though, strictly speaking, a causal relationship between the reforms and the subsequent agricultural performance cannot be established beyond *all* doubt, there are good and sufficient reasons to believe that the two are related. Productivity emerged as a victim of massive upheaval, violence, and insecurity engendered by such reforms.

It is of particular interest in view of this relationship (between Communist agrarian reforms and productivity) to consider land reforms carried out under the auspices of democratic political systems. A case in point is the Japanese land-reform program between 1947 and 1950

[31] *Ibid.*, p. 112.
[32] *Ibid.*, p. 116.
[33] *Ibid.*

and its consequences for productivity. The Japanese reform reduced the percentage of arable land in the hands of tenant farmers from 46.3 per cent to 10.8 per cent in a period of three years. But this ambitious program was carried out under elaborate procedural safeguards. The measure was inspired, to be sure, both by the direct and indirect pressure of General MacArthur's Allied Occupation Command.[34] It was nevertheless openly and extensively debated and passed by the Japanese Parliament.

Conforming as it did to the procedural ideals both derived from and consistent with American democratic values, the law was the very antithesis of arbitrary expropriation. It was attacked by Japanese Socialists as too favorable to the landlords and not radical enough. Provision was made for compensation to landlords. Moreover, landlords were given substantial representation on the local Land Committees, which were charged with the execution of the scheme, as well as on the district level and national committees, which oversaw the whole operation.

For example, R. P. Dore notes:

> The government-appointed Central Land Committee, a general policy-making body whose chief function was the scrutiny of administrative orders issued under the Acts, consisted of 8 tenants, 8 landlords, 2 representatives of peasant unions and 5 university professors.[35]

Landlords represented the largest number of chairmen of these committees in 1947.[36] Between 1947 and 1949, landlords presented 95,000 objections to actions taken against them; some 25,000 appeals to district level committees and ultimately 4,000 law suits were processed by the courts, and of these 119 suits alleged "unconstitutionality" of the whole land-reform program.[37] Notwithstanding this landlord litigation, the proportion of arable land under tenancy was reduced by 75 per cent in three years' time. The results were not nearly as sweeping and complete in Japan as they were in China or North Korea. Landlords, as a class, were not wholly destroyed; some of them even managed to dispossess their tenants by taking over the cultivation of the land themselves—that is, by renouncing absentee ownership. But, if the extent of the social revolution resultant from this reform in Japan's countryside was not nearly as complete as on the Asian mainland, the advantages of continuing social and economic relationships were reflected in the peace of the countryside. And

[34] See R. P. Dore, *Land Reform in Japan* (London: Oxford University Press, 1959), Chs. VI and VII.

[35] *Ibid.*, p. 140.

[36] *Ibid.*, p. 159.

[37] *Ibid.*, p. 170.

thence also it was reflected in the increasing productivity of Japanese agriculture. No peasant or worker in Japan paid with starvation for the benefit of a thorough rural revolution.[38] Japan did not pay the price of extreme sociopolitical mobilization incurred elsewhere, either in lives or productivity indices. Whereas Chinese agricultural production in the 1960s was insufficient to insure the nutrition of the people at levels of the 1930s,[39] in Japan remarkable nutritional advances were made in the wake of land reforms. Between 1949 and 1953, the levels of consumption of agricultural products (with the 1934–1936 average as 100) rose from 88.3 in 1949 to 131.0 in the rural areas and from 65.0 to 94.0 in urban areas.[40] More impressive gains have been recorded since 1953.

From the standpoint of agricultural productivity, reforms undertaken on the Japanese pattern, with American inspiration and backing, have similarly correlated with fairly spectacular successes in Taiwan, and with somewhat more mixed economic results in South Korea.

Democracy, unlike communism, cannot be said to have one distinctive attitude on the land question, let alone a policy. Democracies may or may not support land-redistribution programs depending on their particular economic conditions and in the last analysis on the disposition of their electorates. Their systemic attitudes may be said to be pragmatic and flexible, not fixed. Where they further significantly differ from the Communist systems is that, insofar as they do implement agrarian reforms, their procedural characteristics tend to reduce overt conflict and violence. This appears to have some favorable economic consequences of its own. Democracies in general also have a tendency to devote considerable public resources to the support of various kinds of public service activities that aid private enterpreneurs including farmers: through research, education, public works projects, and the like.[41]

[38] *Ibid.*, p. 173. "... the amount of blood spilled per acre was remarkably small. Altogether only 110 incidents between landlords and tenants involving physical violence were reported in the two years 1947–48, and not one life was lost."

[39] Lord Walston, *op. cit.*, p. 83.

[40] Klein, *op. cit.*, Table 16, p. 234.

[41] See Charles M. Hardin, *Freedom in Agricultural Education* (Chicago: University of Chicago Press, 1955), on some interesting aspects of the American experience. Professor Hardin notes that, in the United States, federal domination has failed to follow the federal dollar because of a jealous regard for the maintenance of local control, at the grass roots; any such effort "... would be publicized immediately and countered by the enormous resistance which land-grant institutions... can muster in the general public, alumni, and supporting groups." P. 28. Traditional autocracies not only often fail to give such help but hamper or destroy the communications infrastructure that guards the independence of recipients.

Among non-Communist autocracies, the pattern of land-related attitudes is even more variable than among the democracies. At one extreme we find innovational autocracies whose reformist characteristics approach—even if they do not match—the degree of agrarian change sponsored by Communist regimes. At the other extreme are the traditionally oriented regimes whose land policies are characterized by opposition and/or indifference to land-redistribution schemes; and these provide a very low level of publicly financed services to the farmer.

An example of the first kind was offered by the Egyptian UAR under Nasser's rule. Except for substantial holdings of the former royal family (178,000 acres), UAR reform involved payment to the former owners for lands taken over. Within three years of Nasser's seizure of power, by 1955, some 250,000 acres of land (roughly 20 per cent of the arable area of the country) was redistributed to some 69,000 families of small holders.[42]

An example of the second type of autocracy was described by the United Nations' *FAO Mission for Nicaragua* in 1950. Here, the agricultural economy was not merely based on sharp, long-standing inequalities between relatively few rich landlords and a mass of impoverished tenants; agriculture was largely left to the private devices of the individual proprietors. The public interest expressed through governmental and/or voluntary technical, scientific, advisory, or administrative bodies—and concerned with the over-all problems of land technology, of conservation, sanitation, pollution, reforestation, and the like—was hardly felt at all. This lack of public welfare programs in agriculture was only partly, and in a secondary sense, a function of Nicaragua's economic underdevelopment. It was in the first place the function of political direction (or misdirection) of resources. As the UN mission observed:

> Expenditure on agricultural improvement in 1946–48 amounted to . . . 1.5 per cent of total Government expenditure. [This] ratio is low compared with many countries that are less dependent on primary production and the disbursement has also been, in part, technically ineffective. Large sums have been advanced as credits to producers, but without appropriate safeguards.[43]

This strange imbalance in public spending on land-related improvements was taking place in a period of prosperity—thanks to the rising prices of coffee in the world markets—in a country whose economy was almost totally dependent on agriculture. There is every indication

[42] See Doreen Warriner, *Land Reform and Development in the Middle East: A Study of Egypt, Syria and Iraq* (London: Royal Institute of International Affairs, 1957), pp. 34–35.

[43] FAO Mission for Nicaragua, United Nations (New York: 1950), p. 13.

that this singular public inattentiveness to the needs of the land and the people living on it reflected far more the indifference of the Nicaraguan oligarchy than the dearth of material resources. The point is not that the country's organization was not efficient in dealing with its various problems by the criteria of the more technologically advanced nations, or that it was different. It simply did not exist. And its nonexistence was part and parcel of an oligarchic acquiescence in the management and the perquisites of status quo interests come what may.

There is at least a *prima facie* case to be made, on the basis of the performance of all Communist states so far, that the impact of Communist rule on agriculture has been adverse. No Communist regime has as yet succeeded in producing remotely spectacular agricultural output. On the contrary, the Communist states have fallen far behind the production advances achieved in many nonrevolutionary economies. They have not done as well as the nations of Western Europe and North America and have done less well than such states as Israel and Japan, whose per capita incomes are in the category of the USSR, Czechoslovakia, and East Germany. (See Table 20.)

Table 20
Comparison of Selected Crop Yields in East and West Germany
(100 Kg units per 1 hectare or 2.5 acres of land)

	Wheat	Rye	Barley	Oats	Mixed Grain	Maize	Sugar Beets
East Germany	37.8	26.6	34.9	31.4	27.4	23.7	333
West Germany	41.2	32.4	36.2	33.6	32.8	47.2	470

	Potatoes	Onions	Tomatoes	Cabbage	Cauliflower
East Germany	205	236	173	304	229
West Germany	301	229	430	358	220

	Green Beans	Green Peas	Cucumbers	Dry Beans
East Germany	62	52	128	14.1
West Germany	106	107	218	27

This table is based on FAO, U.N. Production Yearbook, Vol. 22, 1968, pp. 36-70.

To say that the agricultural sectors of the Communist economies have been deliberately depleted, drained, and denied capital investments in order to finance spectacular advances in industrialization is a partial explanation of what has happened; it is not an adequate justification in economic terms. If we choose to designate Soviet economic advances in the fifty-year period since 1917 as spectacular, we must also acknowledge that twentieth-century Japan and Germany have made analogously spectacular advances. Yet they, and other fast-developing countries, have combined industrial and agricultural growth in which the Communists have remarkably failed.

One can only speculate on the causes of the chronic agricultural crisis under Communist regimes. Some attribute it to an innate incompatibility of Communist collectivism with the incentive psychology of farmers. It is sometimes believed that poor agricultural performance reflects either indifference toward productivity on behalf of the State (rather than for one's own benefit) or insecurity in the case of East European farmers who live in constant dread of collectivization. Some see the causes as less fundamental (the regimes have not yet spent enough on this sector of the economy). Some see them in extraneous factors, as for instance in the case of USSR: poor climate and topography in most areas under cultivation. Some see it as a problem of administration with faults attributed to overcentralization and rigid price and tax policies.

Not all Communist states have pursued a single land policy; but all Communist regimes have shared a common ideological platform that consigns the farmer's property to eventual oblivion. In those periods and places where the Communist regimes have attempted to implement their ideological aspirations, economic and human losses have been prevalent. And there is some evidence that as radical policies have been eased—in Russia, Poland, and Yugoslavia, among several examples—there have been favorable changes in agricultural productivity. This was the experience of the Soviet Union under NEP; by 1928, Russian agriculture had advanced to peaks of performance never attained before and not to be matched until 1955. The crucial point about Communist agricultural policy is that its basis is not to be found in the search for prosperity or even industrialization. It is rooted in a dogmatic political-ideological commitment against the institution of private property in land. Its ultimate justification and criterion is found in the collectivist reshaping of society, not in the mundane, pragmatic satisfaction of people's wants.

It is of interest to note that taking into comparison two great periods of world industrial expansion (1870–1913) and (1950–1960), the most spectacular percentage growth of GNP per head of population was achieved by Japan.

According to Peter Wiles, the figure was 3.0 per cent for Japan between 1870 and 1913, as compared with 2.3 for Sweden; 2.2 per cent for the United States; 1.8 per cent for Imperial Germany. Russian expansion was only 1.1 per cent per capita. In the 1950s, Russia—under Communist rule—achieved a growth rate of 5.5 per cent; but Japan—under the most democratic political system in her history, and with no traumatic upheavals in her countryside—advanced to an 8.8 per cent per capita growth between 1953 and 1963.[44]

The unique results obtained by Soviet policy were not economic but social; the policy achieved drastic changes in the social physiognomy of the nation not uniquely successful increases in industrial-economic might. To the latter end it was probably not merely superfluous but quite probably detrimental.

The social revolution carried out, partly through such economic measures, was reflected in the findings made in the early 1950s by G. K. Schueller in his study, *The Politburo*.[45] These showed not merely a great change in the socioeconomic background of Russia's rulers since Tsarism, but also a great chasm in social status as between the prerevolutionary leadership of the party and the postrevolutionary leadership. The former consisted predominantly of persons of middle-class origin who had studied at universities, lived abroad, and engaged in literary work. The latter were persons of low social origin, with no higher education.[46] By the late 1950s and 1960s, the Soviet leaders began to reflect the educational as well as social revolutions of the Soviet society of the past half century. They became predominantly persons with higher technical and university education but of overwhelmingly peasant and worker family backgrounds.[47]

Few contrasts could be more striking than the evolution of leadership positions under the Nazi regime in Germany. It was explored by Maxwell Knight in his study *The German Executive 1890–1933*.[48] Knight showed that Hitler's cabinet more than doubled the percentage of aristocrats within it in the period 1933–1945, as compared with the democratic Weimar Republic of 1918–1933, and decreased the percentage of the working-class elements.

Classified by family backgrounds, under the Empire, between the

[44] Wiles, *op. cit.*, p. 98.

[45] Hoover Institute Series B, No. 2 (Stanford, Calif.: Stanford University Press, 1951). *Cf.* J. B. Moore, Jr., "The Communist Party of the Soviet Union: 1928–1944: A Study in Elite Formation and Function," *American Sociological Review*, Vol. 9, No. 3 (June 1944), pp. 267–278.

[46] Schueller, *op. cit.*, pp. 32–33.

[47] See Grey Hodnett "The Obkom First Secretaries," *Slavic Review*, Vol. 24, No. 4 (December 1965), pp. 636–652, and Table 4, particularly. *Cf.* A. Doak Barnett, *Communist China: The Early Years 1949–55* (New York: Praeger, 1964), p. 56, on the vigorous efforts to make the ruling CCP proletarian in a predominantly peasant milieu. See also, John W. Lewis, *Leadership in Communist China* (Ithaca, N.Y.: Cornell University Press, 1962), p. 108, Table 1, on social backgrounds of the CCP members in 1956 and 1957; in the latter year it was 66.8 per cent "peasant"; 13.7 per cent "worker"; 14.8 per cent "intellectual"; and 4.7 per cent "other," according to official data.

[48] Hoover Institute Studies, Series B, No. 4 (Stanford, Calif.: Stanford University Press, 1952).

years 1890–1918, 64.5 per cent of the Kaiser's cabinet members were aristocrats; 35.5 per cent were of the middle class; and there was no representation for labor. Under Weimar, the ratios changed to 11.5, 78, and 11 per cent, respectively; under the Nazis they became 27, 70, and 3 per cent, respectively.

Based on a classification by occupations rather than family backgrounds, Hitler more than doubled the percentage of men drawn from the military and from business. He appreciably decreased those drawn from the professions such as law, journalism, medicine, science, and education. Although he somewhat increased the number of farmers (from 7 to 12 per cent), he decreased the share of workers from 11 to 3 per cent.[49]

There is no evidence that we know of that denies the factual validity of a recent statement by William M. Mandel:

> There is nothing in the Soviet Union like the range from people sleeping in doorways to others who have one mansion in Hyannis Port, another in Florida, a $40,000-a-year Manhattan penthouse, a ranch in the West and a home on the Riviera. . . . *No* Soviet industrial "tycoon," including the man who heads the steel industry, bigger than U.S. Steel, nor the head of the petroleum industry, bigger than Standard Oil, nor the head of the merchant fleet, bigger than Niarchos' or Onassis', earns even $15,000 a year, although that is no money at all by the standards of the wealthy in underdeveloped, poverty-stricken countries like India or even Ghana. Nor does any Soviet Party or government official, including the premier, earn that much. Nor does any movie star. A handful of the most creative people do: a few authors, some scientists, and musicians and dancers who perform abroad.[50]

Many issues posed by this relationship, nevertheless, still remain open: Is economic equality in any degree desirable? Is the measure of equality brought about under communism worth the sacrifices

[49] See *ibid.*, pp. iii–viii. See also Donald R. Matthews, *The Social Background of Political Decision Makers* (Garden City, N.Y.: Doubleday and Company, 1954), Ch. IV, on British decision makers (for example, Table 10, Members of British Cabinet 1801–1935, and so on).

[50] "Reflections on the Soviet System: Toward a More Human and Equal Society," in Samuel Hendel and Randolph L. Braham (eds.), *The U.S.S.R. After 50 Years: Promise and Reality* (New York: Alfred A. Knopf, 1967), p. 200. *Cf.* William Ebenstein, *Today's Isms* (Englewood Cliffs, N.J.: Prentice-Hall, 1958), pp. 54–55, and particularly pp. 49–51. Nothing that Professor Ebenstein has to say about the disparity of differentials between skilled and unskilled workers in the USSR as compared with the United States bears on the preceding statement. The proposition advanced by Ebenstein that in Communist states "the income spread between the different classes has been steadily widening" is now both obsolete so far as it goes and is not directly relevant to the issue of disparities between Communist and non-Communist states.

apparently required to achieve it?[51] Finally, has this equality, in terms of incomes, been linked with other undesirable social manifestations?

The chief of Soviet steel or oil industry may be more "equal" vis-à-vis his employees as far as remuneration is concerned. But he is more of a monopolist in the USSR—the *sole* employer in a whole industry —than his U. S. Steel or Standard Oil counterpart in the democratic West.

Democracies have occupied a middle ground between the innovative Communist systems and the traditional oligarchies. They have been unable, if not unwilling, to follow either extreme of policy: utterly demolish the haves or permanently subjugate the have-nots.

As we have noted earlier (see Chapter 4), the techniques and the rules of democratic politics with their emphasis on persuasion and organization have given the well-to-do considerable advantages; these have historically helped them to significantly offset the mere power of numbers on the side of the poor. In terms of the social derivation of their political leaders, at least, all democracies show a certain lag, in the sense that their electorates tend to choose for office not their equals but their superiors—if not directly superior in wealth then at least in those qualities that money is most likely to buy. On the other hand, as with a number of other differences that we have explored in earlier chapters, there is an important sense in which the differences among the democracies tend to be narrower. No category of the population in any democracy falls into a *de facto* "outlaw class," as once landlords in Russia or Jews in Germany were. *Legal* and *de facto* disabilities—as between poor and rich, haves and have-nots, those who are socially or ethnically or otherwise in the mainstream, and those who are "marginal" or a minority—are kept sufficiently *distinct,* so as to allow a reasonable measure of hope for self-improvement to virtually all persons in society: an open horizon for the future.

To be sure, the patterns of social mobility, upward and downward, are, like virtually all social trends, also heavily influenced by industrialization. But, with all due allowance for the factor of industrialization —with its international tendency to convert farmers into workers and to replace individual entrepreneurs with a bureaucratic managerial stratum—politics has continued to play a major role in shaping the mobility patterns of all extant societies.

Democracy as a political system has certain procedural implications

[51] For a discussion of the sacrifice of the goals of economic development to the values of racial and ethnic equality in Africa, see Donald Rothchild, "African Nationalism and Racial Minorities," *East African Journal,* Vol. 2, No. 8 (December 1965), pp. 14–22. See also his "Ethnic Inequalities in Kenya," *The Journal of Modern African Studies*, Vol. 7, No. 4 (December 1969), pp. 689–711.

for any and all kinds of social reforms. As we have noted earlier, its mechanics and institutions are geared simultaneously to the values of consent and due process for all actual and potential participants in public decision making. Because of these values, social reforms enacted by democratic regimes cannot be brought about in a summary manner—that is, without discussion, argument, and deliberation. They cannot be brought into being without the opposition to them being heard, nor implemented in such a fashion that the political and civil rights of the minority opposed to reform can be denied.

The foundation stone of the democratic system is in the uninterrupted genuineness of the power of the electorate. That power cannot be vitiated or foreclosed; if it were, the system would cease to be democratic. For the British Labour Government of 1945–1951 to have nationalized certain industries was perfectly legitimate and consistent with the democratic values of the system, so long as the electorate was not being denied the opportunity of changing its mind on another occasion at some future date, and so long as the "losers" and the advocates or sympathizers of the "losers" (that is, the former owners and their conservative defenders) were not denied the rights of equal citizenship with the "winners" or the gainers.

Reform within the context of an autocracy, however, can readily assume a summary form, either through violence or even legally, in the narrow sense that the ruler's fiat may be embodied in a decree that may have a legal form and be binding on the courts. Eichmann's Final Solution could be regarded as a social reform, as indeed it was by the precepts of Nazi ideology. It was also legal in the sense that it was based on the authentic decrees of an authority that German courts at the time recognized as the supreme legislator of the Reich. But because of the closed process through which it was elaborated, and the finitely arbitrary procedure through which it was implemented, the tragedy of genocide was as far removed from the operational values of democracy as any action of a public authority could be.

Nevertheless, the procedural conveniences of a well-entrenched autocracy provided Hitler—and Eichmann—with undeniable advantages in the realization of their social reform. No one could publicly say "nay" to them without running the risk of forfeiting his life; there was no need to publicly explain and justify actions that could never have been explained or justified publicly either in Germany or elsewhere. Thus, Hitler could proceed farther and faster in his chosen field of "racial reform" than he conceivably would have been able to do with all these impediments in full force.

CHAPTER 9
JUSTICE AND POLICE POWER

COURTS and police generally distribute different kinds of justice in political systems—or subsystems—in which the political participation of the citizenry is widely diffused and effective, and in which it is drastically limited and lopsided. The relationship between the citizen and his system of justice entails a number of operational features that can be discussed here under two headings: *procedure* and *substance*.[1]

Procedural aspects of justice are those that, in common American and Anglo-Saxon usage, are generally subsumed under the term *due process*. The question here is, regardless of the character of the laws, how are they enforced on the citizen? At one extreme, we may find that the laws are bad in the sense that they embody norms widely different from the expectations and demands of the populace; or in that they are extremely harsh or unduly restrictive; or in that they possibly are grossly unfair in the treatment of some citizens, or some interests in the system, as opposed to others. But, we may nevertheless find that, given any or all of these defects, the administration of justice is efficient, quick, cheaply and equally available to all citizens,

[1] On the subject of political manipulation of the judiciary, see Otto Kirchheimer, *Political Justice* (Princeton, N.J.: Princeton University Press, 1961).

fair and equitable to all—*insofar* as the law provides for it—and scrupulous of the citizen's rights and the security of his person and his property.

On the opposite side, we may find justice that is eminently equitable in the substance of its laws—judged by any of these standards—and yet eminently unsatisfactory in its actual enforcement. Is the citizen subject to arbitrary arrest and detention? Do police officials carry out raids, searches, and seizures without judicial authorization? How honest and efficient are the judges? Are the citizen's rights to a fair and speedy trial maintained? Can the citizen always be represented by an attorney? Can he always present his side of the case? Are judicial proceedings subject to public scrutiny and review where the citizen, or his attorney, claims denial of rights and a miscarriage of justice? How equitable is the penal system?

Problems of this latter sort relate more to the administrative and procedural side of the law than to its substance. Ideally, the most effective system of justice is based on just laws, justly and efficiently executed. In practice, whatever standards we may choose for the measurement of justice and right, wide disparities between law on the books and law in application to actual cases are commonplace.

At the outset of our discussion here, we shall make two clarifying observations: The differences to be detected in the judicial outputs of different political systems cannot be realistically examined in terms of absolutes; they can be examined only in degrees. Many an innocent man has been condemned before the most learned and dispassionate judges under circumstances embodying the most far-reaching protections of his rights. On occasion, justice may also be rendered under circumstances in which we might least expect it, possibly by chance, and actually in spite of official efforts to thwart it. Nor can we assume that the political determinants of the judicial process and of its outputs are "the only ones that count." The influence of purely economic or technological factors on the system of justice can be readily appreciated insofar as the training and equipment of a police force are concerned, and insofar as the general and professional education of the judges, of prison administrators, and ultimately even of the whole public, to the extent that jurors are employed in the courts, are concerned. The quantity and the quality of the whole system are dependent on how much wealth is made available to support it. This in turn depends to some extent on the total resources. And this gets us back to the basic question of how much and what kind of justice the rulers are willing to support.

If we start at the totalitarian innovative-mobilizational extreme, we find that the individual's welfare is seriously undermined in both the substance and the procedure of law. It is undermined first of all by the nonrecognition of the fundamental equality of all persons before the law. It is eroded by the deliberate confusion of individual and collective responsibility; by the denial of political recourse and public scrutiny of the regular judicial process; by the arbitrary nature of police and prison administration; and finally also by the resort to *ad hoc*—virtually private—secret proceedings in lieu of and apart from the organs and processes of ordinary judicial authorities.

In the totalitarian regimes, law and law enforcement serve as instruments of far-reaching social engineering by the rulers and are permeated by an officially sanctioned "subjectivity."[2] This subjectivity enjoins judges, policemen, and administrators to regard themselves as, above all, front-line fighters for the realization of the political objectives of the regime. These objectives, not the case before them, they must regard as paramount. Independence and impartiality as judicial values are either completely denied or grotesquely minimized. The principle that justice be rendered to persons on the basis of law and the facts of the case, without regard to extraneous considerations, is publicly decried as nothing less than treasonable.

Vigilance against the foe—who must be exterminated—and the successful achievement of dictatorial objectives can never be allowed to be compromised by the claims of an individual. Individual rights are subordinated to the higher, transcendent interests posited by the regime in such a way that, as a rule, the individual may obtain satisfaction through legal proceedings only if, and to the extent that, his claims do not clash with public policy. The latter may *never* be sacrificed to the former. The former must *always* be sacrificed to the latter. In cases in which public officials believe that the conduct or the thinking, or possibly even the mere existence, of the citizen poses a threat to the security or other politically "vital" interest of the regime, they may take action against him. This action, from arrest to execution (or release from punitive confinement), may be carried out wholly outside the regular judicial apparatus. Arbitrary and secret proceed-

[2] Although information on this subject is obviously scarce, usually carefully concealed and scattered in official budgets, the police systems of the several modern autocracies, Fascist and Communist, appear to have drawn and manipulated vast sums of money. Robert Conquest, *The Soviet Police System* (New York: Praeger, 1968), estimates that the police apparatus in the USSR consumed 1.1 billion rubles or 2.0 per cent of the national budget in 1934; in 1950 the police absorbed 21.1 billion or 5.2 per cent of the budget, and 14 billion rubles or 2.7 per cent in 1954, p. 38. In 1941, 1.2 per cent of the USSR industrial production originated in police-operated enterprises. The goods included furniture, ironware, cameras, shoes and construction machinery, p. 85. Cf. Robert M. Slusser, *The Soviet Secret Police* (New York: Praeger, 1957), pp. 96–179. Although he does not give any figures, Edward Crankshaw, *Gestapo* (New York: The Viking Press, 1957), pp. 88–96 and pp. 132–144, describes the great magnitude of secret police operations in Nazi Germany.

ings, in lieu of an open judicial process, are not accidental among these regimes, even if the *actual use* of such proceedings, and the severity of the punishments meted out in them, varies from time to time. Totalitarian regimes could hardly hope to change the world around them and to mold men to their preconceived images without manipulating the law to their purposes.

The openness and predictability of the legal system are sources of security and continuity in any society. People, as individuals and in the organized groups that they form, generally know what kinds of activities are "crimes," how they will be punished, and what the sequence of accusation, trial, sentence, and execution of the punishment is likely to be. They know what recourse is open to them and what lawful limits exist for their activity. The answers to any of these questions in nontotalitarian regimes, even if in some cases beyond "what everyone knows" through everyday experience, are readily available to every attorney and ultimately to any interested citizen who can read the printed page.

The absence of such openness and predictability, however, allows totalitarian regimes to pulverize actual and even potential opposition among the population. It instills a sense of fear, suspicion, and isolation in the individual that makes him a pliant tool of the dictatorship and weakens his links to private and group interests that are not officially sanctioned and favored. The individual under the innovative totalitarian system of justice can never be sure that what was not a crime yesterday may not become a crime today. He does not know what the rulers may construe to be a "political security matter" rather than an ordinary legal matter. Even if the use of the procedure is rare, the citizen can never forget the possibility of being arrested and banished to prison, even executed, without anyone knowing about it—except for the "authorities," of course. The latter, too, are a mystery. Would they strike because of a careless remark about someone or something? Would they act on the advice of an informer whose identity may never be known and whose veracity cannot be challenged? The arrest could take place anywhere, at any time of the day or night, with no opportunity even to inform one's family or to obtain legal aid. And the captors, prosecutors, judges, and executioners would always remain mysterious shadowy figures—nameless, faceless officials of the "secret police."[3]

One of the ways in which the deliberate augmentation of fear and insecurity has been promoted by totalitarian mechanisms of justice

[3] For a vivid documentation—from the testimony of victims, observers, and participants—about summary justice on a mass scale under the innovative-mobilizational Castro regime in Cuba, see *Cuba and the Rule of Law*, International Commission of Jurists (Geneva: 1962), Part IV.

has involved pledging by the released, or "rehabilitated," victims that they would never disclose what had happened to them on pain of punishment to themselves and to their families. Historically, the Nazi Gestapo, the Italian Fascist OVRA, and the successive Soviet institutions (Cheka, GPU, NKVD, MVD, and KGB) have made the preceding practices virtually standard procedure. The methods that they institutionalized in the interrogation, detention, imprisonment, and even the execution of persons fall readily into the category of what the United States Constitution prohibits under the clause concerning cruel and unusual punishment, unpredictably and arbitrarily dispensed.

What we have described so far deals with "justice" dispensed through the subterranean channels of the police apparatus—relatively extraordinary even in innovative-totalitarian systems. The operation of this part of the judicial system could be said to have historically fluctuated depending on the intensity of the policies pursued by the totalitarian rulers.

In Germany in 1934, "justice by terror" became singularly salient as Hitler moved to liquidate assorted, and in some cases only potential, opposition to his newly established power within the Nazi movement itself. Analogously, Stalin's drastic purge of the Communist party in Russia in the mid and late 1930s saw an enormous enlargement of the role of the secret police and the essentially terroristic enforcement of justice. With the Nazis, the program of extermination of the Jews and the supervision of the concentration camps were largely handled by extraordinary guardians of justice—the Gestapo and the SS. *Ad hoc* "justice by the gun" was in the forefront of the Soviet liquidation of Russia's rural middle class.

On the other hand much, and at times most, of the judicial process in all the Communist, Nazi, and Fascist states has remained within the framework of courts and judges established by law and operating within reasonably well-articulated rules and procedures. We may at once hasten to say that the contrast between justice meted out by these courts and by the courts of the most effective Western democracies is narrower than between the extremes of rule by law and rule by terror. But even among these relatively regular and open mechanisms of justice, important practical differences can be noted.

The substance of the law under these regimes has been one of the sources of inequity to every man in court. For example, with respect to basic, constitutionally guaranteed rights among Communist states, we find a qualification on their applicability that commands the judges to protect such rights *only* if they serve the interests of the working people in the construction of a Socialist and Communist society. These same rights are denied by law, explicitly and implicitly, to those whose political purposes in availing themselves of them—that is, rights pertaining to the free exercise of speech, association, or religion, for example—are opposed to the political purposes of the regime. The effect of such a qualification of rights is to deny them precisely to those who are most in need of them!

In all the innovative-totalitarian systems the judge is expected to be an ideologue of the regime, be it Marxist-Leninist, Fascist, or Nazi, not a mere legal expert. As such, even in the regular courts and with ostensibly objective, codified written rules to follow, he must apply subjective justice. He ought not give equal consideration to the enemies of the State and the people *and* to the supporters of the Leader or the party. If need be, the law must punish the innocent for the acts of the guilty. It must deny redress to those who are politically impure. It must punish even if there is no crime in a strictly legal sense because the "healthy racial instinct of the community," or the Fuehrer's will, or the interests of proletarian dictatorship demand it. The law can afford to bear a semblance of impartiality, objectivity, and predictability *only* when the person or subject before it is such that the totalitarian leadership does not wish to interpose policy on law. This may be either because the regime considers the nature of the case to be politically nonsensitive; or because in a particular case it wishes to stage a show of judicial objectivity for the benefit of an international public; or finally because it wishes to accommodate certain interests whose support it values.

Impartial justice may be frequent in so-called civil cases—that is, those among private citizens rather than between the citizens and the State. Thus, the Soviet citizen who sues his neighbor for the theft of his personal property or other personal damage may generally get reasonably speedy and effective redress in the courts, *provided* that his neighbor is not a significant party functionary. In some areas of law, such as those pertaining to marriage and divorce, for example, the regime may be willing to rely on the written law and the routine determinations of the judges. In some cases, as for instance when the Soviet regime was anxious to show the United States and world opinion that it was giving a fair trial to the U-2 spy pilot, Francis Gary Powers, the punitive objectives may be subordinated to the display of equity in the proceedings. In the Nazi experience, the trial of Georgi Dimitrov in 1934 on the charge of plotting the Reichstag fire was aimed at creating widespread domestic and international credibility for the hoped-for verdict through the openness and the procedural correctness of the whole affair.

Finally, as Ernest Fraenkel described it in *The Dual State*, autocratic-totalitarian regimentation may leave certain areas of life more or less legally intact—that is, leave them to the ordinary, already established judicial processes and norms—partly because this is indispensable to an effective functioning of some very necessary institutions—in the Nazi case, it was the private economic sector. Lawlessness and insecurity with respect to fulfilment of contracts, for example, would have jeopardized the operation of business firms and thus also of the whole German economy. The willingness to maintain a *de facto* rule of law for some segments of the community under its sway may also be construed as a concession to the power of interests whose support the regime needs.

It is quite likely that had Hitler immediately extended the same justice on the same scale to the businessmen, landlords, generals, and bureaucrats of the Third Reich that he extended to Jews, Marxists, and assorted liberal opponents of his regime, he would not have survived the 1930s.

In 1934, the Nazis established so-called People's Courts, which preempted jurisdiction in virtually all sorts of political cases from the regular courts of justice. Decrees passed as early as May and October of 1933 prepared the ground for the Nazis' new political courts in that they made the most wide-ranging, and often trivial, acts and utterances fall within the definition of "treasonable offenses." At the apex of the People's Courts structure, The People's High Court was established. Made up of two Nazi judges and five Nazi laymen, it represented the highest and last instance of appeal from the People's Courts. All of these courts constituted a veritably classic illustration of legalized illegality, in that their proceedings and decisions were predicated solely on the desirability of destroying the enemies of the regime. There was not even any institutionalized pretense that the judges and the accused were meeting in court on the common ground of a law binding equally on both. The People's Courts were in fact agencies for meting out politically desirable punishments with a dosage of fanfare and publicity designed to intimidate other actual and potential foes.[4]

In addition, of course, the Gestapo performed a complete set of judicial functions from arrest, detention, interrogation, and sentence to the execution of that sentence in a clandestine, secretive fashion. There was no judicial or administrative recourse against it or review of its actions; its powers combined those of judge, jury, jailer, and hangman in one agency. Political recourse was possible against the Gestapo's actions through Himmler, Hitler, Goering, and their lesser adjutants for those with "inside connections" and influence, of course. The concentration camps with their millions of victims were adminis-

[4] See William L. Shirer, *The Rise and Fall of the Third Reich* (New York: Simon and Schuster, 1960), p. 269.

tered by the SS in collaboration with, but apart from, the Gestapo. These camps to the average German citizen were forbidden soil. Consignment to them, the treatment of prisoners within them, and possible release from them could not be negotiated through action in courts, judicial or administrative.[5] The physical and psychological impact on the victims of this Nazi machine of political "justice" has been amply enough explored in trials like the one at Nuremberg in 1946 and numerous ones hence.

With respect to criminal law, and particularly to crimes against public property and public officials, totalitarian codes of law have been distinguished by the vastness—and vagueness—of their sweep. The effect has been to make even relatively trivial and in some cases unintentional acts by individuals harshly punishable as crimes against the State. Under Soviet codes:[6]

> Any act shall be considered a crime against the administration if, while not directly aiming at the overthrow of the Soviet authority . . . it nevertheless leads to a disturbance of the regular activities of the organs of administration or of the national economy and is accompanied by opposition to the organs of authority and obstruction of their activities, disobedience to the laws, or other activities causing a weakening of the power and authority of the government. (Article 59).
>
> Thus, if a driver has been absent from work for several hours during harvest time he can be punished either for "nonfulfilment of his obligation under a contract with a public institution" (deprivation of liberty for a period of not less than six months, Article 131 of the Penal Code) or for counter-revolutionary sabotage (deprivation of liberty for a period not exceeding ten years, Article 59, 3c).
>
> If a worker or peasant, after having lost his patience and self-control, attacks his boss he can be punished for insulting a representative of authority in the course of execution of his official duties (deprivation of liberty or forced labor for a period not exceeding six months, Article 76) or for an act of terrorism (the supreme measure of social defense: death by shooting, Article 58, 8).
>
> If a hungry Soviet citizen should express his disappointment in an empty store and say that there are some people who are supplied with everything, he can be sentenced for an act of hooliganism (deprivation of liberty for a period not

[5] See Joseph Tenenbaum, *Race and Reich: The Story of an Epoch* (New York: Twayne Publishers, 1956), pp. 163–172, for the early years. *Cf.* Eugen Kogon, *The Theory and Practice of Hell* (New York: Twayne Publishers, 1951).

[6] George C. Guins, *Soviet Law and Soviet Society* (The Hague: Martinus Nijhoff, 1954), p. 311. Some of the penalties enumerated here have been lessened since; the elasticity of the legal definitions has remained.

exceeding three months, Article 74) or for an act of anti-Soviet propaganda which must be punished as one of the major crimes against the Soviet state (Article 5, 10).

Great latitude to the judiciary in ascertaining the evidence of the commission of treasonable acts has been characteristic of totalitarian regimes. Provisions explicitly allowing the punishment of persons other than those committing the crimes or having verified prior knowledge of them have also been sanctioned.

Thus, the regular courts have operated under a system in which the law itself has been at once harsh and broadly structured in a catchall fashion, backed up by injunctions to the judges to apply it subjectively. The safeguards of this subjectivity have come from a number of positive sources including indoctrination of the judiciary through training, personnel selection, and exhortation by party organs. It has also been punitive. The principle of judicial independence—that is, security of tenure in office subject to legal proceedings—has been removed and in principle denied by the totalitarian regimes whether Communist, Nazi, or Fascist. The judge has been enjoined not only to be subjective but has been defined as an integrated tool of the regime, removable as readily as any public official.

The separation-of-powers concept has been rejected. No special sanctity has been recognized in the law, greater than or different from other branches of State administration. The conception that judges must be made secure in positions of such independence that they can protect the rights of citizens *against* the power holders, if need be, has been explicitly rejected. Such judicial checks and counterchecks as have been established in the Communist states have little in common with promoting true judicial independence. The separation of the offices of the Prosecutor General from that of the courts does not render judges independent either of the Prosecutor General or the ruling party. It is more in the nature of multiplying channels of control culminating in the hands of the ruling oligarchy. The status and conditions of employment of judges and of the secret police are not significantly differentiated. Both categories are equally discretionary insofar as the regime's ability to remove or regulate is concerned. Employees must please the office of the Prosecutor General and of the police apparatus outside of his jurisdiction far more urgently than the public at large. Above all, they must please the controlling party leadership.

In the practice of Communist regimes, even regular courts of original jurisdiction are manned in part by laymen, so-called people's assessors, who are generally party nominees. The assessors have powers equal to those of the professionally trained judge. They may not only intervene in all the proceedings of the court but may outvote the professional judge on all decisions respecting procedure, determination of guilt, and sentence.

If we may thus conclude that the regular portion of the judicial machinery is apt to dispense lopsided justice to the citizenry, our conclusion must be strengthened by a consideration of the recourse available *against* the judiciary. The only channels through which defects in the law itself or in its administration can be denounced and changed are controlled by the ruling oligarchy. The laws and the judges are virtually immune from public attack and censure by anyone who is not of the ruling party. Redress against a bad law or maladministration of justice cannot be made through publicity in the press or action in the legislature, except and insofar as the party sanctions it. To the extent that the initiative for such censure or corrective reform does originate outside the top leadership of the party, it represents the party's own sounding out of the public. There is no forum or channel through which attempts to remedy existing abuses could be not merely voiced but used to rally popular support in opposition to the wishes of party leaders. This tends to make the legal system far more rigid in its adaptability to popular demands and expectations than is the case among the democracies.

Among the latter, the norms or general rules of the law and of its administration are more open to public scrutiny and to reform "from below," or "from the outside," by virtue of the political mechanisms that exist and are available quite apart from the machinery of justice. The legislature is not the forum of one party, a mere sounding board for the dictator of the day. The press and news media are analogously available to many different interests outside of the actual government; they are not simply the mouthpieces of the leader. Judges and courts realize that public opinion cannot be disregarded because (1) it cannot be muffled and (2) it can have legislative-administrative consequences if sufficiently aroused.

On the other hand, against this more generalized responsiveness assured by publicity, we find democratic judicial machinery more insulated from the everyday pressure and manipulation by the political leadership in control of the executive. Large-scale public criticism of a law may force its repeal or amendment; and disclosure of judicial corruption may force commencement of legal proceedings against the offending judge. But no amount of public criticism, discussion, or indignation need jeopardize the physical security of a judge, his office, or even his salary and conditions of employment within certain well-defined limits. Changes in the status, functions, or remuneration of judges and court officials would in all effective democracies require the publicized and orderly process of legislation or trial. They could never be carried out as on-the-spot, prerogative, discretionary acts of the executive.

Thus, with the democracies, we have a reversal of the totalitarian model: less pliability at the top (that is, in the subservience of the judiciary to the executive) and more responsiveness at the bottom (that is, in the degree of vulnerability to demands voiced in legislative assemblies, news media, and by the public at large). In these two respects, the system of justice under democracy is as different from the totalitarian as is its whole bureaucratic apparatus: significantly shielded at one end, relatively open at the other.

Democratic justice combines responsiveness to public opinion in both substance and procedure with considerable safeguards of rights inherent in each person as a citizen and individual. The latter aspect of democratic justice transcends all constitutional formalities. In all systems in which the democratic electoral process is effective, the judiciary stands watchdog over the rights of participants, to insure the continued openness of the system; and in all of them it is sufficiently shielded from arbitrary control or restraint by the majority of the day, or the government of the day, to enable it to fulfill this crucial function.

In polities that are imperfectly democratized or frankly oligarchical, under autocratic, dictatorial regimes, the legal systems represent a different range of characteristics. Among regimes that for one reason or another are "aspiring democracies"—that is, possess the outward trappings of democracy but very limited actual diffusion of popular participation in the political process—justice reflects the anomaly. Its distributive effects are generally schizophrenic and hypocritical. The differences between such systems and the genuinely effective democracies relate less to the substance of the laws than to their enforcement or procedural aspects. A basic difference between effective democracies and the oligarchical quasi-democracies might be expressed in this way: the administration of justice in the former is frequently better than the written rule on which it operates; in the quasi-democratic oligarchies, the practice is nearly always worse than the rule.

Among the democracies, Britain has no statutory equivalent of the American Constitution's First Amendment safeguarding freedom of the press and of speech. A number of specific ordinary laws proscribing seditious speech passed by Parliament during some of Britain's past wartime emergencies have never been repealed. If the judiciary were so disposed, these statutes could theoretically be invoked not only to stifle virtually every form of expression but also to restrict and suppress every conceivable form of public assembly and association. In fact, the actual administration of the law by British courts is so scrupulously solicitous of the right of free speech that there is hardly a political system on earth that excels the British on the score of allowed freedom of expression. Another illustration of this superiority of practice to the letter of the law is provided by Ireland. Its 1937 constitution, in codifying certain common-law rights, imposed a number of modifications of language on them such that, theoretically speaking, these rights could be readily enough abridged or denied by the State. Thus, the right of association was reaffirmed but declared subject to control "in the public interest." The right of free speech was analogously qualified by the proviso that it should not be misused "to undermine public order or morality or the authority of the State."[7] Such provisions could be readily enough applied by a willful, irresponsible, or autocratic judiciary to crush public liberties. In fact, however, just as in the British experience this has not been the case.

On the other hand, the legal situation in most Latin American states has been the exact opposite of the examples just cited. Individual rights are spelled out in great detail and most Latin American constitutions abound in them. In 1959, one authority on the subject estimated the average Latin American constitution to be thirty-five pages long, as compared with the thirteen pages of the United States Constitution. Cuba's basic law under Batista and for the first year of Castro's rule was the longest at sixty-eight pages![8] Generally, the major constitutional loophole has been a device called the declaration of state of siege, enabling the chief executive to suspend temporarily all constitutional guarantees. In practice, even apart from resort to the declaration of siege:

> The judiciary, like the legislature, is subordinate to the executive, numerous constitutional provisions to bulwark the power and independence of the courts to the contrary notwithstanding. In fact, the courts of Latin America are even less effective than the legislature in limiting the authority of strong presidents. ... [Only] routine matters in the lower courts, and other cases in which the executive manifests no interest, are usually free of political interference.[9]

Interesting parallels may be found between justice notoriously dispensed in the more oligarchical subsystems of the United States and the *de facto* oligarchies among the Latin American republics. Beyond a façade of constitutional niceties and even elective judgeships, American cities with large, politically inert, or politically unassimilated populations, immigrant and nonwhite, have experienced a

[7] See Alfred G. Donaldson, *Some Comparative Aspects of Irish Law* (Durham, N.C.: Duke University Press, 1957), pp. 164–167.

[8] J. Lloyd Mecham, "Latin American Constitutions: Nominal and Real," *Journal of Politics*, Vol. 21, No. 3 (1959), pp. 258–275.

[9] *Ibid.*, p. 269. See also, Helen L. Clagget, *The Administration of Justice in Latin America* (New York: Oceana Publications, 1952). "The guaranteed individual rights [are] enumerated in the first twenty-nine articles [!] of the Mexican Constitution in much more detail than is found in the Bill of Rights of the United States Constitution...." P. 136.

grossly unequal and sometimes brutal administration of justice. Among the majority of the states below the Mason-Dixon line, the system of justice has grotesquely failed, during most of this century, to live up to the ideal of equal treatment for all citizens. Everywhere gross discrepancies in the political participation patterns have been correlated to gross discrepancies in the treatment meted out by courts, police, and prisons. In the Latin American republics, the flagrant *de facto* disproportion in political participation has had an analogous impact on justice. Wealthy oligarchs have been able to assure themselves lenient, considerate, and ultimately preferential treatment at the hands of a judiciary that they could readily control and whose personnel they substantially furnished.

The treatment of the poor peasant or worker at the hands of Latin American judges and policemen has been far less favorable, and far more harsh, than the treatment meted out to the poorest strata by the courts and police in Sweden or Switzerland. Nor have the advantages of the very rich in the latter nations ever been so flagrantly disproportionate as they have been in Latin America, or in the American South, or in the urban enclaves.

But, by the same token, the less well-to-do elements have hardly constituted an effective, articulate public opinion to be reckoned with in these areas where they have suffered the worst abuse. The *de facto* political capabilities of the midwestern farmer and the southern sharecropper, or the Latin American peon, have been very different. The aspiring quasi-democracies are less responsive to the demands of their populations in the substantive aspects of their legal systems than the effective democracies, but they are even less responsive in terms of the application and enforcement of the laws.

But, within a political framework where an autocracy's traditional right to rule is not seriously challenged, the legal system can dispense with hypocritical subterfuges of ineffective democratic controls and of rights that exist on paper only. It can also compensate the citizenry for its substantive inadequacy or rigidity by the procedural advantages of administration and enforcement. Where its rule is secure, thanks either to popular apathy or consensus obtained by prescription, the traditional autocracy can "afford" to allow judges and courts to be reasonably independent in interpreting and applying the laws. In fact, it can rely on the open, predictable, and, within the limits of the law itself, fair administration of the judicial system as a principal bulwark of its popularity and power.

A traditionally enforced legal system in which the population knows what to expect is one of the more attractive stabilities of traditonal autocracy, a selling point, as it were, with the people. The apparently fixed character of the autocracy's rule assures the related stability of its laws, which protect the people in their particular fashion and are seemingly unaffected by the changing vicissitudes of the surrounding world. In the modern era, these have been the seeming advantages of the legal systems of such diverse autocracies as Imperial Germany and Imperial Ethiopia—out of the reach of popular whim, to be sure, but not unreasonable, dishonest, or particularly oppressive in their application and made additionally attractive by long usage: in each case a legal system both singularly well known and predictable.

But, given the autocratic control of the norms and the machinery of justice, *social* changes prompting people to desire—in turn—*legal* changes may not be brought as readily as in the democracies. The traditionally oriented autocracy of Saudi Arabia provides an illustration. The highest source of law there is officially viewed as the Koran. Legislation and adjudication are both regarded essentially as interpretations of and adaptations to the basic principles of Islam and the Prophet. Customary law and royal decrees are seen as operative and valid insofar as they conform to the fundamental Moslem religous law of the land. With respect to all disputes, including those over trade, water, pasturage, land, ownership of stock, and other essentially secular problems, the power of ultimate decision rests with the King, who

> . . . in rendering his decisions is guided if not governed by the customary law which provides [standards for] his authority, even though his powers involve the right to impose extreme penalties and his decisions are final and not subject to appeal.[10]

In thus relying on custom and religion, the Saudi monarchy has managed to realize some significant legal values for the population under its rule. The following extensive quotation from Lipsky's *Saudi Arabia* is an excellent description of these:

> One of the most notable achievements of the late King Abd al-Aziz Ibn Saud was the establishment and maintenance of security and organized justice in an area which had previously known little of either except on a limited, local level . . . constant intertribal raiding for livestock and other loot and conflict over grazing areas or water rights characterized the life of the nomadic bulk of the population, and crimes against the person and property were rampant and generally unpunished in the urbanized parts of the peninsula.
>
> . . . Ibn Saud undertook to stamp out banditry and raiding and to reduce the bloodshed arising from blood feuds by bringing tribes more and more under the authority of his central government. He made travel safe for pilgrims and others throughout his territory and harshly repressed crime in the settled urban areas. At the same tme he made the nomads, whose judicial practices had traditionally been based on customary law, increasingly subject to the Sharia.[11]

[10] George A. Lipsky, *Saudia Arabia* (New Haven: Hraf press, 1959), pp. 112–113.
[11] *Ibid.*, p. 124.

The Sharia, or religious law, was itself in large measure a product of Arab custom. What the absolute monarchy accomplished in twentieth-century Saudi Arabia was to bring all its subjects within the pale of effective enforcement of that law backed by the ultimate sanction of royal power. The exercise of this power is generally understood to involve the attribute of consultation with royal advisors, a fatherly concern for the people, and other manifestations of deference to the traditional judicial role of a sheikh. The administration of justice today is carried out in part by royally appointed judges (*cadis*) and in part also by local chieftains subject to the King—the emirs and the tribal sheikhs. Saudi administration of justice has a reputation for dispatch, effectiveness, and an essential fairness even among foreign observers.

Substantively, however, notwithstanding the impact of Western influence and the impact of change in other countries of the Middle East, the law leaves much to be desired.

> The lack of distinction in decree legislation between simple and criminal negligence makes imprisonment virtually mandatory even for relatively minor violations.
>
> Theft is punished by cutting off of a hand in serious cases . . . whipping is the standard penalty for drunkenness.
>
> Punishments, including execution by the sword, are generally carried out in public, but foreigners are apparently no longer as welcome to witness the proceedings as in the past.[12]

Stoning to death continues to be the legal punishment for those found guilty of adultery. There is no right of *habeas corpus*, although release from jail pending trial may be arranged at the discretion of police chiefs.

> Theoretically, all residents of Saudi Arabia are equal before the law and are subject to both Sharia and decree law. In practice, however, members of the royal family and other prominent persons are seldom brought to trial, and all but minor cases involving foreigners are generally referred directly to the district or regional emir, who tends to give them special consideration. In the past when serious cases have involved American employees of Aramco, the Company, with the approval of the Saudi authorities, has quickly discharged and deported the accused employee after the trial has taken place.[13]

It may be reasonably conjectured that many citizens of Saudi Arabia today, particularly under the impact of cultural, social, and economic changes taking place within their immediate and proximate environ-

[12] *Ibid.*, p. 123.
[13] *Ibid.*, p. 122.

ments, oppose the legal system to which the monarchy subjects them. But within the framework of their current regime, even the capability of manifesting displeasure to the ruler is severely limited. Short of the King's own disposition changing, only a revolution could bring about substantive legal reforms in Saudi Arabia.[14]

The advantages of traditional-autocratic and democratic justice can be matched by the innovative-mobilizational regimes in at least several important respects. The experience of the Communist states after World War II indicates that such states can provide the machinery of the courts and make it available to the citizen more quickly, more cheaply, and with fewer procedural obstacles to the prosecution of his case than has been the practice in many democratic constitutional states (notoriously in Britain, for instance). We may observe that the provision of justice through so many courts to an increasing number of people, as in the case of Russia and China, under a strikingly increasing complexity of social and economic conditions, reflects a political allocation of resources to the public sector not to be found among the politically entrenched but socially quiescent traditional oligarchies or among the more socially balanced and cost-conscious democracies. The advantages of cheap and speedy legal recourse in some areas of the law—those regarded as nonsensitive by the regime or those selected for special handling by the courts—are offset, however, by the greatly increased prerogative, discretionary aspects of the system—those connected to the administration of politically "sensitive" questions.

So long as no political checks exist on the exercise of power by the ruling parties in the Communist systems, the reforms of the post-Stalin era curbing the secret police, the use of torture, assassination, and slave labor camps can be regarded as putting these devices into abeyance or minimizing their use. No citizen living under these regimes can be quite sure that any or all of these procedures may not suddenly reappear—perhaps in only a few cases, like his own, if not on a mass scale.

So long as the administration of justice, like all other things, stands beyond the reach of the legislative and communication organs of public opinion, only the ruling oligarchy (that is, the party leadership) can decide what is to be done, and only it can really know what is actually

[14] In Ethiopia, most new laws require the approval of at least one of the legislative bodies (Senate or Chamber of Deputies) before promulgation by the Emperor. On the other hand, the appointment and removal of judges and other principal administrative officers lie wholly within the imperial prerogative, and although the power has apparently been used with discretion, the procedure is a closed and summary one. W. E. H. Howard, *Public Administration in Ethiopia* (Groningen, Djakarta: J. B. Wolters, 1955), pp. 103–107.

being done. There can be no opposition to and no exposure of a slippage back to terrorism unless the party permits it to manifest itself. Assurances by party leaders that the bad old days, whether in Russia, Hungary, Poland, or China, will never return again do not yet have the institutional safeguards that would make them wholly credible. Among Communist leaders who most solemnly eschewed terrorism for a number of years before actually using it against opponents within and without the party was, after all, the arch terrorist of communism, Stalin.

In appraising current Soviet justice we need not succumb to either of the two fallacies: that the Stalinist system has not really changed since 1953 or that it has been abolished. The facts indicate a middle ground between these extremes and still leave a very considerable gap between justice Communist-style and justice as practiced in the effective democracies.[15]

When Khrushchev made his celebrated attack on the Stalinist legacy at the Twentieth Congress of the Soviet Communist party in 1956, he set off a chain reaction of developments in all the Communist states. It is noteworthy that in condemning the use of terror and torture under Stalin and the latter's last police chief, Beria, Khrushchev deplored the use of terror because it was aimed against Communists. He recognized the usefulness and desirability of terror when directed against the party's true enemies, in the interest of the Communist revolution and the maintenance of party rule, as presumably Lenin had used it. Khrushchev indicated that the time had come to return the sword of proletarian revolutionary justice to its sheath, not to break it or foreswear its legitimate use.

These statements presaged something of a middle-ground approach to the reform of Soviet justice that followed Stalin's death and the campaign of de-Stalinization. Among the more important reforms, the security secret police have been deprived of the independent power of investigation, with all its consequences in terms of detention, interrogation, and the like. Such procedures now require the supervision of the Prosecutor's office. Special courts, which, under a 1937 statute, were empowered to try cases of serious anti-State crimes in secrecy and without rights of counsel or appeal, have been abolished. The

[15] See Harold J. Berman, *Justice in the U.S.S.R.* (New York: Vintage Books, 1963), pp. 67–68: "despite the very substantial changes . . . the Soviet legal system remained Stalinist in its basic structure and its basic purposes. The organization and functions of the lawmaking, law-enforcing, and law-practicing agencies—of the legislature, the Procuracy, the courts, the administrative organs, the bar—were not essentially different ten years later from what they were when Stalin died. The main outlines of Soviet criminal law and procedure—civil law and procedure, labor law, agrarian law, family law, administrative law, constitutional law, and other branches of the Soviet legal tree —remained basically the same as before."

jurisdiction of military courts in trying civilians has been limited, although not completely eliminated. Relatives of persons escaping the USSR can no longer be punished for this crime, provided they had no prior knowledge of it and were not involved in it. The notorious use of confessions has been limited in that Soviet courts must now require corroborative evidence in addition to any possible confession by a defendant. The burden of proof of guilt is now placed on the accuser.

One of the widest "nets" in the Soviet legal system has been considerably narrowed in that, "Persons may no longer be held liable for acts of their associates unless they intended those acts to take place."[16] Many acts that were heretofore construed as crimes against the State, such as labor absenteeism, have been removed from the criminal code. There has been liberalization in the administration of the once dreaded and notorious slave labor camps.

Notwithstanding all these substantial reforms, Communist justice in Russia still differs widely from the democratic models and retains much of its Stalinist residue of several decades. Reform of penal labor camps must not be confused with their abolition. The powers of investigation, arrest, detention, and interrogation, although now shared by the State prosecutors and the police, can still be exercised in a prerogative, discretionary fashion. The prosecutor is not required to present his evidence for initiating proceedings against someone before a court of law. The decision is his own on grounds of his own choosing. The prosecutor's warrant, however, may result in the long-term confinement of an individual, and there is still no *habeas corpus* procedure in the Soviet system of justice to secure the release of a person whose liberty has been taken by a prosecutor's whim or ill-founded suspicion. The search and seizure of a person's belongings, home, or correspondence also continue as administrative acts requiring neither a court warrant nor, in many cases, even the prosecutor's prior approval. Travel within the Soviet Union still continues under *de facto* legal restraints, inasmuch as certain areas continue to be regarded as security zones (notably frontier areas), and the issuance of passports is required for resettlement by a Soviet citizen from one location to another.[17]

Even though the harshness of punishments meted out for certain kinds of crimes, ranging from murder, desertion, and "speculation" or the buying and selling of goods privately in the black market, was lessened in the 1950s, many more severe punishments were added in 1961 and 1962. Soviet law makes the failure to report the preparation or commission of a whole plethora of crimes to State authorities pun-

[16] *Ibid.*, p. 71.

[17] W. W. Kulski, *The Soviet Regime, Communism in Practice* (Syracuse, N.Y.: Syracuse University Press, 1963), pp. 152–154.

ishable by up to several years' imprisonment or exile. Among such crimes are infractions of traffic regulations, speculation, and the pilfering of State or public property. Flight from the USSR is defined as treason, carrying a maximum death penalty. Sabotage, which may also be punished by the death penalty, includes "undermining the Soviet economy . . . with the purpose of weakening [it]."[18]

Among the crimes punishable by death since 1961 are forgery, violations of currency regulations, looting of public property, and the giving or accepting of bribes under some circumstances.[19] Although ostensibly criminal punishment can no longer be imposed except by a sentence of a court, since 1957–1958 Soviet law has sanctioned the exile to compulsory labor in another part of the Soviet Union of persons who are adjudged "parasites" living on unearned income and "leading an antisocial life" by laymen assemblies of their neighbors in the villages or towns where they happen to live. The sentences of exile imposed by one's neighbors may range from two to five years. As Professor Kulski notes:

> The verdict of the assembly needed only approval by the executive committee of the city or district soviet which is an administrative body. There was no appeal to courts. The assembly decided in an open ballot by the majority of those present. As the quorum was the majority of adult residents, the actual voting majority could have been a minority of the total inhabitants. It is easy to imagine that the vote of the assembly might have been swayed by the pressure of the local Party cell or local State officials.[20]

Another similar nonlegal way of punishing persons is maintained in the so-called comradely courts established in various places where people work, study, or live. Specially convoked committees of coworkers or coresidents can sentence one to minor fines, demand public apologies, and issue a verdict of public censure upon one. They can try persons for infractions of labor discipline, such as lateness or drunkenness at work.

If any of these nonjudicial courts decide that the accused person before them has committed graver infractions than those entrusted to their jurisdiction, they can recommend action to the State Prosecutor. The latter is always free to initiate his own proceedings, in any case. In fact, Soviet law still makes it possible for the State to retry persons who have been sentenced already if the Prosecutor believes that the penalty imposed on them was not sufficient.

Even though the Stalinist Soviet Constitution of 1936, still in force, affirms freedom of speech and expression, the 1958 Criminal Code

[18] *Ibid.*, p. 163.
[19] *Ibid.*, p. 167.
[20] *Ibid.*, p. 176.

makes it an offense to engage in agitation, propaganda, or dissemination of information "discrediting the Soviet State and social regime."

> The distribution for the same purposes of slanderous and concocted rumors . . . as well as the distribution or preparation or storing for the same purposes of literature having such a content—shall be punished by deprivation of freedom for from six months to seven years or by exile for from two to five years. The same acts committed by persons previously sentenced for especially dangerous anti-state crimes, or if committed in wartime, are punished by deprivation of freedom for from three to ten years. (Article 7)[21]

Actually, the criminal code is consistent with that master provision of the Soviet constitution that makes it clear that all the numerous individual and group rights provided in it may only be used in the furtherance of, and not against, the party and its regime (Article 126). Parallel qualifications of analogous rights are included in all the constitutions of the other Communist states.

The totalitarian State, with its vast mobilization of men and resources for political objectives, can and does actually provide effective justice in *some* areas of the law in which the adversaries are private parties, and in some cases, at least, even where one of the adversaries is a public official. What it has yet to provide are safeguards for *any* citizen whose adversary is the "interest of the State" as defined and understood by the rulers. In the last case, the character of totalitarian justice has least generally applicable dependability as an impartial umpire and a shield capable of protecting the accused from the wrath of the rulers. The salience, or relative significance, of this aspect of the legal system in terms of its total impact on the population varies with the circumstances of the time and the whims of the rulers.

Reviewing the procedures employed in Russia to create a totally socialized economy, Stalin once remarked that it was not possible to make an omelet without scrambling some eggs. The decisions with respect to the omelets and the eggs, as in Stalin's day, continue to be made in utmost secrecy by relatively few individuals within the central organs of the ruling parties in the Communist world.

A citizen in an effective democracy may frequently find the cost and the time involved in the prosecution of his case against another individual or against a private or public corporation discouragingly excessive. Thus, even in the most effective, long-established democratic regimes it is undoubtedly true that it is easier to obtain justice for the well-to-do than for the poor; for the man who has the resources to hire attorneys and investigators and to give freely of his time than for one who cannot, and ultimately also for one who is capable of

[21] *Ibid.*, pp. 163–164.

understanding the law and of conducting his own defense than for one who is not.

Yet, even the poorest and least learned of citizens in an effective democracy can have confidence that he will not be indefinitely detained on the mere whim of a policeman; that he cannot be sentenced to jail or penal servitude without the sentence of a duly constituted court of law whose proceedings, and verdict, may be reported in every news medium in the land and are subject to appeal; and that his property may not be wrested from him without an appeal to the law. And he enjoys this basic security of life, limb, and material possession in the courts regardless of the identity of his adversary. He knows that if he has a grievance it can be publicly ventilated and, if need be, made a *cause célèbre* even if, and perhaps even because, it may embarrass, weaken, and ultimately unseat those in power, whoever they may be.

Moreover, he knows that if the rules or procedures applied in his case are widely felt to be unfair, to represent an actual or potential threat to the safety and welfare of other citizens, they may be politically changed through legislative and administrative reforms of the law. This is more than he can generally expect under any autocracy, traditional or innovative, quiescent or mobilized. To be sure, the so-called right of petition may be said to exist in some form, however minuscule, marginal and sublimated, in every conceivable political system, in the sense that the aggrieved may at least sometimes express their disappointment or displeasure directly to the courts, to the police, or ultimately to their rulers. But where it cannot be manifested openly, publicly, and where the means of redress are wholly at the discretion of the power holders as a matter of "grace," the difference in degree may well be seen here as a difference in kind.

This basic distinction in the position of the citizen in the courts vis-à-vis the State has yielded historically paradoxical results.

A German businessman, for example, whose political behavior was, from the Nazi point of view, appropriately correct could receive profit-making aids and concessions from his government (including the use of free slave labor from the conquered territories) that could not have been obtained in any democratic political system. He did not have to worry about strikes in his plant because the party prohibited this, in law and in fact. In some cases the party even assured him an iron-clad monopoly for his product at a guaranteed price. But all of these advantages would represent no value at all to the businessman if he displeased the party politically. He would then become as much an outcast as any other oppositionist, and the sanctity of his life, let alone his property, could not be protected from the grasp of the Gestapo or successfully defended in any court of law.

At the other extreme of policy, we find Socialist parties ensconced in power by the electorates of democratic regimes pursuing policies widely regarded as antibusiness, publicly committed to an egalitarian levelling out of wealth and the destruction of the power of the privileged few. But, as in the case of the British and Scandinavian experience, no businessman need lose a night's sleep about the safety of his assets from arbitrary seizure and expropriation. The property of a maverick landlord or entrepreneur in a totalitarian or autocratic regime, even one that is *generally* favorable to the upper classes and the rich, is never as safe from sudden confiscation as it is within the framework of an effective democracy, even if the government in power happens to be politically hostile to the rich.

In substance, then, we could describe the advantages that accrue to the citizen of a democracy from his legal system in two ways: There are the tangible protections to be found in the law and in the way in which the law is applied by the judiciary. There is also an intangible but highly significant by-product of the realization that rules protective of the individual exist and are in fact being applied. The by-product is a general feeling of personal security among the people.

In most societies, including even totalitarian ones—that is, autocracies that maximize innovative-mobilizational tendencies—the majority of the population probably never experiences any substantial, direct contact with the courts and the penal administration. Even though virtually any person may be expected to have had some exposure to policemen, a majority may never have experienced arrest, interrogation, or detention by the police. The security, ease, and confidence with which the ordinary man goes about his business in the shadow of the law, and of the law-enforcement apparatus, is generally based on expectations drawn from the experiences of others and from the mechanisms of justice in the society as a whole.

In an effective democracy, the citizen does not live out his life in dread of the agencies of justice. It would seem preposterous to him to hide from the view of policemen, a precaution he might frequently consider wise in the totalitarian systems. Nor would he think it unwise to talk to simply anybody at any time for fear of being reported to a secret police. Ultimately, these so-called intangibles of personal security are probably so essential to a reasonably autonomous, spontaneous, and anxiety-free existence that in their impact on the people they outweigh the codified and procedural tangibles of the law.

In terms of our discussion so far, it would appear that the extension of democracy in any community would be conducive to increased personal security for the average individual in the courts and in his relationships with law-enforcement agencies. Conversely, the opposite political tendency would be reflected in the diminution of that security. If we correlate the processes of law reform and of democratization both contemporaneously within subunits of nations—as in the United States—and historically within whole nations, we are confronted by a great deal of empirical evidence in support of this proposition.

Even in autocratic Prussia of the nineteenth century, the emergence of the so-called *Rechtsstaat* out of the more crude and arbitrary *Polizeistaat* was a significant corollary and sequel to the political-constitutional reforms of 1848 extending suffrage and parliamentary participation in government.[22] In Britain the extension of political rights to the middle class and to the workers was closely linked to the successful campaign for legal reform that improved the British administration of justice in many respects: it extended recourse to courts; it lessened the harshness of punishments meted out for relatively trivial offenses; and it encouraged humanitarian reforms in prison conditions, among many others.

The process of democratization in Latin America at present is also significantly correlated to such reforms. One of the striking current illustrations of it is Venezuela, which in 1961 observed its first on-record presidential succession through the peaceful and legal election process. The legacy of justice under dictator Jimenez, ousted in 1958, had been a compound of terroristic abuse of the individual combined with a contemptuous neglect of all the regular agencies of justice, courts, and prisons. The succeeding administration of Romulo Betancourt has not merely done away with the secret police but has set Venezuela on a course of thorough—and expensive—improvement and modernization in the whole apparatus of justice.[23]

For those whose citizenship is recognized as only partial and distinctly second class, justice is generally an enforced system of discrimination. At its worst, it may represent no more than brutal police rule; at its best it is still flagrantly discriminatory.

Based on the premise of racialism, the political development of South Africa in the last several decades has proceeded in two contradictory directions: The franchise among whites has been extended, so that women for instance were granted suffrage in 1930 and all qualifications on male suffrage for whites were done away with in 1931. But the disenfranchisement of the native Indian and colored population

[22] See H. G. James, *Principles of Prussian Administration* (New York: Macmillan, 1913), pp. 154–155. See also, B. Chapman, *The Profession of Government* (London: Allen and Unwin, 1959), p. 183. *Cf.* F. A. Hayek, *The Constitution of Liberty* (Chicago: University of Chicago Press, 1960).

[23] See Robert J. Alexander, *The Venezuelan Democratic Revolution: A Profile of the Regime of Romulo Betancourt* (New Brunswick, N.J.: Rutgers University Press, 1964), Ch. 22.

has not only been maintained; it has even lost the last vestiges of its token respectability of minuscule, indirect representation.

While the apartheid regimes of Malan, Verwoerd, and their successors have maintained an outward pretense of separate, rather than subordinate and inferior, development of some races as compared with others, unequal power has been translated into unequal justice.

Since 1911, nonwhites have been legally barred from holding skilled jobs in the mining industry. They have been restricted in their freedom of movement in changing employment. Since 1913, they have been restricted in the right of land purchase. Under the so-called Native Administration Act of 1927, last amended in 1956, a minister's order could be issued for the deportation of "any African to a certain prescribed place, if this African according to the Minister's opinion promoted hostility between white and black."[24] In 1952, this law was supplemented by another that now empowers the government to exile or resettle not merely individuals but whole tribes and parts of native African tribes. These laws were buttressed by a 1956 act that specifically denied legal recourse to the victims of such political-administrative measures. In 1953, African trade unions and strikes by Africans were prohibited. In addition, several enactments curtailed the rights of nonwhites to welfare services provided by employers and the State; among these were old-age pensions, aid to the blind, unemployment insurance, and safeguarded conditions of work and employment in agricultural and industrial enterprises. In 1959, nonwhites were banned from the hitherto mixed or at least "open" South African universities.

These enactments are merely some of the substantive legal disabilities and limitations imposed by the minority white rulers on a majority nonwhite population. Much more could be added to this not simply in terms of laws but in the administrative enforcement of them, the treatment of the "inferior races" by the police and the courts, and the deprivations inflicted on the population by harsh and arbitrary penal institutions.

Because the number of persons in the politically nonparticipant and discriminated categories has been so large, the oligarchic governments of South Africa have been understandably and conspicuously nervous about any agitation or any organization that would mobilize the resentments of these masses against their political, social, and economic masters.

This concern with security in a society so numerously repressed has led to curtailments of the right of association and expression not

[24] K. L. Koskam, *Apartheid and Discrimination* (Leyden: A. W. Sythoff, 1960), pp. 62–63.

merely for the nonwhites but for Europeans suspected of dangerous revolutionary attitudes as well. Among other measures, South Africa has recently enacted Communist control legislation so sweeping that it allows the banishment from place of residence and confinement to a specified area of any individual who merely *in the opinion* of the Governor General or the Minister of Justice is a Communist, with no further or greater burden of proof or recourse.[25]

Examples of the South African experience have been duplicated elsewhere: on a lesser scale even in the subunits of the American political system. The Southern black, long considered a noncitizen for all practical purposes, rarely enjoyed even minimally equal-though-separate justice at the hands of white officialdom. The political mechanisms of democracy were generally understood to be applicable to whites only, and in states in which blacks constituted a very sizeable portion of the total population, the rights of the relatively privileged white citizens were seriously qualified by what might be termed "the rules of the powder keg." A nonblack was always more likely to be well treated by the local sheriff, the courts, and the prison officials than the black, but certainly not much better if he happened to exercise his rights of free speech in behalf of the black's cause.

In the American political system, however, the capacity of the subunits to limit political participation and thereby also its social, economic, and legal advantages on the basis of racism has been limited by the more democratically organized and superior power of the Federal Government. In fact, it would hardly be rash to speculate that as the democratization of the institutions of the Federal Government increases, through such devices as reapportionment and an ever-larger share of representation in the Congress to urban areas, the pressures on the deviant discriminatory subunits will magnify.

In the context of this chapter, we note the evident contrast between the equity of justice disbursed by the more democratically constituted Federal Government and that disbursed under the auspices of *de facto* political oligarchies, rural and urban, state and local.

To a large extent, the differences among these law-enforcement systems have their political coordinates: in the degree of popular participation in the mechanisms that fund, appoint, and control the legal systems; and no less importantly in the greater openness and ready accessibility to a greater range of interests at the federal level.

The Congress itself may still overrepresent, and traditionally has for a long time overrepresented, rural over urban communities, but the latter have always had a significant voice there. The Presidency has

[25] *Ibid.*, pp. 56–57. *Cf.* Edgar H. Brookes and J. B. Macaulay, *Civil Liberty in South Africa* (London: Oxford University Press, 1958), pp. 22–24.

been even more sensitive to the political power of the urban centers.

Some ethnic minority groups have had virtually no significant representation, let alone political power, in many of the states. But inescapably they have had *some* representation and *some* weight on the composite federal level over a prolonged period of time, along with the obvious interest to use the great powers at the center to improve or safeguard their positions in all possible respects.

In consequence of this, more eyes have been focused, more intently, on what is being done or not being done by Washington than on any state capital in the federal system. The executive agencies of the Federal Government, judicial as well as administrative, could not afford to mistreat *any* person as readily as some state systems could mistreat certain, to them politically inconsequential, categories of persons and citizens.

To the degree to which racism is a discount of the American people's commitment to democracy, it has not been historically as strong and as salient in all the subunits of the system. Therefore, it has never been quite as strong and salient at the federal level as it has among *some* of the subunits. This has had distributive consequences for persons coming in contact with federal agencies. The different mix of values in Washington has been progressively reinforced toward more democratic norms by the character of the structure and of the process of politics there.

A continuing handicap of democratic justice, at all levels of government and among many otherwise diverse political systems, has been the problem of costs. In the perennial debate of democratic politics between those who wish to maximize public services and those who prefer to minimize spending and the ensuing fiscal burdens to themselves, justice has often suffered. Inadequate funds devoted to the training, equipment, and maintenance of police forces; insufficient courts to handle the needs of litigants; overcrowded, understaffed, and antiquated prison and penal institutions have all characterized a number of democratic polities in modern times.

These inadequacies of resource allocation have tended to hurt most the poor, the illiterate, and the economically underprivileged strata in the democratic societies. These people could not afford to purchase the personnel and the time often necessary to vindicate their interests in the courts of law. Those who could afford them, when necessary, have resisted increased taxation in order to provide adequate legal services to those who could not. In consequence, without the existence of diabolical plots hinted at by Marxian critics of democracy, the man at the bottom of the social pyramid has been, willy-nilly, the principal victim of the inadequacies of democratic justice. We have already noted that, other things being equal, he has also been least effective in using the political mechanisms of democracy for the defense of his interests.

The differences between the political capacities of the rich and the poor have been rendered much more narrow in Switzerland and in Scandinavia than in Britain, the United States, Ireland, and Uruguay. Education, diffusion of popular culture, widespread trade union membership, prevalent conditions of health, individual security, and the availability of leisure time have all served to heighten the political capacities of the so-called lower strata of countries such as Sweden, Norway, and Denmark. Social democratic regimes have historically contributed to this in Scandinavia and in turn made the leverage of the relative have-nots on the total political system stronger. Among other policy results this has brought into being a machinery of justice for the very poor in Sweden that is more generous and considerate than that in the United States.

Notwithstanding these significant differences among the democracies, they share a legal system supportive of the security of persons and property from secret, arbitrary, and nonlegal infringement common in the so-called totalitarian and autocratic regimes past and present. They also share the characteristic of popular recourse against and control of law and its enforcement, which is generally lacking under oligarchical rule. Innovative autocracies, including Communist ones, make far greater use of law for reshaping society in a direction chosen by the ruling oligarchy, and tend to make greater resource allocations to legal-punitive purposes than do other regimes.

CHAPTER 10
BUREAUCRACY AND PUBLIC SERVICE

IN most nations of the world today government is the biggest single employer and the biggest single purchaser and purveyor of goods and services in society. In the larger, economically advanced systems—as in the United States—governments employ literally millions of persons: soldiers, policemen, firemen, postal clerks, teachers, social workers, scientific advisers, building inspectors, administrators, engineers, judges, attorneys, and countless other employees in even more specialized and esoteric fields.

Naturally enough, the relationship between this vast body of governmental servants and the people at large has a pervasive impact on the life of every member of society. Government employees whom the citizen meets in his daily pursuits and in his locality are to him "government personified." It is within the power of this government to make the citizen's life more comfortable, richer, and more secure; alternately, government can make it a nightmare of terror, burdens, and vexation. Watchdogs may sometimes be wolves and guardians may turn out to be robbers.

In appraising the impact of bureaucracy on society as a whole, so many considerations are involved that no single scale of measurement can possibly be enough to tell us if the given bureaucracy is "good" or "bad." Broadly speaking, public services can be expected to live up to criteria of high professional competence: efficient performance of duty; honesty; reliability; prompt, fair, and impartial service to all; and consideration and even courtesy to the public and to each individual who may come in contact with government.

Some of these, and many other evaluative criteria of service, obviously may be more readily achievable in a rich, literate, industrialized nation than in circumstances of widespread poverty and illiteracy. If this indeed is the case, we could regard economic development as *one* of the determinants of the quality of a bureaucracy. For example, one could expect public employees in Western Europe today to include more professionally trained and technologically efficient functionaries than among the newly emancipated nation-states south of the Sahara. But, granted this, what of the *political* determinants of the bureaucracy?

Bureaucracy, like the judiciary, may be more or less sensitive to public opinion; more or less independent of the government of the day; and more or less arbitrary in its treatment of people.

Autocratic bureaucracies and legal systems vary, but among the innovative-mobilizational regimes they tend to be open toward the top and closed toward the bottom: they are subject to massive direct manipulation by the rulers but are far less sensitive to popular pressures from below. To be sure, democratic bureaucracies are also controlled by and accountable to political officials, but they are generally more thoroughly protected from direct personal reprisals by rulers, while their policies and procedures are more amenable to public pressures.

In terms of the dichotomy between democracy and authoritarianism, the crucial distinctions relate not to efficiency or to technical competence but to accountability and control primarily. Bureaucratic establishments in the democracies tend to be open to public scrutiny and are subject to ultimate modification and change by organs closely linked to public opinion. These are characteristics that, admittedly, they possess only to a high degree—not in any absolute sense.

In the twentieth century, the expansion of government services brought on by wars, efforts to deal with economic crises, and popular demands for various welfare services from the State have greatly augmented the scope of bureaucratic operations. These demands have rendered the control and accountability of the whole administrative machinery—in virtually all political systems—more difficult than heretofore. For example, the desire for profitability in public enterprise in countries where there was widespread nationalization after World War II has been reflected in a considerable delegation of authority to "experts"—a maximum of leeway, hopefully, for a maximum of efficiency. The increased technological complexity of the war establishments has resulted in increased status for scientists, engineers, technicians, and planners. The adequate performance of their functions has required a good deal of discretion and independence. It has also become increasingly difficult for laymen—politicians and the public alike—to judge competently about the issues and problems implicit in the work of such experts.

The central problem of bureaucratic responsiveness in a democracy is the cleavage between the center and the periphery, or, put in different words, the conflict between responsiveness to the presumed wishes of a whole electorate and to its different particular segments.

The bureaucrat owes his service partly to those with whom he comes into immediate contact—for example, in a work place, a school, or a geographic locality. But he also owes his service to a larger public that presumably is entitled to maintain, direct, and control the whole service of which he is a member.

Where the center and the segments are not *homogeneous* in their demands on the bureaucrat, he must become a broker of conflicting needs and aspirations. Frequently, he may be tempted to respond more to his immediate local constituency than to a more general, sometimes tenuous, and almost abstract, public opinion embodied in election results or legislative resolutions.

Occasionally, it may take extraordinary exertion at the national level to counter specific, local pressures on a bureaucracy, as in the case of public regulatory agencies that often become spokesmen for the regulated rather than their regulators.

No uniform solution for these conflicts is possible in a democracy without sacrificing essential procedural rights of individuals and groups to defend what they regard as their interests. The preferences of a national majority cannot always correspond to the preferences of the inhabitants of each township or every given professional association. Apart from the question of procedural rights, it may not be physically or economically feasible to elicit compliance by force. Negotiation, compromise, and adaptation of a general policy to a specific situation may be all but indispensable. The values implicit in a democratic bureaucracy combine respect for the interests and the rights of particular client groups balanced against a sensitivity to the opinions of the electorate.

The nature of the equilibrium thus achieved in any democratic system at any given time varies. The rights of some clients may be less than equally respected; the wishes of the electorate may be, in some cases, at least, ignored. But in the discrimination among different client groups, and in the insensitivity to public opinion, there are degrees of difference worth noting. The accountability of a democratic bureaucracy rests on the values of the system: toward individuals, toward groups, and toward public opinion.

The democratic bureaucracy is one ultimately open to challenge, scrutiny, and, if necessary, change by a very wide range of interests operating through legislative organs, the political executive, the media of public opinion, and, most recently in several democracies, through the mediation of the so-called Ombudsman.[1]

Before analyzing these control mechanisms let us compare the responsive democratic bureaucracies with their authoritarian counterparts. In political systems where democracy is not, in fact, firmly established, bureaucracies tend either to (1) a position of corporate independence approaching that of "a state within a state" or (2) they are primarily the tools of a controlling oligarchy.

The first situation is likely to arise in all those political systems that are democracies outwardly, or constitutionally, but where, for specific historical reasons, democratic governments have not been able to function. Basic social and political dissensus may inhibit the formation of a powerful executive or a reasonably united and coherent legislative representation out of such elections as do take place. It may also be the resultant of popular apathy, inertia, and parochialism in situations where democracy is not "congruent," to use Almond and Verba terms, with the political culture of the population, as in the Latin American republics or some of the newer nation-states of Africa and Asia. In the second case, the bureaucracy's position is likely to reflect the general monopoly of power of the autocrats who are the policy makers of the system.

In both cases, the bureaucracy may still realize significant service values to the population at large. But in neither case is it as generally responsive and subservient to the injunction of the people's will. The values of the two spheres or worlds—bureaucracy and society—may coincide only at times that essentially represent the oligarchy's or the bureaucracy's own choosing.

Under either alternative, the bureaucracy itself is likely to become from time to time an open contender for supreme power in the system. This tendency is most likely to be expressed through the armed forces. The armed forces' virtual monopoly of the means of coercion gives them an advantage over other possible power claimants.

[1] See David B. Truman, *The Governmental Process* (New York: Alfred A. Knopf, 1959), Ch. 12, pp. 352–394, on how limiting the size of an attentive public can affect (narrow down or enlarge) the policy-making process. Among the interesting American case studies analyzing the process and consequences of expanding the attentive public on an issue of policy, see John R. Owens, "A Wildlife Agency and Its Possessive Public," in Frederic C. Mosher (ed.), *Governmental Reorganizations* (Indianapolis, Ind.: Bobbs-Merrill, 1967), pp. 103–149.

The military's motives and its disposition to intervene in politics—either to dictate policy or take over—are not very different from the motives and dispositions of other segments of the bureaucracy. The military establishment in any political system tends to develop its own corporate identity and orientation based on a particular mode of life, hierarchy, and the traditions and rules under which it has developed and that regulate its behavior. The sense of identity, and conceivably apartness from the rest of the body politic, may be reinforced by the unique social, cultural, and economic backgrounds of its leaders. Finally, the Army's orientation with respect to things political is likely to be shaped by its functional purpose and the attempt to adapt to the successful execution of its missions—in sum, by its professionalism.

Admittedly, the general's or colonel's preoccupation with the tasks at hand—the training and deployment of men and weapons—may be both exacting and time consuming, so that he may tend to look inward and have little concern about ordinary civilian affairs. But that represents only one side of the coin. The soldier's professional preoccupations cannot in the long run ever remain wholly apolitical, because the preparation and conduct of war are ultimately political problems. The military is involved in politics when it makes claims on the national budget, when it demands the stockpiling of strategic raw materials, and indeed when it demands decisions by politicians, in foreign or domestic affairs, that it claims to be necessary to the successful execution of the armed forces' tasks or possibly even to the very preservation of the armed forces' existence.[2]

As specialists in their field, the military leaders may believe that they alone are competent to judge on such matters as the size, organization, recruitment, and equipment of the forces. In their professional capacity they may be impelled to establish national security as they see it—economically and socially as well as militarily, in the narrow sense of the word. They may seek to convince the civilian authorities that only in the context of certain policies can they guarantee victory. Such views are all consequences of professionalism, yet they have often led the military to try to intervene in politics.[3]

It is understandable that the *motives* for a military seizure of power may exist at any time, anywhere, so long as men crave power, and that at least some of the circumstances favorable to the execution of a military coup could arise under any political system. An example of

[2] Interestingly, the demand for an early armistice pressed on political superiors by German and French Army commanders in 1918 and 1940, respectively, rested on the same premise: that a quick cessation of the fighting was necessary to preserve the Army as an organized force capable of deployment against domestic unrest.

[3] S. E. Finer, *The Man on Horseback: The Role of the Military in Politics* (New York: Praeger, 1962), pp. 26–27.

this would be a disruption of the ordinary processes of law and administration engendered by war or civil strife, making the Army the sole force capable of restoring and maintaining order. Out of a combination of personal ambition and favorable circumstances, military rule could thus emerge.

In fact, however, effective democracy—the ultimate foundation of all authority in public opinion and the participation of the citizenry in government—is the *only* kind of legitimacy for which neither the military nor any other bureaucratic component can ever hope to substitute itself. Popular recognition of any oligarchial legitimacy—traditional or innovative—necessarily implies that the citizen accepts a passive subject role for himself.[4] He submits to policies and regulations that are not of his own making, even if presumably only so long as the *source* and *mode* of that authority is X but not Y, Q, or Z. The successful substitution of one oligarchical authority for another in the context of a subject political culture might involve more a change of symbols and personal identity of rulers than of the actual *mode* of governing. It need not require the creation of new political roles for most citizens or the destruction of the old, as a transition from oligarchy to democracy inevitably would.

Under every form of autocracy, government is outwardly bureaucratic, whether it is government in the name of the Tsar, Emperor, Duce, or the General Secretary of the party. Insofar as the citizen is concerned, policy decisions come down to him from the officials. Whether the bureaucracy is a party, or a State bureaucracy, or a mix of the two, may well be beyond the ken of the man in the street. In any case, he expects government decisions to come from the officialdom. Under circumstances of traditionally very limited popular participation in policy making and policy implementation, the military bureaucracy need not have great trouble in substituting itself as the power of the State.[5] So long as the participant roles and capacities are scarce, or nonexistent, the military's task is relatively simple. The viability of a military coup and of a consequent dictatorship can be turned into a calculus of a general's will to power, propitious circumstances, and adequate deployment of force to secure the mechanisms of government. This would be true even where the population was relatively literate and politically mobilized, simply in the sense of having considerable information and awareness of government and of political affairs.

In Imperial Germany of 1916–1918 *de facto* military rule under Hindenburg and Ludendorff was accepted for many months without

[4] *Ibid.*, pp. 87–89.

[5] See Samuel P. Huntington's article, "Patterns of Violence in World Politics," in *Changing Patterns of Military in Politics* (Glencoe, Ill.: Free Press, 1962).

eliciting any outward difficulty. The Army there had always been so close to the imperial throne—and the people sufficiently at arm's length—that given the obvious emergency situation of the war, Army rule appeared quite natural and legitimate. After all, it would have been difficult to tell even before 1914 whether certain aspects of German policy were the initatives of the Kaiser or of the military. Similarly, the Tsar's rule in Russia before 1916 presented both an outward façade and an underlying *reality* of bureaucratic power. Was the Tsar's will his own, or that of his bureaucrats, or perhaps both, and if so to what extent each? The resolution of such matters might well trouble scholars, let alone the average Russian of that era.

Even though a military coup has never yet succeeded in the USSR, China, or any of the Communist states, we might venture to guess that its likelihood is far greater there than in Great Britain, Switzerland, or the United States. If in 1957 Marshal Zhukov had taken adequate measures to "persuade" his 15-odd fellow members of the party's Presidium that he should be designated their First Secretary, the very process of government established by the party, with its emphasis on obedience to central directives, party unity, secrecy, and unanimity, would have facilitated swift and complete control by the leaders of the armed forces. The latter would probably have presented themselves to the Russian public as defenders and guardians of the party's *true* interests, in other words not only as Communists but even as "purer than pure." And under the Soviet system of rule there would have been few opportunities to investigate and challenge the central leadership of the party.

Analogously, for any well-established but autocratic royal dynasty—like Emperor Haile Selassie's in Ethiopia in 1960, for example—the threat of a military coup is always in the background. The dynasty may be held sacred, and royal rule may be widely revered, but might not the Army argue that the incumbent had become "incapacitated"? Perhaps it could be made to appear that he had *asked* his commanders to forestall a nefarious plot against him, and asked them to take over the actual control of government to *prevent* a coup.

All of these vulnerabilities of being a plaything to the military and the bureaucracy only the effective democracies can wholly discount. To be sure, in all systems the military and the bureaucrats are certain to be among the more important pressure groups of politics. But where the notion of legitimacy is identified with widespread political participation of the citizenry, no professional oligarchy could establish its rule: first, because it could not be camouflaged; and secondly, because it would be so unacceptable in the light of prevailing political norms that no *junta* could establish the minimal degree of responsiveness from the society as a whole necessary to make its rule effective.

If American or British generals wanted to prepare a military coup they could discuss it with one another at much less risk and cost than their Nazi or Soviet counterparts. But their long-term prospects of holding power, once seemingly gained, would be far more discouraging.

Within this range of deviation from the responsive democratic model toward corporate autonomy and finally the tool of an oligarchy, the practical consequences to the man in the street range from occasional inconvenience and frustration to major assaults on his security in person, property, and every conceivable right. These variations in bureaucratic behavior can be observed *within* a single nation-state over a long period of time, as well as *among* contemporaneous political systems.

Historically, France and Germany illustrate the variation *within* single nation-states. In France, a large bureaucracy had been brought into being under the Bourbon monarchy. At the time of the French Revolution, it was subject to the directives of King Louis XVI but not to any agencies of popular control. In the succession of regimes that France had had between 1789 and 1871, no democratic, or even quasi-democratic, system lasted long enough to provide the bridle of popular control on the large and cumbersome structure of French administration.

The first genuine attempt at such control could only have come under the Third Republic, which achieved formal constitutional consolidation between 1871 and 1875 and lasted some seventy years until France's defeat at the hands of Nazi Germany in 1940. Nevertheless, the sequence of political development in France had been such that by the time the Republic came into being, French bureaucracy had two centuries of existence behind it, with well-developed political and corporate traditions in its background. To the high civil servant of nineteenth-century France, the democratic republic could well seem—and to most of them it did seem—a transient upstart. Political writers began to speak of the radical tradition of the French Republic confronting the older, conservative one of the French State.

For most of the nineteenth century the dichotomy of outlook and orientation between these two traditions was everywhere evident. The republicans were proponents of universal suffrage, parliamentary government, political and civil liberties for the individual, separation of Church and State, and anticlericalism. The civil service leaders were overwhelmingly conservative, royalist, and clericalist in their views, looking upon the Republic as an aberration from which they, the true, dedicated, professionally competent men, would save France—if necessary, in spite of herself! A dramatic illustration of these divergent political worlds in conflict was provided by the Dreyfus

Affair, which occupied French and world attention from 1896 until 1906. Here some of the ideological premises of both sides at last confronted one another openly in the courts of law and before the bar of public opinion: the honor of the Army and its integrity in the face of cosmopolitan, "un-French" influences such as the abstract rights of the individual—to quote from the Declaration of 1789—as a man and as a citizen.

Although the democratic Republic in France seemed to make headway against the entrenched power of the bureaucratic state, outwardly at least, it was in fact weak and divided in the face of a powerful and long-established machine. French military, diplomatic, and colonial officials and the chiefs of administration at home continued, by and large, to be hostile to and alienated from the institutions of democracy that the Republic outwardly maintained. They may have lacked sufficient popular support to destroy the Republic, as General Boulanger had attempted at the close of the nineteenth century, but they continued in place. It was they who by and large furnished the support for Marshal Petain—himself a representative of the State tradition—when the latter constituted the autocratic and reactionary regime at Vichy from 1940 to 1944.[6]

In the two postwar decades many of the leaders of the Army wanted to pursue a colonial and Algerian policy of their own and were not prepared to tolerate either weakness or confusion among their nominal superiors in Paris, or what they regarded as worse still: betrayal through capitulation to rebels. The inability of the democratic French Republic to control its servants was a continual source of danger to its very survival. In fact, the French armed forces supplied the principal momentum for the destruction of the parliamentary democratic Fourth Republic in 1958.[7] Any citizen who had a stake in the maintenance of democracy in France—for whatever reasons—could not, of course, be indifferent to this. But such dangerous bureaucratic malfunctions could be regarded as occasional—more analogous to volcanic eruptions, under proper circumstances—rather than constant sources of vexation or danger to the citizenry.[8]

[6] See E. Strauss, *The Ruling Servants: Bureaucracy in Russia, France and Britain* (London: Allen and Unwin, 1961), pp. 211–217.

[7] On the Army as catalyst of the 1958 upheaval in France, see Alexander Werth, *The De Gaulle Revolution* (London: Robert Hale, 1960), p. 176; and Philip M. Williams and Martin Harrison, *De Gaulle's Republic* (London: Longmans, 1961), p. 51. See also Dorothy Pickles, *Algeria and France* (New York: Praeger, 1963), p. 60.

[8] See Henry W. Ehrmann, *Organized Business in France* (Princeton, N.J.: Princeton University Press, 1957), pp. 58–100 (Ch. 11) and pp. 210 and 489–490. *Cf.* J. D. Kingsley Davis, *Representative Bureaucracy* (Yellow Springs, Ohio: Antioch Press, 1944), p. 274. Heinz Pol, *Suicide of a Democracy* (New York: Reynal and Hitchcock, 1940), p. 21; André Simon, *J'accuse* (New York: Dial Press, 1940), Ch. 8.

In fact, the dispensation of justice—or settlement of claims against the bureaucracy—by the French Council of State has been so effective that one recent American study conceded the superiority of the French system of special administrative law and administrative courts over the traditional Anglo-Saxon model of control of the administration through the ordinary courts applying the common law.[9]

On the other hand, in the area of implementation of policy and legislation—where the ordinary citizen could not simply sue the bureaucrats on the relatively narrow grounds of illegality—the French bureaucracy has done less well. Among the fields in which it has notoriously sabotaged central directives, in addition to military affairs and financial administration (see Chapter 4), have been social welfare legislation enacted by the Popular Front government under the Socialist Prime Minister, Leon Blum, and from time to time before World War II various aspects of France's official foreign and colonial policy.

Prussia and Bismarkian Germany of 1871–1918 furnish additional examples of bureaucratic establishments that were generally legalistic rather than arbitrary and discriminatory in their proceedings. Broadly speaking, the *law* and the *policy* represented the decisions of the autocracy. The execution or implementation of these, however, was generally safeguarded in such a way that the ordinary citizen could appeal for redress to the bureaucrats, if he felt that they were misapplying the law or the orders of their political superiors. If the citizen had good grounds for his case, he was frequently accommodated. Legalism and efficiency had become so firmly embedded in the Prussian civil service—which was a product of some three centuries of development by the early 1900s—that cases of arbitrary violence, arrest, seizure of property, and the like were relatively rare in the federal, Hohenzollern, Prussian-dominated German Empire.

The top administrative posts throughout the Prussian and German federal bureaucracy, whether military, diplomatic, civil, or judicial, were heavily dominated by representatives of the landholding Junker nobility on which the autocratic power of the Prussian King, and simultaneously the German Emperor, chiefly rested. Toward the end of the nineteenth century, the virtual monopoly of key administrative posts by the Junkers was somewhat diluted by the admission of other, West and South German, nobility, as well as the upper middle class.

Those social strata in which maximum opposition to the autocracy existed, however, and that represented the bulk of the Empire's population—the lower middle class, the workers, and the peasantry—re-

[9] Bernard Schwartz, *French Administrative Law and the Common Law World* (New York: New York University Press, 1954), p. 125.

ceived virtually no representation in the administrative machinery of the governing system. Ingeniously enough, such control as these social classes might possibly have exercised through the central parliament, the Reichstag, was nullified by the delegation of various administrative functions to the states. The latter, beginning with Prussia herself, were generally more autocratic in their political structures and allowed fewer opportunities for participation to elected representatives of the people than did the federal system.[10]

The various branches of the German bureaucracy developed an *ésprit de corps* of their own, with long-established conservative and reactionary biases and traditions analogous to those of the French. But where the French bureaucracy was severed from its original autocratic masters by the upheaval of 1870, in Germany the over-all leadership continued in the hands of the Prussian King and the relatively small monarchical cliques allied with him in the other constituent states of Germany. Thus, notwithstanding the whole Prussian tradition of bureaucratic legalism, the man in the street was exposed to certain kinds of bureaucratic abuse that only effective popular control could have forestalled.

The conduct of the armed forces was a case in point. Since its heyday in the seventeenth century, the Prussian Army was a branch of government service under the King's personal command. The attempt by the Prussian legislature in 1862 to control military spending was successfully defied by Bismarck, and thereafter royal control of the armed forces was never seriously challenged. Where the King could not, or would not, set the initiative or the limits, the Army's commanding officers were a law unto themselves.

When, in 1913, the German military arbitrarily arrested and held in custody a large number of persons in the Alsatian villlage of Saberne, the Reichstag censured the Kaiser's Chancellor, von Bethman-Hollweg, by 293 votes to 55—with no consequences whatever. In fact, the colonel responsible for actions that the representatives of the German people overwhelmingly condemned as an outrage was rewarded with an imperial decoration! If the French Army in 1958 was a state within a state, the German Army in 1914 was rather *the* state within a state.[11]

Would the outcome of such an affair differ under a democratic polit-

[10] The elections to the federal Reichstag were based on universal male suffrage since 1867—that is, the establishment of the North German Confederation preceding the Second Reich. Unlike the Prussian Landtag and other German state legislatures, the Reichstag was not elected by taxpayer estates that gave the wealthy few a disproportionate share of the representatives. Reichstag representation was, however, distorted by malapportionment, and the Reichstag itself was in many crucial respects a very ineffective legislative body.

[11] See Koppel S. Pinson, *Modern Germany* (New York: Macmillan, 1955), pp. 288–289.

ical system, with ultimate government accountability to the public? In October 1962, in democratic West Germany, the then Defense Minister, Franz Joseph Strauss, secretly arranged for the midnight arrest of Rudolf Augstein, publisher of the news magazine *Der Spiegel,* for the search and seizure of the magazine's files, and for Augstein's detention without bail on a charge of treason.

These and related actions of the West German police and officialdom resulted in a major political uproar in the parliament and the press. With the tide of public opinion turning against the initiators and condoners of this midnight raid (only too reminiscent of Nazi Gestapo procedures) the federal cabinet resigned, and Chancellor Adenauer dropped Franz Joseph Strauss from the new cabinet, which had replaced the previous one. This occurred, interestingly enough, in spite of the fact that the coalition cabinet of 1962, of which Franz Joseph Strauss was a member, had a comfortable majority in the Bundestag over the opposition Socialists. But with an election to face in 1965, no West German government could have remained indifferent to the public reaction that had thus manifested itself.

Whether the West German Federal Republic, with barely twenty years of effective democratic mechanisms behind it, can develop and maintain a responsive working relationship between the demands of public opinion and the agencies of the State remains to be seen.[12] We do know that when the mechanisms of autocratic rule crashed at the end of World War I, the bureaucratic apparatus did not readily associate itself with the Weimar experiment in democracy. The German Army Officer corps, in particular, remained dubious and hostile toward the new regime, and evidenced successively by the activities of the Freikorps, the abortive Kapp Putsch of 1920, General Ludendorff's support of Hitler's attempted coup in 1923, and by the attitudes of such Army chieftains as Generals von Blomberg and von Fritsch in the early 1930s, to name but a few.[13]

The political systems in which the bureaucrats have most conspicuously tyrannized and abused the citizenry on the largest scale and with least recourse for those aggrieved have been the totalitarian systems of modern times. Within these, the machinery of government and its sphere of action have been greatly extended, with the simultaneous removal of the legal and prescriptive checks to which the bureaucracy has been generally subject in the traditionalist states. In order to bring about desired changes in the societies around them, the

[12] For an account of the *Der Spiegel* case, see Otto Kirchheimer and Constantine Menges in *Politics in Europe* (New York: Harcourt, Brace and World, 1965), pp. 87–138.

[13] See, for example, John W. Wheeler-Bennett, *The Nemesis of Power: The German Army in Politics, 1918–1945* (New York: St. Martin's Press, 1954), pp. 157–286.

Nazis, the Fascists, and the Communists have sought to limit the autonomy of the bureaucratic apparatus vis-à-vis themselves as policy makers, and cut down on the "impediments" of legality: due process and all such safeguards that would in any way hamper the effectiveness, speed, or thoroughness of their measures.

In the process the inhabitants of these systems have been intermittently subjected to harsher rule by bureaucrats than ever experienced by the people of Imperial Germany or Royal Prussia. These new systems legitimized a capricious absence of rules and safeguards in the administrative process, at the pleasure and discretion of the political leadership, and did it to such a degree as to suggest a parallel with organized crime or banditry embodied in a State.[14]

This did not mean, of course, that the bureaucrats *always* operated without any rules to guide them, or that there were no successful appeals against their dispensations and authority from among their publics. Such a condition would undoubtedly have carried with it total chaos. What it did mean was greatly increased *discretionary* authority and *more* frequent incursions of the political masters into every realm of administration in a prerogative and arbitrary fashion.

Thus, for example, the Nazi regime increased the bureaucracy's power to make decisions arbitrarily by the abolition of the administrative court system in 1939. These courts had existed not only under the Weimar Republic but since 1875 under the Empire. The Nazis, however, made the local administrative chieftain, the Landrat, a one-man tribunal, whose decisions could be appealed only in extraordinary circumstances—to an official directly above him. Thus, as Herbert Jacob concluded:

> These measures completely swept away the system of judicial restraints on Prussian field officials which had existed for half a century. Henceforth, the Landrat was legally responsible only to his administrative superior, the District Officer. Quasijudicial administrative tribunals no longer restricted his scope of action.[15]

While the local bureaucrat thus became more powerful vis-à-vis his public—the inhabitants of his area of jurisdiction—limitations were imposed on the exercise of these increased powers from the Nazi party officialdom and the Nazi central authorities in Berlin. Certain functional, as distinct from geographic, areas of responsibility were put in the hands of the Nazi party rather than those of the State officials. And, however powerful a bureaucrat might be in his own

[14] On the Nazi State as a non-State—that is, a community ruled by lawless predators, see Franz L. Neumann, *Behemoth* (New York: Oxford University Press, 1942).

[15] *German Administration Since Bismarck* (New Haven: Yale University Press, 1963), p. 126.

district, he could not be safe from the retribution of the Gestapo should he seriously displease the influentials in the party.

Nevertheless, the impact of the Nazi regime was such as to not only greatly increase the power of officialdom over the citizenry, but to bestow that power substantially upon the bureaucrats of the old regime. As David Schoenbaum puts it in his recent study:

> The effect, in terms both of personnel policy and constitutional development, was that the Party as such was not integrated in the affairs of State. In part it was superimposed on them, in part excluded from them altogether. . . . Even after all patronage debts were paid, political enemies eliminated, and ideological goals—such as the elimination of Jewish officials—achieved, the loss in Prussia, the hardest-hit of the States, was only 25 per cent, in the rest of Germany 10 per cent. . . . In 1937, 81 per cent of all Prussian civil servants were Party members but only 48 per cent of them had joined the Party before 1933. In the rest of the Reich, the comparable ratio was 63 per cent and 11 per cent.[16]

A similar impact of increased bureaucratic powers, combining mostly old and some new officialdom was felt in Italy under Mussolini's rule in the 1920s and 1930s. In Nazi Germany, some district officials were leaders of party and State simultaneously, although most of their bureaucratic staffs and officials were regular pre-Nazi and non-Nazi civil servants.

Mussolini, however, continued to maintain complete separation of the party and State bureaucracies to the last. Each hierarchy was distinct and responsible to a different set of officials in Rome. In maintaining two nation-wide bureaucracies, Mussolini gave formal supremacy to that of the State. A circular issued by the Duce on January 5, 1927, made the Prefects virtual local replicas of the national dictator's powers. In formally subordinating the officialdom of the party to the officialdom of the State, Mussolini ran the risk of conflict and subversion.

> The problem was partly eased by the gradual appointment of Fascist generals and Party leaders to the prefectoral posts. In the early years of the regime, few career Prefects were dismissed or voluntarily resigned. Many Prefects shared the sympathy for Fascism, in its conservative aspects, which prevailed in the Court, and among other high state functionaries, large landowners, industrialists, the aristocracy, and many of the liberal politicians. The position of the Prefects in the early years was not enviable, but with the trend toward "normal-

[16] *Hitler's Social Revolution* (Garden City, N.Y.: Doubleday and Company, 1968), pp. 204–205. See also Paul Seabury, *The Wilhelmstrasse* (Berkeley: University of California Press, 1954), pp. 161–162, on the German Foreign Office personnel under nazism. At the end of 1937 out of 92 top departmental officials, only 33 were party members, and of these only seven had joined the NSDAP *before* entering the Foreign Office.

ization," and indications of increasing prefectoral power and prestige, Party members began to press for prefectoral appointments. The first group of Fascist Prefects, all generals (sic!) was appointed in 1923; every year afterward a new infusion by Party elements took place so that by the mid-thirties about half of all Prefects serving in the provinces were from outside the regular career service.[17]

Ten years after the original decree vesting administrative supremacy in the Prefects, Mussolini confirmed the traditional bureaucracy in its share of power by requiring that "three-fifths of all Prefects on the rolls be taken from the career service of the Interior."[18] And, again in analogy to the German Nazi experience, the Fascist regime maintained various field agencies additional to and outside the scope of prefectoral supervision. Such agencies included old-age and disability-insurance administration; war invalids' assistance; poor relief; and workmen's compensation, as well as branch offices of the central ministries in Rome locally staffed by Fascist appointees. And like his German counterpart, every Italian bureaucrat was spied on, informed on, and terrorized by the secret police and the party organs reporting through their own separate channels to the Duce in Rome.

In Italy, there continued to exist bodies advisory to the Prefects and formally, at least, expressive of local opinion. But before fascism these bodies were elective; under fascism they were appointed by the Prefect himself with the approval of the Ministry of the Interior, and the Prefect's choices were predictably politically limited and biased.

> Most of the *Presidi* and *Podesta* were in practice chosen from among the traditional aristocratic and bourgeois ruling classes, thus excluding the representatives of the peasants and industrial workers from the major source of governmental-administrative power that they had been able to win since the unification of the country.[19]

The regimes of Hitler and Mussolini succeeded to power with substantial support and a reservoir of good will in the bureaucratic machinery of Germany and Italy, respectively. Among the armed forces, the police, the judiciary, and the diplomatic service, sundry officialdom of the Germany of 1933 and Italy of 1922, Hitler and Mussolini had many supporters. These officials helped the new dictators to power overtly in some cases, and merely by benevolent neutrality in other instances. Thus, both regimes could and did regard various segments of the bureaucracy as adjuncts and allies in maintaining power. Neither Hitler nor Mussolini could have dispensed with the support of

[17] See Robert C. Fried, *The Italian Prefects: A Study in Administrative Politics* (New Haven: Yale University Press, 1963), p. 183.

[18] *Ibid.*, p. 185.

[19] *Ibid.*, p. 204.

the armed forces whose power vis-à-vis their own was in each case very considerable indeed.

In contrast, Communist take-overs were overtly directed against virtually all the forces of the then status quo, Army and bureaucracy foremost among them. Far from courting the bureaucrats as Hitler did in the 1920s, in 1917 Lenin promised them ultimate extinction at the hands of organized workers in *State and Revolution* and scores of other pronouncements and publications. Moreover, Communist victories were achieved in the face of widespread destruction of the bureaucratic machinery of the old regime—the armed forces in particular. The bureaucrats were in each case badly weakened enemies, not powerful allies. Finally, we must also consider the comparative social-reformist aspirations of these movements. Fascism and nazism dismissed the ideal of far-reaching economic betterment for the underprivileged as an idle dream and an essentially worthless aspiration. They were contemptuous of the ideologies that exalted the "full belly" or material satisfactions for the poor. To be sure, both nazism and fascism made much use of radical language in their propaganda, freely adapting the verbal violence of embittered Marxian working-class parties. The sum and substance of their proposals for reform of Germany in 1933 or Italy in 1922, as enunciated by the authoritative leaders, however, were very much less sweeping than the Communists'. The leaders stood committed to forging national unity and national power. Egalitarian reforms were at best incidental to this purpose. Like the spokesmen of nineteenth-century reaction, they dwelled on the virtues of heroism, unity, struggle, and grandeur and not on the satisfaction of the needs of the atomized components of society—the individuals. For these reasons also, fascism and nazism could be more readily satisfied with the routine performance of bureaucratic functions by an inherited, as it were, bureaucratic apparatus.

Such modifications in structure, personnel, and procedures as were carried out by Hitler and Mussolini in peacetime, before 1939, were far more piecemeal and partial in nature than those made by Lenin and the Russian Communists after 1917 during a corresponding period of time. The aspirations of communism made it impossible to acquiesce in the continuance of government machinery by the same old hands, under the same old rules, and through the same old institutions. First of all, such continuance would have spelled drastic vulnerability to the Communist regime in terms of overthrow from within or counterrevolution. For given the nature of Communist objectives and program, would not Tsarist bureaucrats sabotage and undermine them if they could?

Thus, the Communists moved to eliminate the risks in all directions:

institutions, procedures, and personnel. We may note, however, that even in the case of the Russian Communist revolution, political factors leading to change were always subject to environmental restraints. Innovation and upheaval were checked by a calculus of necessity. Political reliability in the bureaucratic cadres was needed and was being sought, but so also was a minimum of professional-technical competence. The new Red Army could not really operate effectively in the field, as Trotsky found out, without competent officers. Men had to be trained to read maps, decipher codes, and know something about weapons before they could really fight. And while Communist-taught proletarian officer schools were being hastily organized, the Red Army continued to use Tsarist officers under the surveillance, to be sure, of the political commissars of the Communist party. Analogously, the dispossessed owners of industrial and commercial establishments throughout Russia were being frequently pressed into service as managers of the enterprises that they had once owned.

In variously modified forms, these drives for change in the bureaucratic apparatus, and the restraints on such changes, recurred under all of the Communist-led regimes of Eastern Europe and Asia after World War II. The resulting pattern of bureaucratic performance in the Communist systems, as compared with the Fascist and the Nazi systems, was to increase the over-all proportion of innovation in personnel, methods, and structures of the former regimes.

Although the rule of the Communists has tended to replace and weaken the autonomy and the integrity of the old bureaucracy more, the total power of the bureaucrat (old or new) versus that of the citizen at large was greatly increased in all these systems.

If we look upon the bureaucracy in the modern total States from the standpoint of the average citizen, as a consumer of their services, we should find that those services have tended to be offered less in response to local need and more in response to either central government or autonomous bureaucratic authority, and sometimes to a combination of both. We should also find that the services have tended to be performed in an arbitrary, often capricious, and "let-the-public-be-damned" fashion, with little recourse for the citizen who may have suffered in the process and wishes to obtain redress.

Current illustrations of citizens' mistreatment at the hands of an innovative-autocratic bureaucracy are provided in the nationalized economies of the USSR and Eastern Europe. For the housewife and the shopper in government-run stores, the indifference, poor service, and occasional abuse faced across the counter of the grocery store represent historic and tangible expressions of a basic political situation. In all these cases the bureaucrat is not subject either to an ultimate or immediate popular control and can well afford to be indifferent, harsh, arbitrary, and capricious toward his public. He is likely to be thoughtful, considerate, and responsive only insofar as his clientele has preferential access to the rulers. The bureaucracy has acquired an immunity from public exposure and criticism, utterly inconceivable under democratic regimes. The results have been genuinely paradoxical. In virtually any individual case the bureaucrat would not merely be removed from his job, but he would forfeit his life and his liberty if he seriously displeased the ruling tyrant; the vengeance of a Hitler or a Stalin was incomparably more arbitrary and brutal than that of a Wilhelm II. Simultaneously, however, the bureaucrat was assured that no complaint against him could possibly become a matter of public knowledge or public controversy—unless the ruling party wanted to make it such. Thus, for example, even in those cases in which appeal procedures were *not* abolished in Nazi Germany—for such complaints as personal mistreatment, unlawful seizure of property, and so forth—the citizen could not mobilize public opinion on behalf of his cause. He stood before the courts or the administrative authorities alone, hat in hand, to receive such consideration as they might deign to give or refuse. No media of communication would report the facts of his case; no opposition spokesman in the national parliament or in the local legislature could take up his cause. His only possible leverage could derive from "inside connections" with the party. Barring these, he was alone.

From time to time, Communist party organs of Russia, China, and the other People's Democracies conduct campaigns against alleged bureaucratic wrongdoing. They may occasionally publish letters from irate citizens denouncing the bureaucrats. But all such criticism is invariably very carefully screened and limited. Often, it does not even reflect the grievances of the people, but rather the grievances of the party and the displeasure of the dictator. For the ordinary man, reading his daily newspaper, the denunciations of the bureaucrats for failure to implement the latest six-year plan in a more enthusiastic and energetic fashion sound hollow. They are not *his* grievances, and they do not concern *him* nearly as much as the police, administrative, or economic abuses that the party organs do not mention because the disclosures would compromise the regime. Instead, the regime may allow some subliminal shadow-boxing in which the citizen's real grievances against his government functionaries are harmlessly deflected by selective and relatively innocuous denunciations—even humor—directed at bureaucratic red tape, foot dragging, and the like.

In the democracies the bureaucrat's life and his job are safer; they are protected by many safeguards, not the least of which is public opinion. On the other hand, the bureaucrat's policy can rarely, if ever, be hidden under a rug and remain impervious to the expressed wishes of the community he serves. No aggrieved citizen needs to stand alone before the agencies of the State in a democratic political system—regardless of whether these agencies are judicial, administrative, or openly and overtly political.

In some respects, the controls over bureaucratic performance in the effective democracies have always been very much alike—even the same. The operation of administrative organs has been legally sanctioned, funded, and audited by legislative bodies. Even though these bodies could not, generally speaking, act as courts watching over bureaucratic behavior in this or that particular instance, they could always make changes in the rules and the structure of bureaucratic operations if they regarded them as unsatisfactory. In conjunction with the executive—or, as in the American experience, apart from it—the legislatures could undertake to investigate specific bureaucratic operations, publicize and expose them if they wished, and exercise the power of legislating remedies for the abuses. And although the legislatures of modern democracies do not wholly replicate the functions of courts, they are forums in which, as classically in the case of the British House of Commons, grievances against particular instances of administrative misconduct can be aired by representatives acting on behalf of their constituents. Such grievances, if serious enough, are almost inevitably seized on by all those who have a political axe to grind. All the organized interests that directly or indirectly are involved in elections are also potential participants in the discussion of individual grievances, insofar as these either affect their own rights and interests or are used to promote political ends. If a scandal or the discovery of some gross mismanagement or abuse of power can be made to reflect discredit on one's political opponents, in government or outside it, such a discovery is not likely to be quickly buried or forgotten. One of the salient operative features of all democratic systems is that the bureaucracy cannot hide behind the shield of (1) general and complete censorship and/or (2) procedures of redress and appeal that are in practice so private that although they may or may not give relief to specific individuals they offer little security to the public as a whole.

Nevertheless, it would be physically impossible for parliamentary bodies, however ardent in defense of individual liberties, to give attention to *all* those cases in which individuals feel they have been mistreated by government. And there is, increasingly, a serious problem of competence on the part of the legislators, cabinet ministers, and other political spokesmen in attempting any systematic or thorough review of administrative acts, a problem analogous to that of ordinary courts, not really familiar with all the technical aspects of administration.

Because of this difficulty, a new institution has come into use among the modern democracies, adapted from the Swedish example of 1809—the Ombudsman.[20] The duties and the legal competence of the Ombudsman vary among the several systems in which the institution has been adopted.[21]

In Sweden, the Ombudsman may investigate administrative as well as regular court proceedings and decisions of every kind; he may do so on his own initiative, or on the basis of a complaint from any interested citizen. The steps undertaken by the Ombudsman involve no costs to the citizen; nor do they require representation by an attorney or even, in most cases, the citizen's own actual participation, beyond a letter of complaint. The Ombudsman may publish the results of his investigation; and he may advise or admonish administrators and judges. Moreover, he may order the prosecution of bureaucrats (including judges) if he thinks that to be warranted by misconduct in office seriously prejudicial to an individual or to the public interest. He does not, however, *decide* any cases.

The Ombudsman annually reports to Parliament, which elects him to his office for a four-year term, supervises, and, if necessary, criticizes his activities. The Swedish Ombudsman is wholly independent of the executive, judicial, and administrative branches of the government. His tenure of office, his salary, and his conduct are legally and politically at the pleasure of the national legislature, as provided by law.

In other countries in which the institution of the Ombudsman has been adopted, his powers have been more restricted. In New Zealand, for example, the so-called Parliamentary Commissioner does not oversee the work of the regular courts of justice but only of the administrative agencies; and he cannot initiate prosecutions of officials. He can merely recommend action either to the administrative authorities involved, or to the cabinet minister in charge of that particular branch of administration. And if he is not satisfied with the ministerial response, the Commissioner may then report and appeal to Parliament.

Although the functions and the responsibilities of the Ombudsman differ from place to place, the redress-of-grievance and the watchdog functions that are performed—in Sweden and New Zealand, as well as in Denmark, Finland, and Norway—have much in common. They are all anchored in the ultimate authority of the representatives of the people—that is, of Parliament, and beyond it in public opinion. Notwithstanding all the differences of jurisdiction, the effectiveness of the

[20] The Swedish word *ombud* refers to someone who acts as spokesman for another.
[21] See Donald C. Rowat, *The Ombudsman* (London: Allen and Unwin, 1965).

Ombudsman in each case depends much less on the ultimate sanction of legal proceedings than on recourse to the judgment of the people.

The Ombudsman is, in each case, empowered to look into all of the information available to the bureaucracy and to make public disclosure of such information to other administrative organs: to the courts, to ministers of the government, to news media, and finally to Parliament, subject to safeguards protecting national security and privacy for the participants.[22]

Ulf Lundvik, a Swedish judge and former Deputy Ombudsman, has expressed the underlying common denominator of such activities in these terms:

> The publicity given to the Ombudsman's activity should not be looked upon merely as a consequence of old Swedish traditions. For the proper functioning of the Ombudsman system a considerable amount of publicity seems indispensable. The Ombudsman's decisions on questions of principle would lose most of their importance if they were not brought to the attention of all those officials who may have to deal with similar questions. Furthermore, no Ombudsman would be able to discharge his duties effectively without the confidence of the people, and in order to gain that confidence he must exercise his activity openly and not withhold his decisions from the scrutiny of the public.[23]

It is interesting to note that in the Swedish experience, the institution of the Ombudsman has grown actually more effective under conditions of increasing governmental growth—that is, of great multiplication of government agencies, personnel, and activities. In the nineteenth century, when parliamentary government in Sweden was based on very restricted suffrage and the King still not only reigned but also ruled, cases of flagrant abuse and transgression of the laws on the part of the bureaucracy were far more frequent, despite the fact that "government" was then a far more limited and far simpler operation that it is now. But in the nineteenth century, many victims of administrative abuse did not as yet constitute an effective public opinion—their views, and the views of others like them, did not particularly matter to the bureaucracy because they possessed little, if any, political leverage through the legislative and executive branches of the political system.

However useful the institution of an Ombudsman may have been, or is, under conditions of pronounced oligarchy, it is far more effective when combined with wide diffusion of popular power. A case in point is that of Yugoslavia, which has recently created an Ombudsman. No

[22] In Denmark only the Ombudsman's decisions or opinions are made public, whereas in Sweden virtually any documents involved may be made public as well.

[23] Rowat, *op. cit.*, p. 50.

Communist system in history, including the Yugoslav, has as yet acknowledged the objectivity of law or of its administration. No Communist system has acknowledged the equal rights of all persons, regardless of their political opinions, their political affiliations, or even their social origins, to equal consideration by the organs of the administration of a Communist-ruled state.

In a variety of ways the primacy of the party and the overriding public importance of building a Socialist and then Communist society, for and by the toilers and under the leadership of their party vanguard, have been distinguishing features of all the avowedly Communist regimes to date. It is hardly likely that party rule could be long maintained under conditions of genuine equality for Communists, non-Communists, and anti-Communists alike.

Possibly, the Ombudsman could prove to be a forerunner of the liquidation of one-party rule in Yugoslavia. More likely, he will serve in traditional Communist fashion in the role of a minor lightning rod for popular discontent. He may rectify minor abuses and even provide the party, like the Prosecutor General of the USSR and other Communist systems, with an additional avenue of control and supervision of the bureaucracy. The least likely alternative, compatible with the maintenance of Communist rule, would be for the Ombudsman to protect anti-Communists from arbitrary arrest, detention, trial, and more generally from persecution and discrimination at the hands of the State.

Apart from the intentions and inclinations of Marshal Tito and his party colleagues, the Yugoslav Ombudsman cannot find in the political infrastructure of the system around him those independent and even oppositional organs of opinion—in the press, in the legislature, in the political parties, and in the organized interest groups—that would give wide publicity to his findings and recommendations, should they clash with, or compromise, the position of the ruling party.

On the other hand, in effective democracies such as Britain or Switzerland, the values promoted by the Ombudsman in Scandinavia are already realized to a far greater degree then they are in Yugoslavia, without the Ombudsman! Unless wrongdoing can be genuinely publicized, and the bureaucracy has something to fear from an aroused citizenry, its incentives to reform and virtue must remain necessarily limited. The bureaucrat's eye will still be fixed largely on the party, not on the public. If, however, through genuine diffusion of popular power and means of expression, criticism can be effectively secured and translated into various tangible consequences for the bureaucracy, no single institutional device, like the Ombudsman, is indispensable to it.

Another aspect of bureaucracy's impact on society that is closely related to the democratic-authoritarian dichotomy is the representativeness of the bureaucratic establishment. The representative character of the bureaucracy may be seen as a political issue to the extent that we can establish links between *who* the bureaucrats are and *what* they do: between the policies and the dispensations and the political, social, economic, or cultural characteristics of those making them. Still another political issue, however, is posed by the bureaucracy as an important source of employment and career opportunities giving an equal chance to all to participate in the administrative side of politics.

Not all democracies have had equally high marks in achieving representative bureaucracies. But with respect to criteria of openness based on political affiliation as well as social or ethnic background of entrants, only the democracies have made it a major issue of policy to achieve such openness and representativeness in their systems.

Autocratic bureaucracies have generally operated under discriminatory recruitment policies, both explicitly and implicitly. Discrimination has been established either directly with formal *exclusions* of certain classes of citizens, as under Soviet and Nazi laws, or by the delegation of the recruitment function to the bureaucratic agencies themselves. In the process, the subject of popular access to the bureaucracy is outwardly a nonsubject among the traditional autocracies such as, until most recently, modern Spain or Ethiopia.

In autocracies—such as the USSR or People's China—in which the recruitment of bureaucracy does receive public attention, its discriminatory character is explicit in the effort to secure the services of certain elements to the exclusion of others: workers and peasants but not bourgeois; Communist and nonparty people, but not those professing adherence to "reactionary and bourgeois ideologies." Again, the identity and number of those discriminated against vary from one dictatorship to another. What is common among them is the denial of universal access to the public service to all citizens.

The exclusion of the bourgeoisie in Russia or of Jews in Germany or of Protestants in Spain have in each case been officially regarded as exemplary and laudable actions, hopefully to be continued into perpetuity. The relative exclusion of workers' sons from the bureaucracy in Great Britain has been not only officially lamented and deplored but has drawn measurable effort to end it.[24]

[24] On some of the problems of recruitment and service, see Victor A. Thompson (ed.), "Bureaucracy in a Democratic Society," in *Public Administration and Democracy* (Syracuse, N.Y.: Syracuse University Press, 1965), pp. 205–226; on Britain, see Fabian Society, *The Reform of the Higher Civil Service* (London: Gollancz, 1947); R. K. Kelsall, *Higher Civil Servants in Britain from 1870 to the Present Day* (London: Routledge and Kegan Paul, 1955); and E. N. Gladden, *British Public Service Administration* (London: Staples, 1961).

Summing up the discussion of this chapter, we may say that the citizen as a consumer of bureaucratic services receives the most considerate and unarbitrary treatment where he "counts" politically—that is, in the effective democracies. This generalization can be qualified by the recognition that the capacity of the bureaucracy to give efficient service is clearly also related to its material and intellectual resources.

In countries in which democracy has not been firmly established, the citizen's treatment by the bureaucracy is likely to vary widely. In the totalitarian autocracies of the twentieth century, bureaucratic rule has been emancipated from traditional and legal restraint to such an extent that the citizen is deprived of safeguards successively available from (1) the substantial autonomy and possibly traditional professionalism of the bureaucracy characteristic of many politically unstable or divided regimes; (2) the restraints of custom and law characteristic of traditionalist oligarchies; and (3) the recourse to the lever of popular will characteristic of the effective democracies.

Finally, we note that in all autocratic systems the bureaucracy is regarded not as a representative of the whole society but rather as a special governing force. Its recruitment is confined to certain politically and socially acceptable strata of society in such a way as to make it a pillar of the oligarchy—analogous in views to the rulers and pliant and quiescent toward their directives. The scope of recruitment of a bureaucracy among the democracies is generally wider and therefore also culturally, intellectually, and socioethnically more representative of the citizenry. But even among the autocracies, recruitment of the bureaucracy may have unintentionally upsetting political consequences to the extent that the requirements of modernization—the technological and economic needs of survival—necessitate an expansion of entry opportunities beyond the prudent dictator's own best preference.

CHAPTER 11
CONCLUSION: POLITICAL VALUES AND POLITICAL CHANGE

IN the preceding chapters we have examined different political systems from the standpoint of the values that they distribute to their populations. In a sense, one might say that this is what politics is all about. The comparisons we can make among different polities, however roughly and imperfectly, can help us understand "who gets what, when, and how," given a particular form of political organization in a given society. Unless we supply our own values to the appraisal of the comparisons, however, we have no way of calling X good and Y bad or worse. Without reference to our own particular values, it is impossible to decide, for example, which regime promotes human values better, or is more just and equitable in terms of the welfare of its people. Nor can we even make judgments about which values correlate with success, and which with failure, because such appraisals also need criteria for deciding just what it is that success implies for a political system. Perhaps not everyone would agree with us on criteria of this kind. The same facts may well mean different things to different people.[1]

[1] *Cf.* Theodore J. Lowi, *The End of Liberalism* (New York: W. W. Norton, 1969),

Our discussion has focused on the value-distributions or attributes, as it were, of three principal kinds of political systems: We have analyzed the attributes of democracies, with special attention paid to those well-established regimes that have maintained their process-and-structure democratic characteristics since before World War II. And we have considered the attributes of autocracies of two basic orientations: the innovative-mobilizational, particularly the Communist as the most extreme form of these, and the traditional-quiescent.

We have noticed an important distinction between *all* autocracies, however, and *all* democracies. It appears that the autocratic regimes, whatever their particular predominant tendencies, are more likely to undergo sharp and sudden oscillations of policy outputs, or values distributed, because of the more limited nature and size of their controlling publics. Democracies involve political processes so open and widely based that their policies are likely to be more fixed or inelastic, other things being equal. Autocracies embark on occasional zigzags—more often, more steeply, and in more policy areas—because basically the rulers are watched and controlled by fewer people through more cumbersome control mechanisms. This elasticity of autocratic government can and often does produce apparent anomalies, as when traditional rulers, within what appear to be traditionally autocratic systems, occasionally pursue very mobilizational, avant-garde, progressive policies in various fields: historically, men like Bismarck, Joseph II, Peter the Great, and currently some modern rulers of Afghanistan, Kuwait, Iran, Ethiopia, and Paraguay, among others.

To be sure, we can speak of fairly persistent output profiles among various political systems. These enable us to distinguish, for example, Portugal or Spain from any Communist regime on the basis of six or seven output indices at any time during the last twenty to thirty years. But the variety and complexity of system attributes cannot be minimized, and much more numerous and refined analytical tools would be necessary before one could achieve an automatic computer read-out on just what kind of political system X or Y *really* represents; or how and when it critically changes from one to another. Even our fairly rudimentary discussion here indicates the existence of political subsystems that are difficult to categorize, such as the Nazi and Fascist autocracies combining innovative-mobilizational with traditional-

pp. 293–297 for a summary critique of liberal, pluralistic interest group democracy in the United States. The difficulty with concretizing the notion of a truly satisfactory democracy or indeed a truly satisfactory political system is best expressed by Lowi when he says that "Poverty is all relativity." See p. 214. On this issue, as on all others, no distributive pattern, *per se*, can answer the question of what *ought* or *will* satisfy or dissatisfy people.

quiescent attributes. Lack of adequate information has prevented us from enriching our conceptual models more fully with the experience of relatively new nations such as Indonesia, Burma, Kenya, or Pakistan. Finally, certain trends and tendencies in social and economic development are found to be characteristic of all polities in the modern world, suggesting important intersystem influences and worldwide trends but also a certain discounting of these trends depending on the particular political order of a given society.

Because the values of autonomous political participation—for individuals and groups alike—are maximized in the democracies all their resource distributions discussed here (tax burdens, investments, culture and education, social welfare, manipulation of individual status and wealth, justice, and treatment by the bureaucracy) fall within a narrower range of variation than can be found among divergent types of autocracy.

With respect to the distributive aspects of participation, it is clear that different kinds of involvement in politics by individuals are not only *means* but they may be valuable as *ends* in themselves. The development of civic orientation or capacity may be regarded as a cultural, educational, and moral asset. It may also be a psychological "good." Traditionally oriented oligarchies discourage political involvement; totalitarian-mobilizational regimes promote it differently than democracies, with less emphasis on autonomous individual roles.

Where democracies carefully safeguard the right of petition and the right of association, all authoritarian regimes control, restrict, and inhibit it—although significantly different approaches characterize the status quo traditional autocracies and the totalitarian, or mobilizing, states. Labor unions are effectively restricted in a variety of traditional regimes much more so than churches and employers' associations. Innovative regimes restrict organized groups more than traditional systems do, and Communist regimes exceed the Nazi and Fascist ones in direct group controls. The effectiveness of group claims on government is affected by these system attributes. The range of permissible group claims narrows down as totalitarian aspirations of autocracy rise.

Tax and budget policies of the democracies, examined in terms of income and outgo, reflect the tendency to balance a wide variety of interests with greater resultant equity for the claims of constituents. The costs of government tend to be more evenly distributed in political systems that make it effectively possible for most significant group interests to assert and pursue their claims in relative equality, unhindered by legal or nonlegal obstacles and prohibitions. Confiscation is not a significant resource intake among the democracies. However, in the effective democracies, with a high degree of individual and group security, the privileged elites show a capacity for influencing governmental action well beyond their mere power of numbers. And this tends to mitigate egalitarian tendencies by significant assertions of special individual and group interests.

The actual effective share of national wealth devoted to public welfare purposes has generally tended to be smallest in traditional autocracies. Under authoritarian regimes where the oligarchies are ideologically oriented to preserving the status quo, great inequalities are endemic in terms of consumption taxes, rate structures, assessment, and collection and enforcement procedures, all of which tend to be discriminatory against the have-not elements. Allocations to public health, education, and popular culture are conspicuously low. Bureaucratic and military allocations are likely to be more generous. In the authoritarian systems whose oligarchies are ideologically oriented to a change of the social structure, notably the Communist ones, welfare spending tends to be much more generous; democracies fluctuate between these extremes. Autocratic budgetary allocations involve secrecy and concealment.

Under autocratic regimes there tends to be limited group access in the formulation of economic policy enabling the innovative, and particularly the Communist, systems to follow policies restrictive of consumption and geared to forced industrialization. Traditional oligarchies, however, protect relatively lavish private consumption patterns of established elites. Economic policies and policy-making organs of democracies tend to be more responsive to popular opinion, including both its relatively privileged as well as underprivileged strata. The gulf between the "in's" and "out's" appears to be deeper in the authoritarian regimes, particularly among the innovational-mobilized systems. This distinction affects the administration of economic policy as well as its formulation.

Great quantitative encouragement of public education on a mass basis at all levels, within the constraints of available wealth, is generally characteristic of Communist autocracies. Considering their resources, effective democracies probably have been next in rank in affording educational opportunities to the masses of the people. Considering the diversity of educational offerings, however, and the encouragement and support of private education, we find that effective democracies give a fuller expression to diverse popular aspirations and wants.

Traditional autocracies are not interested in costly and politically explosive expansion of education, particularly at higher levels. Fascist regimes, true to their avowed principles, fear and restrict intellectual education, whereas Communists pursue both industrialization and political safety through the creation of substantially new intellectual-technological elites bred in their own image. All autocratic regimes use censorship and curriculum controls to secure themselves the "right kind" of educational system. Discrimination and restraints characterize both the admission of students and the management of teaching staffs. Publicly financed diffusion and subsidies of popular culture media are characteristic of Communist regimes far more than of other systems.

Among authoritarian regimes, welfare programs range from being nonexistent to highly developed ones. In those generally subsumed under the quiescent autocracies there is a reliance on traditional charities and self-help, with indifference frequently to have-not suffering. Among the totalitarian and especially Communist regimes, many legal and administrative safeguards are lacking, and discriminatory practices in the administration of otherwise generous assistance programs are frequent. Social welfare policies tend to be highly politicized—that is, used as tools for introdoctrination or control of the populace by the rulers. In the effective democracies, concern with costs, tax burdens, and bureaucratic controls frequently acts as a counterweight to the speedy expansion of social welfare programs; policies are generally responsive to popular demands, however, and provide extensive legal and administrative protections of individual and family interests.

The democracies have been characterized by policies of aspiration to open up access to decision-making jobs and to public careers within their respective societies, although with mixed results. In traditional oligarchies, and Nazi-Fascist dictatorships, such policies have been conspicuously slower and more limited. Certain social groups, including workers, peasants, women, and racial minorities, among others, have been the most seriously disadvantaged.

The progress of social reform in the democracies has been slowed by the striving for legal-orderly changes that would safeguard the rights of individuals (as in nationalization) and minimize dangers to popular consensus. Innovative-mobilizational and Communist autocracies have frequently implemented the more radical policies of equalization and replacement of old elites, but unlike the democracies they have carried them out at the tangible cost of individual safeguards, national consensus, and frequently with the ruthless sacrifice of the economy. In the process, new privileged elites have replaced the old ones, although the pale of opportunity for the previously disadvantaged—as in Russia or China—has been often dramatically widened. The extension of opportunities to new social groups has been accompanied by sharp organizational and political *restrictions*, a cutting down on the number of channels and on the variety of ideological-cultural traditions through which individuals could ascend in the social hierarchies.

In terms of justice and police power, democratic systems are less prone to intervention from "above" and more open to demands from "below." These factors contribute to the psychological value of individual (and group) security.

The discretionary power of State organs, in war or peace, against the individual or private associations is generally greater among the authoritarianisms. Traditional dictatorships oriented to the maintenance of the status quo are less given to terror or extralegal expedients in the exercise of police power as compared with the totalitarian-mobilizational systems.

One of the key differences between the democracies and the authoritarian states is found in the publicity of judicial and police proceedings. The openness of the judicial as well as of the administrative mechanisms makes for great, even paradoxical, system differences: with *individual* private property safer in Socialist Britain than in Nazi Germany, Trujillo's Dominican Republic, or authoritarian Paraguay!

In the twentieth century there has been a greatly increased total impact of government and politics on the citizenry. In the democracies there are extensive legal and administrative safeguards against bureaucratic abuse, with many open channels of appeal and redress. The effective diffusion of popular power through political parties, interest groups, and elected officials provides controls of the bureaucratic establishment at the summit of power; and publicity and openness of procedures allow for the weight of public opinion to be felt in the exercise of bureaucratic functions from below. The total power of the bureaucracy, vis-à-vis the citizen, is generally greater under all authoritarian regimes, although among these regimes there are significant variations.

In the traditional oligarchies the bureaucracy may be limited in its roles and have a rather stable, autonomous, and appropriately traditional character of its own. In totalitarian regimes the bureaucracy is a greater or lesser amalgam of the inherited old regime and new (party or movement) components; but in any case, the total range of its powers is inevitably expanded.

Given these broad value-orientations, how do they relate to the problem of maintaining and/or changing political systems?

What is called the viability of political systems is in large measure simply a function of their *acceptability*—that is, the degree to which they coincide with the value-dispositions of the members of a given society. These dispositions vary both in time and place. Even the recognition of so-called common social problems requires common values.[2] In any polity, even the most stable, the order of values is

[2] See the interesting discussion on people's perceptions of change in D. A. Strick-

likely to undergo some shifts over prolonged periods. We do not have a general elite key to such change. Which members of the society have to change their minds about political values in order for a system to cease being viable or, conversely, perhaps, for it to become viable?

The viability of all political systems requires, in the last analysis, certain kinds of dispositions on the part of the people living within them. Gabriel Almond and Sidney Verba have grouped these under the term *political culture*. Democracy requires the widespread acceptance of participatory values. Even if not *all* its citizens believe in the utility, or even the possibility, of self-government, *many* must believe in it for the system to be practically operative. The norms or attitudes required can certainly be taught to a population through the various avenues of political socialization, and they can probably be initiated, augmented or stimulated to a large extent by external agencies—as in Western Germany after 1945, for example, through the efforts of the Occupying Allied Powers. But as *values* they cannot be easily forced on people. Periodic elections and a formal machinery of government can be established by decree, but it is extremely difficult to force men into the roles of eager and watchful critics of government. Forcing them to be independent, autonomous, and critical is a task beyond the capability of physical compulsion. One can readily enough restrain, stop, and prohibit people's actions through force. Making them thoughtful and even enthusiastic about public affairs—which is a significant aspect of democracy—is a far more complex problem. A prevalent state of mind is the ultimate requisite of any viable political system and particularly a democracy. An atmosphere of mutual trust, a measure of security with respect to one's expectations of most other people in the polity, and a modicum of skills in the population are all required to some degree.

Material requisites, however, are, as the case of modern Germany has shown, not enough. Traditionally conditioned attitudes may well be more important. And these are likely to arise only in consequence of a favorable sequence of past political development or historical evolution. They may demand considerable past cohesion, stability, and success in meeting people's policy or output expectations.

Constitutional development is one large part of this tradition. In the case of Britain, for example, democratic values have enjoyed the advantage of prescription—a long life and legitimacy (in the sense of gaining widespread acceptance as being the lawful and "rightful" system of rule for the nation).

Thus we find that in Britain the Glorious Revolution of 1688 not

---

land, L. L. Wade, and R. E. Johnston, *A Primer of Political Analysis* (Chicago: Markham, 1968), pp. 10–13.

only established the sovereign power of Parliament supreme in fact and in law, it also involved the substantial acceptance of that proposition by the monarchy and the mutual reconciliation of royal and parliamentary institutions. Rule by Parliament was henceforth in the name of the King—not against the King. It represented a virtual national consensus so that relatively few Englishmen (among them the so-called Jacobites) questioned the basic premises of the Glorious Revolution in the 1700s. When, more than a century later, in response to the growing complexities of the Industrial Revolution and a growing "welfare and warfare State," Britain developed a massive bureaucracy, the latter grew in the shadow of a well-entrenched parliamentary democracy. The popular right to elect MPs and the right of the MPs to have the last word on the affairs of the Kingdom were hardly new doctrines that needed to prove themselves when Gladstone introduced his Civil Service Reform Act in 1872. The legitimacy of popular rule preceded by many years the development of a powerful bureaucracy in the nineteenth century.

Nor did British democracy cause religious fissures that would make political authority seem spiritually alien and unacceptable to the great masses of the people. Notwithstanding the austere excesses of Cromwell's Puritans, the cause of democracy in Britain never got itself isolated from the preponderant religious sentiment of the people.

In the background of these developments, we may well remember with Lucian Pye[3] that, addressing themselves to the constitutional question—King or Parliament—in the seventeenth century, the British had already had a long experience of national unification and effective central government in England and Wales. When Parliament expanded its electoral base from a few to the many in the nineteenth century, the issue of national unity, even with Scotland, was a long-settled one. And so was Parliamentary supremacy.

All this does not prevent Britain from suffering the impact of value-shattering events, along with the rest of mankind. These may range from economic and military catastrophes to the possibility of, say, diplomatic pressure by some superpower for domestic political change in the British Isles. But long-standing traditions and practices, translated into family, school, church, press, and various informal influences, provide the British people with something of a cushion or a shock absorber against the kinds of challenges to democratic values that have proved fatally irresistible elsewhere.

Illustrative of these are the political systems of France and Germany in Europe, which both have outwardly democratic political structures today. In France the democratic Revolution of 1789 took place against

[3] See his *Aspects of Political Development* (Boston: Little, Brown, 1966).

the background of long-established absolutism. It was more of an "upstart" revolution than the Cromwellian one in England, in that parliamentarism in France had been practically dead for almost two centuries before 1789. It was never as well established in France as it had been under the Tudors in the years preceding the British revolution of 1642. The French revolutionists never succeeded in continuing and combining the older legitimacy of kingship with the newer legitimacy of popular rule. The revolution did not identify itself with or absorb the religious allegiance of the mass of the people who, particularly among the rural elements, continued to identify with Catholicism, the faith of Kings and of adamant opposition to secular democracy for most of the nineteenth century. Unlike Britain, France had had a great bureaucratic establishment long before 1789, under the authority and command of the King. This establishment did not see popular power as its legitimate master. Likewise, Germany, when unified in 1871, possessed neither a well-established tradition of self-government, or basic national cohesion. Germany attempted to solve the problem of worker demands, parliamentary suffrage, and responsible government virtually all at once. Moreover, as in France, a large bureaucracy, civil and military, had grown up long before the claims to popular rule became widespread, under the aegis of absolute Kings.

The twentieth century has been a century of political mobilization, a time when all traditions, values, roles, and statuses have been impacted by rapid and thorough change. The acceptability of the values of a traditional autocracy, and its capacity to endure, rest on the ability either to stem this impact of change, to resist the cultural-political-economic and scientific penetration of an outside world into the traditional society, or to *adapt* gradually to the quickening pace of change. The roots of revolution are not so much in the poverty or the suffering of the underprivileged as in their awareness and politically directed resentment against it. A regime that cannot or will not alter the facts of social life, but cannot prevent the growth of awareness and resentment, sits on a revolutionary powder keg.

The innovative autocracy is a response to pervasive cultural penetration and change; it is best understood in the light of the extensive uprooting and mobilization to new outlooks and new styles of life that have taken place on a worldwide basis. The techniques of modern authoritarian movements—Communist, Populist (such as those of Nasser or Peron or Sukarno), Fascist, or Nazi—are made both possible and also highly desirable to many people by the antecedent processes of social mobilization. The innovative autocracy, as Fromm, Hoffer, Kornhauser, and others have pointed out, is a way of relieving modern man's anxieties and his inability to deal with a runaway world, one that has uprooted all the traditional values and by its complexity has made people feel helpless. It is also a means of realizing output values or expectations that may be or appear to be unobtainable through the agreed-upon procedures of a given society. It may be a way, as in the case of fascism and nazism, of forestalling and controlling the undesirable consequences of social mobilization already consummated in the particular society. It becomes a way of waging counterrevolution against the lower strata.

Democracy's values are not necessarily inconsistent with the processes of social mobilization. In fact, democracy is a singularly adaptable creed because of its secular-pragmatic orientation. It has relatively few sacred cows, and its dominant attitude is "Let us do what the people want."[4]

Yet, without a general sense of popular self-restraint, this attitude is also democracy's Achilles' heel. For if antagonisms and rifts within a society are deeply divisive, an honest election may be seen as untenably dangerous by everyone—even if for different and opposite reasons. It is something no one may be willing to risk. And if the "distributive expectations" of participants in the political process are not moderated from the all-or-nothing ideal of autocratic rule, democracy is doomed. For to allow wisespread and meaningful popular participation in politics is to agree, by implication, that all system outputs will fall somewhere between the extremes of "all for us" and "nothing for them."

Without a climate of mutual trust, consensus on the maintenance of the democratic rules of the game may give way to pressures for various specific claims and gratifications, simply because (1) the rules are not seen as an important enough value in themselves by people in the society, and (2) concomitantly few people believe in the good disposition of others toward this value.

In many areas of the modern world the prevalent predispositions to political change engendered by the processes of social mobilization have been toward innovative autocracy. Mutual trust between elites and masses has been undermined and eroded. Why jeopardize the security of one's estate and one's tax exemption by trusting the masses? Why risk the delay of a radical land reform by allowing participation to the rich and those influenced by them?

Put differently, still, the democratic political system may not be able to supply *clear-cut* allocative decisions where the constituents of the system are deeply and widely divided. What may emerge from democracy under such circumstances is merely stalemate, a heedless drift potentially conducive to dissolution. The recent popular dilem-

[4] *Cf.* Henry B. Mayo, *An Introduction to Democratic Theory* (New York: Oxford University Press, 1960), pp. 248–249, "democracy is a political system . . . providing the machinery and opportunity for individuals to pursue their own private ends." P. 249.

mas of France over the war in Algeria and in the United States currently over Vietnam are illustrative of such issues. In both cases, there have been substantial elements who wished for total victory and others committed to total disengagement. Their differences have been difficult to aggregate inasmuch as neither could be readily satisfied by some sort of a middle course. In France, the inability to evolve an effective Algerian policy under the very open, popularly sensitive political mechanisms of the Fourth Republic paved the way for the return of General de Gaulle in May 1958. Stopping short of dictatorship, the Gaullist solution involved considerable exercise of discretionary power and *insulation* of the decision-making mechanisms from pressures by legislators and political parties.

What might be the effect of a substantial popular "stampede" on some likely issues of the future—for example, ecology or population control? A call for dictatorship? Certainly, autocratic rule could provide the most extreme, immediate measures to manipulate the environment. Communist China has, illustratively, undertaken the total extermination of dogs as consumers of scarce food supplies and as environmental pollutants. Democratic India, in deference to popular traditions, has tolerated sacred cows and even rats, thus sacrificing meager resources of grain amidst widespread human want and poverty. But how trustworthy would the "blank check" of autocracy prove? Once invested with full power, might it not suddenly change course? How well would it apply this power on other issues? Might it not generate such resentment by the arbitrary extremes of its policy as to bring about an ultimate popular conflagration? Might it not increase the economic and social costs of its policies through the passive resistance, alienation, foot-dragging, and sabotage of those whom it coerced and victimized?

In systems such as that of pre-1917 Russia, the autocratic regime previous to the Communists delayed, but was powerless to stop, dramatic social, economic, and cultural changes. It did not succeed in either channeling these changes according to its own designs, or in bringing about a mutual adaptation of values between itself and the people. It was tragically quiescent and ineffective in the face of mounting cries for reform, relying more on repression than on the indoctrination or positive socialization of its subjects. Russia in 1914 was a country ruled by a traditional, status quo-oriented autocracy at a time when economically, technologically, culturally, and socially the values of that system were being undermined by industrialization, new social relationships, increased physical and social mobility (however repressed and retarded by the autocracy), ever-increasing education, literacy, secularization, the permeation of ideologies from outside the system, and many other influences. The eventual change was toward an innovative-mobilizational regime.

In 1943, Argentina was ostensibly a constitutional democracy but in fact was ruled by traditional oligarchs in a diffuse pluralistic system of power. Its traditions of democracy and cultural cohesion were weak. This system, too, subjected to the strains of industrialization in the cities, gave way to innovative-mobilizational autocracy.[5]

The demand for political change inevitably arises in situations where (1) the political system ceases to distribute values in accordance with well-established expectations of various segments of the population; and/or (2) when these expectations themselves change. In either case the system faces a crisis of modernization.[6] When severe and prolonged imbalances develop between the expectations of those who are the consumers, as it were, of political value-allocations, and the nature of these allocations, the crisis of modernization may well turn into a crisis of revolution.

The student revolts of our era are illustrative of some of these problems. The widespread demand for increased participation by students in many countries can be seen, in the United States at least, as a traditional demand for inclusion in the system. Hence they are presumably a demand that the system distribute more rather than different values. In some cases, however, the demands are couched in terms of a new *kind* of participation regarded as hitherto lacking in the system. Under either interpretation, severe crises of traditional authority have occurred.

The establishment of a new political system of power, distributing more or different values, may proceed in a piecemeal and outwardly nondisruptive fashion, or it may occur through revolutionary violence, depending on several circumstances. These involve the *intensity*, all things considered, with which segments of the population desire change; the *rigidity* of opposition to it within the sytem; and the *balance of resources* in behalf of the forces of change. When these factors are maximized, revolutionary upheaval is all but inevitable, even when its initiators are a minority of the population in the system. When they are minimized, accommodative change is possible. Frequently, change in the political system may be engendered by a coalition—deliberate or coincidental—of particular groups or interests each bent on the pursuit of its own particular value-outputs. Democracy could thus be destroyed by a contradictory coalition of landlords and workers, for example, pressing for extreme or at least clear-cut

[5] *Cf.* John H. Kautsky (ed.), Ch. 4, "Totalitarianism and the Future of Politics in Developing Countries," *Political Change in Underdeveloped Countries* (New York: John Wiley, 1962).

[6] See Alfred Diamant, "The Nature of Political Development," in J. L. Finkle and R. W. Gable (eds.), *Political Development and Social Change* (New York: John Wiley, 1966), pp. 91–96.

changes in the hitherto prevailing system and unleashing two, presumably opposite, revolutionary drives. What is of special interest from the standpoint of our study—looking at political systems in terms of the whole profile of their value-outputs—is that change from one system to another, however engendered, usually involves the ultimate substitution not simply of one value for another but in fact of large, interrelated, and reasonably persistent clusters of values. In such changes, many of their initiators are destined to experience both disappointments and surprises.

INDEX

R